ACPL ITEM
DISCARDED

D0824495

6-13-74

Maryland's

REVOLUTION OF GOVERNMENT
1689–1692

ST. MARY'S CITY COMMISSION PUBLICATION NO. 1

Maryland's
REVOLUTION OF GOVERNMENT
1689–1692

Lois Green Carr AND
David William Jordan

CORNELL UNIVERSITY PRESS
Ithaca and London

Cornell University Press gratefully acknowledges
a grant from the Andrew J. Mellon Foundation
that aided in bringing this book to publication.

Copyright © 1974 by Cornell University

All rights reserved. Except for brief quotations in a review, this
book, or parts thereof, must not be reproduced in any form without
permission in writing from the publisher. For information address
Cornell University Press, 124 Roberts Place, Ithaca, New York, 14850.

First published 1974 by Cornell University Press.
Published in the United Kingdom by Cornell University Press Ltd.,
2-4 Brook Street, London W1Y 1AA.

The Maryland Bicentennial Commission and the St. Mary's City Commission jointly sponsored preparation of the manuscript and under-
wrote part of the production costs of the book.

International Standard Book Number 0-8014-0793-1
Library of Congress Catalog Card Number 73-13055

Printed in the United States of America by York Composition Co., Inc.

1807563

To Jack and Kay

1803963

Contents

Map

Tables

Preface

In 1689 three "glorious" revolutions occurred in the English mainland plantations of North America: in Maryland, New York, and Massachusetts. Only fifteen years earlier, a rebellion had disrupted Virginia. The late seventeenth century in America was a "time of troubles," a time of social and political unrest.

There has been much speculation about the meaning of these events, yet little is known about them. This book analyzes the most neglected of the disorders, the revolution of 1689 in Maryland, and attempts to answer certain questions about it: What social, economic, and institutional as well as political developments preceded and followed the overthrow of the proprietor? Who participated in the revolt, and how did the population line up on either side? Was the revolution pervasive and disruptive of social stability, or was it confined to political struggles at the provincial level? How was it related to the stage of social and political organization that had developed in Maryland by 1689?

Well-founded answers to such questions require hard digging in records previously little used. Similar questions need to be raised and discussed for other colonies, including those that did not experience rebellions. It can then be asked what the disorders of the late seventeenth century had in common and why rebellions occurred in some colonies and not in others.

One reason for scholarly neglect of the Maryland revolution is the absence of records. From August 1689 to April 1692, the council and offices of central government ceased to function.

Neither the Associators' Convention, an elected body that met only twice a year, nor its executive committee left journals of their transactions. Records of the Provincial Court, which functioned during the last year of the interregnum, have also disappeared. We are left with records of the local county courts, which are in most instances incomplete, and with letters and reports sent to England and to other colonies.

To put together even a narrative of events from these materials has required intensive study and piecing together of diverse and largely indirect kinds of evidence. What orders local courts received from the convention or its executive committee and how the local magistrates responded become evidence that helps fill out our knowledge of how the interim government operated. Whether debts could be collected, whether taxes were levied and paid, whether the poor received relief, whether magistrates resorted to illegal practices—these provide clues about the maintaining of civil order and local services. Who accepted office and who refused is information that hints at political attitudes. Correspondence with other colonies sheds light on the new rulers and their problems. Petitions and grievances brought by both sides to the negotiations in England are as interesting for what they do not say as for the one-sided arguments they present.

Employing these records, we proposed to find out what happened, how the inhabitants of Maryland perceived what happened, and how the events of the years 1689–1692 affected the course of Maryland history. When details that in themselves tell little are pieced together, a picture begins to emerge of what contemporaries called the "revolution of government."

Late in July of 1689, a small group of agitators and ambitious men raised the militia of the southern counties and seized the proprietary government. The tensions and conflicts between proprietor and colonists that culminated in this uprising had as their common thread anti-Catholic feeling, but this sentiment was not an overriding force that made the revolt inevitable.

Many Protestants supported the proprietor, and Catholic-Protestant cooperation over the years had been on the whole successful. It was a breakdown of leadership, caused in part by the prolonged absence of Lord Baltimore in England, that gave the leaders of the revolution their opportunity.

Except for establishing Anglicanism and excluding Catholics from political office, the overturn of the proprietor and the subsequent assumption of government by the crown did not in themselves produce long-range changes in Maryland. Establishment guaranteed the development of Protestant churches, which had been conspicuously few, while the exclusion of Catholics meant, at least temporarily, expanded political opportunity for Protestants, especially at the provincial level. Crown rule hastened other changes, particularly those that fitted Maryland into an imperial system. Nevertheless, whether or not Lord Baltimore retained control of the Maryland government apparently had little to do with either the direction or the progress of basic social and economic developments.

The revolution reveals much about the sources of stability in a young and growing colony. The absence of disorders once the proprietary government had surrendered suggests elements of stability rooted in established and workable governmental and legal institutions. These were particularly important at the local level, for the central government was in effect suspended for almost three years. Dependable routines and conscientious magistrates were necessary if county courts were to operate effectively under these circumstances, and it is evident that both existed. Together they constituted a force for local stability which forestalled the disruptions that had earlier characterized Bacon's Rebellion in Virginia. The events that took place in Maryland from 1689 to 1692 thus suggest that the habits of behavior and expectation which well-established and workable institutions foster are a stabilizing force in a new and socially mobile society.

We hope, then, that this book will serve as more than just a thorough account of one revolution in late-seventeenth-century America. Perhaps it can also provide a suggestive model for examining the interaction of institutional development and social change elsewhere in colonial America.

The assistance of many institutions and individuals has been indispensable to the making of this study. Morris L. Radoff, Archivist of Maryland, and his staff have collected and preserved Maryland's public colonial records and have created superb indexes for the social historian. Dr. Radoff has criticized the manuscript in several drafts. The staffs of other depositories here and abroad have offered necessary guidance to their collections: the Maryland Historical Society and the Library of Congress in this country; Lambeth Palace, Friends House Library, and the Jesuit Farm Street Residence in London.

At the later stages of preparation fellow students of Maryland colonial society have discussed and questioned our assumptions and hypotheses. Russell R. Menard, Alan Day, Gregory Stiverson, Edward Papenfuse, and Carville Earle will recognize their contributions, the fruit both of daily conversation and of their patient scrutiny of all or parts of the manuscript. Special thanks must go to Russell Menard, who has shared his detailed knowledge of seventeenth-century Maryland leadership, as well as his analytical talents, and to Michael Kammen and P. M. G. Harris, who provided perceptive critiques of the manuscript. For the final product, we take full responsibility.

David Jordan would like to express his particular appreciation to Wesley Frank Craven of Princeton University, who first suggested and then ably supervised Jordan's initial forays into Maryland's colonial history. He also wishes to thank the Danforth Foundation and Grinnell College for financial assistance at critical stages of research. Lois Carr would like to thank Professor Bernard Bailyn of Harvard University for his encouragement at an earlier stage of her share of this work and the St.

Mary's City Commission, State of Maryland, for the released time that made possible the evolution of a book. We both wish to thank the Maryland Bicentennial Commission for the Commemoration of the American Revolution, which made a grant to cover part of the publication costs.

Finally, we wish to make public acknowledgment of debts completely dischargeable only in private. As the dedication notes, these are owing to Jack Ladd Carr and Kay Smith Jordan.

LOIS GREEN CARR
Annapolis, Maryland
DAVID WILLIAM JORDAN
Grinnell, Iowa

Abbreviations

Complete bibliographic information is provided below for items cited in abbreviated form in the footnotes. Unless otherwise indicated, unpublished Maryland records are found in the Hall of Records, Annapolis, and all colonial office materials are in the Public Record Office, London.

AA Land Rec.	Anne Arundel County Land Records
Balt. Ct. Pro.	Baltimore County Court Proceedings
Balt. Land Rec.	Baltimore County Land Records
Cal. S. P., Col.	W. Noel Sainsbury *et al.*, eds., *Calendar of State Papers, Colonial Series, America and West Indies*, 44 vols. to date (London, 1860–)
Cal. S. P., Dom.	William John Hardy *et al.*, eds., *Calendar of State Papers, Domestic Series of the Reign of William III*, 6 vols. (London, 1908–1937)
Cecil Judg.	Cecil County Judgments
Ch. Ct. and Land Rec.	Charles County Court and Land Records
CO5/713–CO5/723	Colonial Office Papers on Maryland
Colonial Period	Charles M. Andrews, *The Colonial Period of American History*, 4 vols. (New Haven, Conn., 1934–1938)
"County Government"	Lois Green Carr, "County Government in Maryland, 1689–1709" (Ph.D. diss., Harvard University, 1968)
DHNY	Edmund B. O'Callaghan, ed., *The Documentary History of the State of New York*, 4 vols. (Albany, 1849–1851)

Dor. Land Rec.	Dorchester County Land Records
Executive Journals of Va. Council	H. R. McIlwaine and Wilbur M. Hall, eds., *Executive Journals of the Council of Colonial Virginia*, 4 vols. (Richmond, 1925–1945)
Fitzhugh	Richard B. Davis, ed., *William Fitzhugh and His Chesapeake World, 1676–1701* (Chapel Hill, 1963)
HLP	Donnell MacClure Owings, *His Lordship's Patronage: Offices of Profit in Colonial Maryland*, Maryland Historical Society Studies in History no. 1 (Baltimore, 1953)
Inv.	Inventories
I&A	Inventories and Accounts
Kent Ct. Pro.	Kent County Court Proceedings
"Mariland's Grevances"	Beverly McAnear, ed., "Mariland's Grevances wiy The[y] Have Taken Op Arms," *Journal of Southern History*, VIII (1942), 392–409
Md. Archives	William Hand Browne *et al.*, eds., *Archives of Maryland*, 72 vols. to date (Baltimore, 1883–)
MHM	*Maryland Historical Magazine*
MHS	Maryland Historical Society, Baltimore
Old Somerset	Clayton Torrence, *Old Somerset on the Eastern Shore of Maryland: A Study in Foundations and Founders* (Richmond, 1935)
PG Ct. Rec.	Prince George's County Court Records
PG Land Rec.	Prince George's County Land Records
Prov. Ct. Judg.	Provincial Court Judgments
Randolph Letters	Robert Noxon Toppan and Alfred T. S. Goodrick, eds., *Edward Randolph: Including His Letters and Official Papers . . . 1676–1703*, 7 vols. (Boston, 1898–1909)
"Royal Period"	David W. Jordan, "The Royal Period of Colonial Maryland, 1689–1715" (Ph.D. diss., Princeton University, 1966)
Som. Jud. Rec.	Somerset County Judicial Records
Talb. Judg.	Talbot County Judgments
Talb. Land Rec.	Talbot County Land Records
Talb. Test. Pro.	Talbot County Testamentary Proceedings
Test. Pro.	Testamentary Proceedings

Maryland's
REVOLUTION OF GOVERNMENT
1689–1692

CHAPTER I

The Background of
the Revolution

In 1689, Charles Lord Baltimore's province of Maryland, with ten counties and some 25,000 settlers hugging the Chesapeake Bay and its tributaries, seemed quite distinct from other American colonies. Maryland alone had a Roman Catholic proprietor who possessed a charter conferring almost unlimited palatinate powers. It alone had a significant Catholic population which held high political offices. Apart from the new Quaker colonies, it had more Friends enjoying religious and civil liberties than anywhere else in America. At the same time among many land plantations were some sixty manors, vestiges of an early seignorial scheme of settlement.

Throughout the seventeenth century, the discontented and the "undesirable" from other colonies had drifted into more tolerant Maryland, thereby creating perhaps one of the most diverse populations in the New World. Significant, however, as the century approached its last decade was the evident erasing of these peculiar characteristics. The manor system had been a futile attempt at social ordering, and manor rights no longer held real meaning, if they ever did. Both geographical circumstances and popular pressures had led to the development instead of local institutions parallel to English quarter sessions and Virginia county courts. An overwhemingly Protestant majority was beginning to chafe at the predominant role played by the Roman Catholic minority, a discontent that threatened the foun-

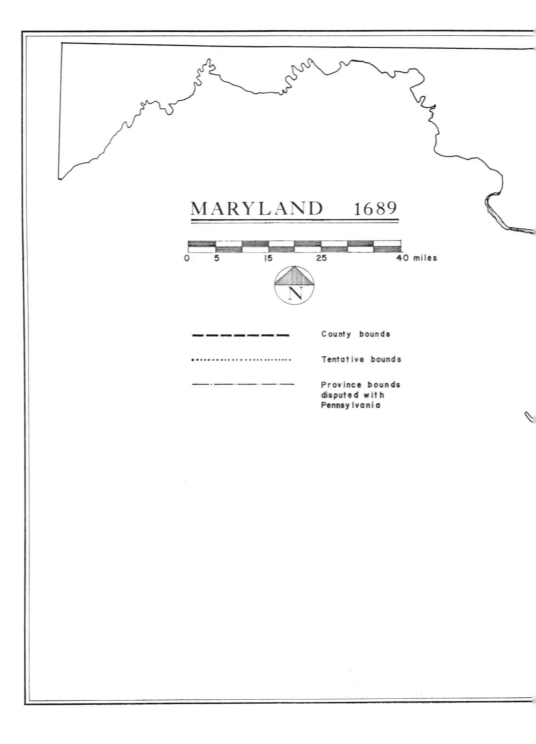

MARYLAND 1689

0   5   15   25   40 miles

N

——— ——— ———   County bounds

·······················   Tentative bounds

——— · ——— · ———   Province bounds
disputed with
Pennsylvania

dations of tolerance; concurrently, the Navigation Acts and
other manifestations of the new English colonial policies were
causing an inevitable clash of royal and proprietary prerogatives.
An economy based on a single staple, tobacco, was obliterating
differences and fostering ties with Maryland's neighbors to the
south, especially Virginia, a royal Anglican colony.[1]

The revolution of 1689, which overthrew the Lord Proprietor and inaugurated a twenty-five year period of royal rule, hastened this process of change. When another Lord Baltimore
regained Maryland in 1715, it was no longer the family enterprise which his grandfather had owned and governed nor was
it any longer a haven for nonconformity; it was an imperial
colony with restrictions similar to those of its neighbors. The
early stages of this transformation contributed to the revolution.
Whether revolution was necessary to complete the change is
one of the questions this book will try to answer.

Maryland had prospered greatly since the first hardy adven-
turers had anchored in the St. Mary's River, a tributary of the
Potomac, late in March 1634. From the beginning water proved
the main determinant in shaping both the pattern of settlement
and the growth of characteristic institutions. "The people there
not affecting to build nere each other," Charles Calvert, the
Third Lord Baltimore, explained in 1678, "But soe as to have
their houses nere the Watters for conveniencye of trade and
their Lands on each syde of and behynde Their houses by which
it happens that in most places There are not fifty houses in the
space of Thirty Myles."[2] By 1689 the population was scattered
north and east of the earliest settlements as far as Pennsylvania,

[1] For this early period, see *Colonial Period*, II, *The Settlements;* Wesley
Frank Craven, *The Southern Colonies in the Seventeenth Century, 1607–
1689*, vol. I, *History of the South*, eds. Wendell Stephenson and E.
Merton Coulter (Baton Rouge, La., 1949); and Newton D. Mereness,
Maryland as a Proprietary Province (New York, 1901).

[2] *Md. Archives*, V, 266.

and boundary conflicts that were to last three quarters of a century had become acute.

A framework for the government of this spreading colony had been provided in the Maryland charter. It granted extraordinary power to the proprietor: He not only owned all the land, but he was the sole source of executive and judicial power. He was to appoint the governor, a council, and all magistrates. He was to establish courts as he saw fit, and all writs were to run in his name. He could create ports of entry for shipping. He could establish an armed force in which all men in the province were obliged to serve, and he could exercise martial law in emergencies. He could even pass ordinances, provided they were not repugnant to English law and did not affect the "right or interest of any person or persons, of, or in member, life, freehold, goods or chattels." Not only could he create manors with powers to hold court-leet and court-baron, but he could make noble titles provided they did not duplicate those of England—a privilege, as it turned out, of doubtful value.

There were three main checks on his power. Only with the consent of an assembly of freemen or their deputies could he pass laws; the laws were to be "(so far as conveniently may be) agreeable to the laws, statutes, customs, and rights of this our kingdom of England"; and Lord Baltimore's settlers were to be considered English subjects with "all privileges, franchises and liberties of this our kingdom of England." On the other hand, no review of the laws by the crown was provided, nor could a judicial decision or act be taken to an English court. Lord Baltimore was the lord and ruler of Maryland.[3]

Nevertheless, provision for an assembly and the requirement that laws must not conflict unnecessarily with those of England

[3] The charter is set forth in Francis Newton Thorpe, ed., *The Federal and State Constitutions, Colonial Charters, and Other Organic Laws of the States, Territories, and Colonies, Now or Heretofore Forming the United States of America* (Washington, D.C., 1909), III, 1669–77 (in Latin), 1677–86 (in English).

ensured that over time Maryland institutions would not differ
drastically from those of the mother country. The proprietor or
his governor ruled with the advice of his council, but the assembly early established a right to initiate legislation and in 1649
gained recognition of its power to levy all taxes.[4] By 1660 it had
permanently divided into two houses, the upper house consisting
of the council, the lower house of elected representatives of all
freemen. Ten years later Lord Baltimore restricted the vote to
freeholders of fifty acres, the usual minimum holding in Maryland, or to men worth £40 in visible estate. These qualifications
were more in line with English precedent than those of earlier
days, although the Maryland franchise remained broader.[5]

   The judiciary also became roughly comparable to that of England. The common law of England was transferred, except as
modified by the Maryland courts and assembly, although the
status of English statutes was in debate.[6] The Provincial Court
was the major court of common law. It exercised jurisdiction

   [4] Mereness, *Maryland as a Proprietary Province*, 223–24; Acts 1650, c.
25, *Md. Archives*, I, 302; Acts 1676, c. 2, II, 548.
   [5] Mereness, *Maryland as a Proprietary Province*, 197, 199; Edward
Porritt, *The Unreformed House of Commons: Parliamentary Representation before 1832* (Cambridge, 1903), I, 20–68. In England, freemen
of the shires needed a freehold with an annual value of forty shillings.
Certain kinds of long-term leaseholds qualified as freeholds, but copy-
holds did not. Borough franchises varied greatly, but only a fifth or so
allowed any large number of inhabitant householders to vote. No study
has yet been made to show what proportion of freemen could vote in
Maryland from 1670 through 1689. Mrs. Carr has shown, however, that
in Prince George's County about 1704–6, two-thirds of the heads of
households had land enough to qualify. In addition, only six out of 300
resident landowners had less than fifty acres ("County Government,"
text, 597–99, 601–2). County rent rolls compiled in 1659 and 1704–7 show
very few parcels of less than fifty acres (Rent Rolls 0–10, Hall of Records, Annapolis).
   [6] Discussions of the transfer of English law before 1689 appear in
Joseph H. Smith, "The Foundations of Law in Maryland: 1634–1715,"
in George A. Billias, ed., *Selected Essays: Law and Authority in Colonial
America* (Barre, Mass., 1965), 98–102; "County Government," text, 86–
92. See also pp. 21–23, 28–29, below.

similar to that of the king's bench, court of common pleas, and exchequer and had sole original jurisdiction over offenses punishable by loss of life or limb.[7] A court of chancery exercised jurisdiction in equity, and by the 1670's what was later called the Prerogative Court had jurisdiction in testamentary affairs. Except that its judge was not an ecclesiastic in charge of an ecclesiastical court, the forms and procedures of this court resembled those of the English prerogative courts and courts of the ordinary, which handled most English probate and administration where there was personalty to account for and distribute.[8]

[7] A commission of February 16, 1665/66 for the justices of the Provincial Court gave them jurisdiction "For the holding of all Pleas touching and Relating unto the Conservation of us, and the Conservation of the peace of our said Province as for the holding of pleas touching our Rights and Revenues and of Common Pleas" (*Md. Archives,* XV, 8). The last commission recorded for the proprietary period, dated August 10, 1685, was couched in the same words (XVII, 432). A description of the Maryland government as of 1715 described the court as holding "Plea of all Actions Real, Personal and Mixt, between Party and Party as well as Debts due to the Crowne & Criminal Matters so that the Court may be well said to be, both Kings Bench, Common Pleas and Exchequer" (XXV, 320). For these three English courts, see William Holdsworth, *A History of English Law,* 16 vols. (London, 1903–66), I, 195–242.

[8] A description of the Chancery Court is given in the Letter of Transmittal of the editors and introductory essays by Carroll T. Bond and J. Hall Pleasants to *Md. Archives,* LI, which reprints the proceedings of the Chancery Court from 1669 through 1679. For the Prerogative Court in Maryland, see Edith E. MacQueen, "The Commissary in Colonial Maryland," *MHM,* XXV (1930), 190–226; Elizabeth Hartsook and Gust Skordas, *Land Office and Prerogative Court Records of Colonial Maryland,* Hall of Records Commission Publication no. 4 (Annapolis, 1946), 81–89.

The Prerogative Court of Maryland had a wider jurisdiction and more effective powers of enforcement than had English ecclesiastical courts. It had jurisdiction over succession to land as well as chattels. In addition, as a proprietary court it could take bonds for performance in the name of the proprietor that could be put in suit in the Provincial Court if executors or administrators proved false or careless. A proclamation of 1681 gave the Prerogative Court powers in contempt similar to those of the Chancery Court (Acts 1681, c. 2, *Md. Archives,* VII, 195–201; XVII,

Scattered settlement early rendered it impractical to administer all provincial affairs from St. Mary's City, the capital on the lower western peninsula. As the population moved north and across the bay, Lord Baltimore's governors by proclamation erected counties, which had their own courts, local officers, and representatives to the assembly. The county courts were in many respects similar to the English courts of quarter sessions, but they early acquired powers that in England belonged to courts-baron, parishes, boroughs, and even the central courts. By 1658 there were five counties: St. Mary's, Calvert, Charles, and Anne Arundel on the Western Shore, and Kent on the Eastern Shore. Five more—Baltimore and Cecil along the northern border of the province and Talbot, Dorchester, and Somerset on the Eastern Shore—had appeared by 1674. These divisions were sufficient to accommodate the growing population for another twenty-two years.[9]

The period from 1660 to 1689 saw a great expansion in the powers of the county courts and their development into local governments. By the 1660's the commissions issued by the governor from which the justices derived their magistratical powers enabled them to hear and determine all offenses for which punishment did not entail loss of life or limb and all personal actions in which the amount at stake was no more than 3,000 pounds of tobacco. In 1679 this civil jurisdiction was expanded to include

---

18). As the Maryland court grew stronger, its English counterparts were losing jurisdiction in testamentary affairs to the English Court of Chancery. See Holdsworth, *History of English Law*, III, 594–95; VI, 652–54.

[9] For the erection of counties, see Edward B. Mathews, *The Counties of Maryland: Their Origin, Boundaries, and Election Districts*, Maryland Geological Survey, Special Publication VI, part V (Baltimore, 1907). "County Government," especially chapters III–VI, discusses the development of the county courts and their officers from 1661 through the first decade of the eighteenth century. C. Ashley Ellefson, "The County Courts and Provincial Court of Maryland, 1733–1763" (Ph.D. diss., University of Maryland, 1963), chapter II, also outlines the seventeenth-century development of the judicial side of the county courts and their officers.

the most important personal actions to any amount, thereby enlarging the role of the justices, already important, in the credit relationships upon which the tobacco economy depended. Two years later the criminal jurisdiction of the country courts was increased to include simple thefts of goods valued at 1,000 pounds of tobacco or less. The effect was to enable the local justices to punish all the offenses that occurred with any frequency in their communities. The Provincial Court, which consisted of the governor and council, had concurrent jurisdiction except in small causes, and had criminal and civil jurisdiction on appeal and error. Since this court did not travel on circuit, however, it was expensive and inconvenient for most settlers. The jurisdiction granted to the local courts gave them major power and responsibility.[10]

During the 1660's and 1670's various administrative powers became firmly and permanently located in the county courts: responsibility for laying down and maintaining roads, licensing inns—called ordinaries—setting some prices for liquors, inspecting weights and measures, supervising relations of masters and servants, appointing guardians for orphans and checking on their welfare, building courthouses and jails, overseeing tax assessments, presiding at the election of delegates to the assembly. Most important of all was the power to raise local taxes to pay

[10] Before 1679 civil jurisdiction was confined to justices of the quorum. Personal actions did not include any involving ownership of real property. For details of court jurisdiction, see "County Government," text, 127–32, 190–202; Ellefson, "County Courts and Provincial Court," 43–49, 110–11. Immediate advantage was taken of the new civil jurisdiction. In Charles County at the August, September, and November courts in 1680, seven actions were either begun or brought to judgment that involved sums of more than 3,000 pounds of tobacco. At the Provincial Court in May and November of 1680, no actions were instituted or tried from Charles County (*Md. Archives*, LXIX, 222ff.; Ch. Ct. and Land Rec., I no. 1, ff. 1–50). Nevertheless, the number of causes tried in the counties probably was not greatly increased. Actions for sums over 3,000 pounds of tobacco were still few. The new criminal jurisdiction was of greater immediate importance. For documentation, see Appendix C.

for "the county charge," granted by act of assembly in 1671. Although there was no express statement that the county courts could decide what money should be spent when no law required or permitted an expenditure, the act was interpreted to allow the justices to determine who should receive poor relief and how much, to establish free ferries, to build bridges, to repair courthouses or jails, and to pay themselves per diem allowances for attending court. The act was to be the basis upon which the local courts expanded powers to make public improvements and provide public services without constant recourse to the assembly for authorization.[11]

These judicial and administrative powers made the county justices powerful men in their communities. The governor and council, it is true, could wield considerable local control: through appointments to the bench; through power to remedy various kinds of grievances, either as an administrative body or as the Provincial Court; through power to sit as justices on any county court. The power to make appointments, however, was undoubtedly curtailed by the shortage of men with sufficient standing—wealth, rank, education—to be commissioned justices. As late as 1689 there were illiterate men sitting on the bench in some counties, and during the 1690's it was still necessary to use the penalties for refusing office to ensure filling these posts with men capable of exercising authority. The chances for exercising power locally through manipulation of appointments were probably not yet great in the more recently settled counties.[12] At the

[11] For a more detailed discussion, see "County Government," text, chapter V. The county courts had already been levying county taxes to support the poor before the act was passed. In the eighteenth century, courts began to obtain legislative authorization for major improvements such as a new court house.

[12] For a discussion of the qualifications of justices for twenty years after 1689, see *ibid.*, 471–76. For illiterate justices, see *Md. Archives*, LIII, 606 (Charles Co., 1665); XVII, 443 (Anne Arundel Co., 1685). As late as 1694 Governor Nicholson hauled recalcitrant men before the Provincial Court for refusing to qualify as justices (XX 225; Balt. Ct. Pro., G, f. 325). See also Craven, *Southern Colonies*, 307–8.

same time, the power to hear grievances and take action to check abuses could only produce remedies after the fact; it did not much curtail the decision-making powers of the local justices. Who could be licensed to be an innkeeper, who could be guardian to an orphan, who could have a road near his house or must allow a road through his cornfield, who must contribute time in local office, who could be supported by poor relief, who was to pay taxes and for what local expenditures—these decisions were rarely challenged.[13] The surest means of influencing them would have come from exercise of the power to sit on the county bench, but the extant records suggest that councillors did not often attend court in most counties.[14] The opinion of any councillor, especially in his home county, or where he owned land, was doubtless heeded, of course. Nevertheless, in most matters that affected the daily life of most inhabitants, the local justices made the local decisions.

Only the sheriff—an officer similar to the English sheriff—carried a competing weight as a local officer. Like the justices he received his commission from the governor. He had sole power

[13] Occasionally the council or the Provincial Court would reverse a local decision. In 1686 the council reversed the Calvert County Court in its determination that Nathaniel Ashcome was liable to service as a constable (*Md. Archives*, V, 466–67). In 1679, the Provincial Court ordered the levy account from Calvert County sent to it for review, but any action taken is not recorded (LXVIII, 226).

[14] Only two counties have reasonably complete records for the whole period, Charles and Talbot (see Note on the Sources). No councillor sat with the Charles court, but Vincent Lowe sat at most courts in Talbot from June 1686 until the revolution (Talb. Land Rec., NN no. 6, ff. 97, 117, 147, 172, 175, 207, 223, 228, 298, 306, 307). Partial records remain for Baltimore, Cecil, Kent, and Somerset counties. In Cecil (1683–89) George Talbot sat at three sessions in 1684 (Cecil Judg., 1683–92, ff. 4–7). In Kent (1677–78, 1683–88) Henry Coursey sat at the levy courts one day in October 1677 and two days in December 1686. In 1686 he was chief judge of the Provincial Court but not actually a councillor (Kent Ct. Pro., I, ff. 32, 228, 229; *Md. Archives*, XVII, 250–53). Not all counties were represented on the council. From 1660 through 1689 no councillor lived in Dorchester, Baltimore, or Kent counties. Only St. Mary's, Calvert, and Charles had regular representation; see Table 1.

to raise the *posse comitatus* when needed to quell disorders. As an executive arm of the governor and council, furthermore, he represented the authority of the central government, even though his functions in this capacity were purely ministerial. In many ways, of course, he was the servant of the county justices. At court order, he delivered judicial process, produced defendants, took custody of prisoners, subpoenaed men for jury services, seized tobacco or goods, collected and disbursed the county taxes. He could be fined or held in contempt for failure to carry out these duties. On the other hand, these same duties gave him great power over individual inhabitants, even if he were careful to stay within the law. He set bail for appearance in civil actions at his own discretion; he granted or refused permission to those imprisoned for debt to live outside the jail; he could break the lock of a tobacco house to collect tobacco owed for taxes; he could grant or refuse credit to men who owed taxes or other debts that he was ordered to collect; he might delay payments to public or private creditors, delay that could be critical to them. Like the justices, he could bind to the peace. Above all, in the exercise of his police powers he could be gentle or brutal, and he might find brutality and terror a handy or even necessary weapon.[15]

Unlike the Virginia county justices, those of Maryland never gained control of the sheriff's office. The twenty-three-year residence in the colony of Charles Calvert, first as his father's governor and then as proprietor in his own right, doubtless enhanced the position of the Maryland sheriffs, who thus represented a resident, not an overseas ruler. It was important to the proprietor, furthermore, to keep firm control of officers responsible for the collection of revenues, for Maryland represented a family investment. Fines and forfeitures the sheriffs collected were pro-

[15] For the sheriff, see "County Government," text, 508–26, 528; Cyrus H. Karraker, *The Seventeenth-Century Sheriff: A Comparative Study of the Sheriff in England and the Chesapeake Colonies, 1607–89* (Chapel Hill, N.C., 1930).

prietary income, as were quitrents they were often deputed to gather. An act of 1662 that gave the county justices power to nominate candidates for sheriff and limited his term to a year was in effect only until 1669. The upper house then refused to continue it on the grounds that it violated Lord Baltimore's charter right to make such appointments at will. The only concession thereafter to local interests was an act of 1678, not revived in 1686, that enabled the county justices to veto reappointments. Thus the sheriff, although he had no decision-making powers, had power and standing that gave him independence of the county justices and a place beside them as a county ruler.[16]

On the other hand, sheriffs were county-based men, who usually had been or would be justices. Not every justice would have a turn as sheriff, as was more the practice in Virginia, but every sheriff was likely to have a turn on the county bench.[17] The profits of office might tie him somewhat more closely than other justices to the proprietary interest, but sheriffs as a group were not basically different from other planters substantial enough to be granted the exercise of authority.

The necessities of administration thus fostered the development of a class of men, mostly Protestant,[18] who might one day have the opportunity to challenge proprietary authority. Never-

---

[16] Acts 1662, c. 17, *Md. Archives*, I, 451, revived 1664, 1666, repealed 1676, 538; II, 150, 197, 544. Acts 1678, c. 6, revived 1681, 1682, 1684, not revived 1686, 1688; VII, 68–70, 215–16, 246–47, 329–30; XIII, 125–26, 141–42, 212–13. Continued efforts by justices and the assembly to gain more control over the selection of sheriffs enjoyed slight success during the royal period. See "Royal Period," 228–31.

[17] For sheriffs of three counties, 1676–1689, see Russell R. Menard, "Major Office Holders in Charles, Somerset and Talbot Counties, 1676–1689," ms., Hall of Records, Annapolis. Xerox copies may be obtained at cost from the Hall of Records.

[18] *Ibid.* At the revolution, 104 justices were sitting in 10 counties, and of these, not more than 17 could have been Roman Catholic. The others were among those that the revolutionary convention appointed (81) or were Protestants loyal to Lord Baltimore (6). See Appendix B, Table B-1, p. 292 below.

theless, these local offices were not the ones that carried the greatest power, nor did the judgeships entail profit-making opportunities. Provincewide powers and patronage were still reserved for the governor and the small circle, mostly Calverts and their relatives, who served on the council. The governor and council constituted most or all of the Provincial and Chancery courts, and the council in addition was the upper house of assembly, and thus also the court of final appeal. The councillors monopolized the lucrative provincial fee-paying positions, including the offices that controlled probate of estates and distribution of land. They held, furthermore, most of the leading military positions. Few colonels in the militia—the highest rank under the governor, who was commander in chief—were not members of the council.[19] Only by serving as members of the lower house of assembly, not yet highly organized and still struggling for status as a legislative body, had the local rulers any opportunity to affect provincial policy and at least attempt to control the fees that made provincial officeholding so profitable.[20]

It was in the assembly, in consequence, that the grievances of this developing county establishment most often gained public expression. As the colony grew, tensions heightened in three broad areas: defense, the economy, and the administration of justice.[21] Interwoven into these conflicts was the battle of the lower house to increase its power, particularly through attempts

[19] Compare, for example, the list of councillors and colonels sent to England in 1681 (*Md. Archives,* V, 309–10). From 1682 to 1689, only three of twelve councillors—John Darnall, Clement Hill, and William Joseph—were not among the chief militia officers of their respective counties.

[20] Mereness, *Maryland as a Proprietary Province,* 176–77. The fee act of 1676, still in effect in 1689, set up a general schedule of officers' fees but allowed the governor and council to establish others (Acts 1676, c. 11, *Md. Archives,* II, 532–37). For councillors in fee-paying offices, compare Table 1 with listings in *HLP,* 78, 122–26, 130, 166.

[21] The most recent discussion of the background that led to revolution is Michael G. Kammen, "The Causes of the Maryland Revolution of 1689," *MHM,* LV (1960), 293–333. Still useful is Francis Edgar Sparks, *Causes of the Maryland Revolution of 1689,* Johns Hopkins University

to limit the proprietor's veto. Growing tension between Protestants and Catholics helped feed a concern that the prerogative powers the proprietor claimed under his charter were undermining the rights his settlers claimed as Englishmen. Vigorous political and constitutional struggles in the assembly—where the upper house was predominantly Catholic and the lower house was heavily Protestant[22]—were among the major events of the decade that preceded the collapse of proprietary authority.

Procedures for enacting legislation must be explained to make sense of the controversies that took place in the assembly. Like the English Parliament, it often enacted laws of importance that were to last only three years or to the next session of assembly, should that occur sooner, when these laws had to be revived to be in force. In Maryland this procedure allowed time to see how well such laws would work, and in addition ensured that the assembly would be called at least every three years. On the other hand, confusion sometimes resulted over what laws were in force. The assembly of 1676 finally made a complete examination of all past legislation and passed an act that listed all the permanent laws in force and repealed all those, both temporary and permanent, no longer thought useful. This was a permanent act assented to by the proprietor, and it simplified matters considerably, but it did not end confusion. For example, in 1678, the assembly inadvertently listed this law of 1676 in the 1678 Act for Revival of the Temporary Laws, thus creating some doubt as to the status of any permanent law and necessitating repeal of the 1678 act for revival.[23] In 1683 the two

---

Studies in Historical and Political Science, series XIV, nos. 11–12 (Baltimore, 1896).

[22] See Tables 1 and 3 and Appendix A. It is generally not possible to determine from the surviving records of the assembly what positions individuals took on particular causes. There is no attempt, therefore, in the discussion that follows to relate religion to support of, or opposition to, the proprietor.

[23] Acts 1676, c. 2, *Md. Archives*, II, 543–50; Acts 1678, c. 15, VII, 82–85; Acts 1681, c. 12, 247 (act itself), 226, 228–29, 234–36, 238, 240, 241.

houses fought so bitterly over the status, permanent or temporary, of an act for wolf-head bounties that no reviving act could pass and the proprietor had to adjourn the session rather than prorogue the assembly in order to keep the temporary laws in force.[24] In following the disagreements of the 1670's and 1680's, this procedural problem must be kept in mind.

Military expenditures were a heavy burden that touched every household and were a source of discontent by the 1670's. The Maryland charter gave the proprietor power to build forts, raise a militia, appoint its officers, and establish martial law when necessary. By 1669 militia companies trained at least four times a year in every county under the general supervision of a mustermaster general, who was paid by a tax of four pounds of tobacco per taxable person. Every man called for training—and all able-bodied men sixteen years of age or over were liable—provided his own sword, gun, and ammunition, but in actual service the province supplied his equipment. The 1660's had seen an increase of Indian troubles, and several expeditions had been sent to the Susquehanna River. To supply them, the assembly had passed an act (1664) to establish a public magazine for arms and ammunition.[25]

The question of how to pay for this military establishment was becoming a pressing matter. At the same time the proprietor, who had invested most of his fortune in establishing Maryland, wanted to obtain revenue from port duties. In 1670 the assembly finally agreed to a duty of two shillings per hogshead of tobacco shipped from Maryland, granted to the proprietor for his life, provided that half be spent for the defense of the province or for other governmental expenses. The bill passed, however, only after being amended to stop taxation for the mustermaster general's salary and for the public magazine. These henceforth would be proprietary responsibilities. In 1674 the

[24] *Ibid.*, 597, 598, 603–05.

[25] Acts 1650, c. 9, *ibid.*, I, 292 (mustermaster general); Acts 1661, c. 5, 412–13 (military discipline); Acts 1663, c. 32, 535–36 (magazine); III, 412–18, 420–21, 431–35, 460–62, 531; V, 22–23.

act was extended to cover the life of Governor Charles Calvert, soon to be the Third Lord Baltimore, and, in 1676, the life of his oldest son. For despite objections soon raised over expenditures for defense, the act brought one advantage to the colonists that they had no desire to relinquish: It required the proprietor to accept payments of quitrents and alienation fines in tobacco at two pence per pound, which by the 1670's was in most years twice the farm price.[26]

The law required no accounting, however, for the expenditures of the shilling per hogshead for defense, and bitter recriminations resulted. Through about 1682 the Indians of the Five Nations—"Cinnagoes" or "Senecas" to the Marylanders—continually raided the weaker Indians of Maryland and Virginia and committed murder and pillage along the white frontier. Taxes to pay for expeditions against the Indians were very heavy during the 1670's, and the colonists began to question where the shilling per hogshead was going. At issue also was the question of how much of the public arms and ammunition should be distributed to the counties rather than kept in a central magazine, where, from the proprietor's point of view, loss and spoilage could be more easily controlled. In the view of many of his subjects, however, a central magazine not only deprived them of quick access to weapons for defense but put control in the hands of Roman Catholics. The militia act of 1678 required more arms to be distributed to the counties, but these were soon felt to be insufficient. Their recall for repair in the spring of 1689 was one of the immediate causes of the fear and suspicion that precipitated revolution.[27]

[26] *Ibid.*, II, 249, 255, 256, 257; Acts 1671, c. 11, 284–85; Acts 1674, c. 1, 386–89; Acts 1676, c. 3, 515–17. The mustermaster general ceased to exist with the abolition of the tax to support him. For tobacco prices, see Russell R. Menard, "Farm Price of Maryland Tobacco, 1659–1710," *MHM*, LXVIII (1973), 80–85.

[27] *Md. Archives*, II, 426–430; VII, 18; XV, 47–50, 56–58, 97–100, 123–25, 181, 186–87, 318; *Cal. S. P., Col., 1677–80*, nos. 12, 310, 1060; *Md. Archives*, V, 136, 137, 310; Acts 1678, c. 2, VII, 53–60; Acts 1681, c. 1, 188–95; *Cal. S. P., Col., 1681–85*, no. 256; *Md. Archives*, VIII, 218, 223.

The early 1680's saw several attempts by the lower house to tighten its control of military expenditures. The first session of 1681 was called to raise funds for a show of force against marauding Northern Indians, but the burgesses refused to advance anything beyond what the militia act then in force allowed, 50,000 pounds of tobacco.[28] They may have feared that such force would be put to other uses, for Josias Fendall had just been tried on suspicion of raising a Protestant rebellion, and anti-Catholic rumors were circulating.[29] In the emergency, Lord Baltimore was forced to adjourn the session. At the end of six weeks a reconvened lower house authorized payment for the expenses incurred,[30] but it had successfully hampered plans for any major expedition beyond the bounds of the province.

In 1682 Maryland envoys to the Five Nations in Albany negotiated an agreement that for the moment brought peace to the frontier.[31] Nevertheless, the lower house in the course of the next two years thought it desirable to clarify its right to approve any taxation for military purposes. Unfortunately part of the assembly record is destroyed, leaving unknown the exact nature of the bill proposed. In 1684 the proprietor refused to accept it, but promised that he would call an assembly to defray the expenses of any war. Although the matter was then dropped,[32] the concern of the burgesses to protect their right to control taxation is clear, and an effort to contain the proprietor's military powers may be suspected. There was unease in Maryland. Only five years later large numbers of the less sophisticated constituents of these men were willing to believe that Lord Baltimore and his council were conspiring with the Northern Indians to destroy Maryland Protestants.

By the 1680's economic problems were becoming as touchy as those of defense. The price of tobacco had been falling since

28 *Md. Archives*, VII, 164; XVII, 40–41.
29 See p. 32 below.
30 *Md. Archives*, VII, 220, 248–52.
31 *Ibid.*, XVII, 208–16.
32 *Ibid.*, VII, 488, 489, 491, 494; XIII, 39–40, 60, 76, 81, 82, 83.

the early 1660's and was ranging from .9 to .7 pennies sterling per pound during most of the 1680's, half of the price obtained thirty years before. In these circumstances, years of large tobacco crops brought discussions of restricted planting and active attempts to control the quality of tobacco shipped. "Towns" were established in an effort to encourage trade by shortening turn-around time for ships and at the same time to attract craftsmen who could lessen colonial dependence upon the English merchants. According to acts passed in 1683, 1684, and 1686, all tobacco for shipping was to be carried to places designated as towns and all goods imported were to be landed there. These acts incurred some opposition, since most planters had a landing nearer than the nearest "town." The lower house did not fight these acts, in part perhaps because many members owned lands on which towns were to be built and would benefit from their success. Friction arose over the acts in the assembly of 1688, however. By then they seemed doomed to be ineffective in bringing towns into existence, and Lord Baltimore had done away with the penalties for loading ships elsewhere in order not to inconvenience shipmasters and merchants. The burgesses objected vigorously to such unilateral dispensing of an act to which the proprietor had originally assented.[33]

In 1688, economic pressures produced an open conflict between the council and the lower house over measures to combat the depression. The council made two proposals, both extensions of policies already adopted. It suggested additional legislation to encourage diversification and hence less dependence on imports and it urged a new coin rating act that would require coin

[33] Menard, "Farm Prices of Maryland Tobacco"; *Cal. S. P., Col., 1681–85*, nos. 448, 507, 656; *Md. Archives*, VII, 448–605; Acts 1683, c. 5, 609–19; XIII, 3–109; Acts 1684, c. 2, 111–20; Acts 1686, c. 2, 132–39; V, 495–98; VIII, 43, 64; XIII, 171–72, 203. Kammen, "Causes of the Maryland Revolution," 311, and Sparks, *Causes of the Maryland Revolution*, 91–92, suggest that lower-house efforts to use passage of this act to bargain with the proprietor for an act for elections indicates opposition. Such an inference is not required to explain the effort to bargain, and later assemblies did not quarrel with the acts for towns.

to be the only legal tender. Inflating the value of foreign coins with respect to sterling was a time-honored device in all the colonies for attempting to attract coins and increase the money supply, and such an act had been in effect in Maryland from time to time since 1671. But these acts had not required that quitrents, taxes, and all debts be paid in coin and had therefore been ineffective. The council was recommending the drastic step of ending the use of tobacco as a medium of exchange. Evidently the proprietor, absent in England and in need of cash remittances, was willing to give up his shilling duty per hogshead of tobacco in return for the right to collect quitrents and fines in coin, especially since the duty was payable in tobacco at more than twice its market price.

The burgesses, meeting with the upper house in grand committee, at first agreed to the whole program, but away from the influence of the councillors they balked. The burgesses welcomed the laws—some revised, some new—to encourage diversification, but would not agree to end the reign of tobacco as a medium of exchange. Instead, they listed as a grievance Lord Baltimore's recent attempts to collect his rents and fines in sterling money.[34]

Other economic issues also created friction at this session. The lower house refused to pass an act prohibiting bulk shipment of tobacco as requested by the crown of England. The London merchants had argued to the Lords of Trade and Foreign Plantations that bulk shipments included too much "trash" tobacco, contributed to market gluts, made smuggling easier, and used fewer ships. The Maryland lower house objected that the colony depended heavily for goods on the West Country shipping that primarily carried bulk shipments.[35] It complained, in addition, that Lord Baltimore had contributed to stifling trade by failing

[34] *Md. Archives*, XIII, 170, 173–74, 182, 185, 203; Acts 1671, c. 12, II, 286–87; Acts 1676, c. 2, 546; Acts 1686, c. 4, XIII, 142–44; Acts 1688, c. 5, c. 7, c. 8, c. 9, 217–18, 220–23; VIII, 64.

[35] *Ibid.*, 198–200; *Cal. S. P., Col., 1685–88*, nos. 1396, 1397, 1489; Kammen, "Causes of the Maryland Revolution," 313–15.

to appoint naval officers for the Eastern Shore and objected to his agreement with merchants and shippers that they would pay the three-pence fee per hogshead (or the equivalent in bulk) at a town, provided they need not actually load or unload there.[36]

More evident sources of discontent in the assembly than economic and military issues, however, were legal and constitutional matters, over which disagreements grew steadily more acute after 1670. Among the most pressing were these: To what extent should English law be transferred? And who should decide which laws extended and to what degree—the judges of the courts, appointed by the proprietor, or the burgesses in the assembly, elected by the freeholders? These problems were especially important to Maryland colonists because Lord Baltimore's charter, although it guaranteed them the rights of Englishmen, contained no provisions for review by the crown of any law or judicial act.

While in England in 1678, Charles Calvert summed up truthfully but incompletely the accepted view of all sides: "Where the necessity and exigencyes of the Provynce Doe not enforce them to make any Particular Lawes They use no other Lawe than the Lawe of England."[37] He omitted to mention, however, what had become the subject of disagreement: whether the judges of the courts had the right to use discretion in applying English law and procedure. When Calvert had left for England in 1676 to take up his inheritance as the Third Lord Baltimore, there had been two laws in effect which gave his judges this power of interpretation. The first, a permanent act passed in 1646, said "All Justice as well Civill as Criminall shall bee administered by the Governor or other Chiefe Judge in Court [i.e., the Provincial Court] according to the sound discretion of the said Governor or other Chiefe Judge and such of the Councell as shall be present in Court or the Major parte of them." The second, a temporary act passed in 1662, had modified this dis-

---

[36] *Md. Archives*, XIII, 171, 172.
[37] *Ibid.*, V, 264–65.

cretion to some degree and extended it to all judges. It stated that "to leave to much to discrecon is to open a Gapp to corrupcon" and required that in civil proceedings where provincial law was silent, "Justice shall be administered according to the lawes and Statutes of England, if pleaded and produced And all Courts to Judge of the Right pleadeing and inconsistancy of the said Lawes with the good of this Province according to the best of their Judgements Skill and Cunning." But this act applied only to civil actions. In 1674 the upper house of assembly had asked the lower house to cooperate in listing English statutes "touching criminal cases" considered applicable to Maryland and in drafting a bill to cover criminal proceedings. The burgesses, however, had felt that such action would deprive them of desirable protections and had asked instead that the act of 1662 be amended to include criminal as well as civil matters. In their view, all, not just selected, "Lawes of England ought to be esteemed & Adjudged of full force & Power within this Province." Such a general extension of the criminal law had probably seemed to the governor and council dangerous to the position of Roman Catholics and Quakers, and no action either way had been taken.[38]

Soon after Lord Baltimore's statement to the Lords of Trade and before his return to Maryland, the assembly of 1678 took steps to make his description more precisely correct. It repealed both the act of 1646 and the act of 1662, and replaced them with an illegal revival of part of an act of 1663. This was nearly a duplicate of the act of 1662, and why it had been passed initially is a mystery. The error had evidently been quickly recognized, for the act of 1662 had been regularly revived, the act of 1663, never. The Second Lord Baltimore had disallowed the act of 1663 in 1669, and the assembly had listed it as repealed

[38] Acts 1646, c. 2, *ibid.*, I, 210; Acts 1662, c. 3, 448, revived 1664, 1666, 1669, 1671, 1676, 537; II, 150, 216, 336, 355, 348, 368 (quotation), 369, 370, 371, 374–75. The 1662 act was not revived in 1674 or 1674/75 in the course of the battle over extension of English criminal law.

in 1676. But in 1678 the Act for Revival listed this act with the following comment: "These words (soe farr as the Court shall Judge them English laws not inconsistant with the Condicion of this Province) . . . are not to stand Revived." Thus did the assembly sneak through, as it were, an implied assertion of its sole power to alter English law to fit the "condicon of this Province," at least in civil proceedings.[39]

This assembly held in the proprietor's absence was of great importance, for it followed an attempted revolt of 1676, and it passed some basic legislation. Among the main grievances of the rebels had been the property qualification for voting first introduced in 1670 and the high taxes paid since by those thus disenfranchised. In a complaint to the crown, sympathizers hinted at popish plots and deplored the state of the Protestant church in the colony. They pointed to severe penalties for sedition against the proprietor and accused him of usurping a position that in their view belonged by right only to the king. The fact that in 1676 the new Lord Baltimore had called only two of the burgesses for each county instead of the elected four had also aroused suspicion that he aimed at a destruction of English liberties.[40] The lower house of 1678, the one elected in 1676 and with all its members called, was probably not much concerned with the disenfranchisement of the poor or with a Catholic conspiracy, but it was certainly sympathetic to many of the other grievances. Governor Thomas Notley and his council were obliged to act with tact.

This assembly attempted to establish two constitutional principles of importance. The first was the removal of judicial discretion in applying English law, just discussed; the second was the establishment of election procedures by act of assembly in-

[39] Acts 1678, c. 16, *ibid.*, VII, 82; Acts 1664, c. 4, I, 487, disallowed 1669, II, 157–58, repealed 1676, 545, revived 1678, 1681, 1682, VII, 82, 214, 245, 328, 436. The Act for Proceedings at Law of 1663 is officially described as having passed in 1664, because the session of 1663 was adjourned, not prorogued, to the following year.
[40] *Ibid.*, V, 134–52.

stead of by Lord Baltimore's prerogative. The act followed the proprietor's writs for election in most details, including the property qualifications, but with one critical difference: Henceforth the writs were to state the date, formerly omitted, on which the assembly was to convene; and the burgesses elected were to appear on that date without further notice. Thus the summoning of all four delegates was ensured.[41]

In addition this assembly helped bring about a major increase in the civil jurisdiction of the county court, thereby decreasing the importance of the Provincial Court manned by members of the council. The lower house several times requested such expansion. In the proprietor's absence, Governor Notley had no power to alter the county commissions, but the pressure thus exercised was successful. Upon his return as proprietor early in 1679, Lord Baltimore created a Commission for the Trial of Causes, which allowed the county justices to hear and determine most actions for the collection of debts.[42] In the meantime, the assembly of 1678 passed an act that allowed the justices to make rules of court. It also passed an act to regulate a procedure for "appeals" so worded that the Provincial Court could no longer consider the merits of a case so brought before it. Instead, like the courts of common law in England, it was to confine itself on review to procedural and legal points. By 1681 the upper house was trying to reverse this provision of the act, but without success.[43]

In general, it must be noted, this upgrading of the lower courts was not the subject of conflict. The new jurisdiction met a need that the proprietor and his councillors recognized, and in any event the number of causes that fell into the new county

[41] Acts 1678, c. 3, *ibid.*, VII, 60–63.

[42] *Ibid.*, 23, 28, 31–32; XV, 253–56.

[43] Acts 1678, c. 7, *ibid.*, VII, 70–71; Acts 1678, c. 8, 71–73 (on appeals), revived through 1688, 216, 247, 330, 438; XIII, 125, 141, 212; VII, 223, 293. The upper house succeeded in insisting that causes it heard on appeal from the Provincial Court be tried on the merits of the cause (224–26, 361).

jurisdiction was not yet large. Serious objections to granting such power to untrained magistrates did not arise for another twenty years, when the amount of litigation for large sums was much greater. Nevertheless, the proposals and legislation of 1678 were the beginning of a long campaign to expand the power and authority of the county rulers at the expense of the governor and council and the central courts—a campaign that long outlived the seventeenth-century proprietary policy of reserving the chief provincial posts for a narrow circle of Roman Catholics and Calvert relatives.[44]

Other legislation of the assembly of 1678 also responded to grievances, although with less basic solutions. A stiff law for Sunday observance satisfied Protestant moralism and incidentally gave the county justices sitting individually their first powers to punish an offense.[45] An act to enable the county court to veto renewal of sheriffs' appointments was a new step toward local control of this powerful arm of the proprietor.[46] Finally, this assembly gave the county courts control of pressmasters, officers first authorized in 1676. Only pressmasters had authority to impress supplies, and then only in time of war and on order of the governor. By act of 1678 the county courts gained the exclusive right to appoint two pressmasters for each hundred.[47]

The most controversial acts of this assembly controlled election procedure and cancelled legislative authority for the discretion of judges in applying English law. These statutes pro-

[44] For this struggle in the eighteenth century, see Ellefson, "County Courts and Provincial Court," 73–92, 116–52; "Royal Period," chapter 5. Appendix C, below, indicates the extent to which the new civil jurisdiction actually expanded county court business at first.

[45] Acts 1678, c. 1, *Md. Archives*, VII, 51–53, disallowed 1684, XIII, 49, 108.

[46] Acts 1678, c. 6, *ibid.*, 68–70, revived only through 1684, 216, 247, 329, 438; XIII, 125; see also p. 13 above.

[47] Acts 1676, c. 8, *ibid.*, II, 557–60; Acts 1678, c. 2, VII, 57; Acts 1681, c. 1, 192, revived through 1688, 247, 330, 438; XIII, 126, 141, 212. A hundred was a subdivision of a county.

vided fuel for conflict that extended well beyond these issues from this time until the revolution of 1689.

The first battles were over election procedure. Lord Baltimore, when he called the assembly of 1681, disallowed the Act for Elections of 1678 and announced that future writs would call for only two delegates from each county. Such action was a slap at the lower house. On the other hand, with this decision he conceded the right of all delegates elected to be called and gave up the opportunities for manipulation that selection of two out of four would have allowed him. In addition, he called all the delegates to this session. No election had been held since 1676, however, and attrition since then had been heavy. The lower house refused to take up any business, even defense of the frontier, for which it had been convened, until writs were issued for holding by-elections to fill vacancies.[48] In addition, the proprietor's effort to exclude John Coode from the assembly for his recent complicity in the alleged rebellion of 1681 probably also failed. Coode was currently free on bail while awaiting trial.[49]

The lower house won the battle for a full assembly but it may have lost a campaign. Lord Baltimore at first had expressed willingness to accept a new act for elections, provided it called for only two delegates per county. The burgesses seem to have been momentarily willing to accept this reduction for the future, but they insisted on a clause allowing the speaker to issue writs of election for filling vacancies, as was the practice in the House of Commons. After bitter words, no act passed. The next year, following a new election, the proprietor refused even to consider an act. Instead he established procedures by proclama-

---

[48] *Ibid.*, XV, 378–79; VII, 120–22, 124–28, 134.

[49] *Ibid.*, 135–39. The precise disposition of the exclusion effort is uncertain, but Coode probably sat in the November session before his trial and he definitely served in the last session of this assembly, April–May 1682. The Provincial Court cleared Coode of the treason charge (V, 329–32; VII, 261).

tion. These were similar to those laid down by the act of 1678, except that only two delegates per county could be elected, and there was added a conciliatory provision that the speaker could request writs of election to vacancies from the provincial secretary, although the speaker still could not issue the writs himself. The lower house was not satisfied. It tried to bargain for an act the following year in return for passage of the act for towns, but without success.[50] Election procedure remained grounded on prerogative, not the will of the assembly.

The proprietor's dissent to the Act for Elections raised the general constitutional issue of his right to veto legislation. It was not a new question, for severe discontent had followed Cecil Calvert's disallowance in 1669 of six laws, some of which had been in effect nearly seven years.[51] The better organized assemblies of 1681 through 1684 attempted to save the legislation of 1678 and to limit the proprietor's veto rights for the future.

The lower house, of course, could not deny Lord Baltimore the power clearly granted by his charter to disallow laws. It followed instead another tack. In 1681 it seems to have argued that Charles Calvert had empowered Governor Notley to act for him, making disallowance of any act of the assembly of 1678 illegal. The house tried to persuade the upper house to agree that these acts could be repealed only with the consent of both houses, as would be true of any act that had received proprietary assent. This approach having failed, the lower house of 1683 tried another. By now the Act of Elections was a lost cause, but others needed protection. An Act to Ascertain the True Force and Validity of the Laws first of all made future dissents impossible once twenty months had passed since enactment of a law; second, it attempted to confirm the perpetual laws of 1678 not yet vetoed. If His Lordship assented to this act of confirma-

[50] *Ibid.*, 120–22, 124, 345, 346, 354, 355, 452, 474, 480, 486–89, 491, 492, 494, 496, 513; XVII, 16–17; Kammen, "Causes of the Maryland Revolution," 298–99.

[51] Kammen, "Causes of the Maryland Revolution," 299–300.

tion he could not later disallow any acts therein mentioned. Not surprisingly, the act foundered on this very point, for the upper house refused to include the vital Act for Repeal, which had rescinded all legislation that gave judges discretion in applying English law. To omit this Act for Repeal, insisted the lower house, was "to leave so many Laws at an uncertainty" as "no ways becomes the Prudence of both houses."[52]

The climax to this struggle came in 1684. Lord Baltimore was about to leave for England to defend his grant from the claims of the Penns. He asked the assembly to settle the laws, permanent and temporary, to its satisfaction before his departure. Both the restrictions on dissents and an act to state a rule of judicature that would clarify the standing of English law at once became major issues. Lord Baltimore admitted that during the debates of 1681 he had agreed to dissent to laws within eighteen months, but he now was unwilling by act of assembly to commit his heirs to less than three years, the length of time allowed for the trial of temporary laws. He also refused to accept any act that extended the laws of England without a clause allowing his judges to determine whether these were suitable to conditions in Maryland. In consequence, no act passed.[53]

Lord Baltimore did more, however. His last act of the session was to disallow all the acts passed in his absence by the assembly of 1678, excepting only those to which he had assented since his return.[54] The temporary laws of that year were thus saved, since he had assented to their revival in later sessions of assembly. These included the acts that allowed the county justices to make rules of court, defined procedures for appeals, and permitted county court veto of sheriffs' reappointments. But the crucial Act for Repeal fell[55] and with it the repeal of the Act

[52] *Md. Archives*, VII, 152–53, 160–61, 235, 236, 508, 510, 512 (quotation).

[53] *Ibid.*, XIII, 31, 33–36, 38–40, 43; Kammen, "Causes of the Maryland Revolution," 303–04.

[54] *Md. Archives*, XIII, 49.

[55] Thomas Bacon in his *Laws of Maryland with Proper Indexes* (An-

for Judicature of 1646. The repeal of the act of 1662 also fell, but it needed to be revived to be in effect. The reviving act for this session had already been passed, however, and without any Act for Proceedings at Law.[56] Thus Charles Calvert unequivocally re-established the power of his Provincial Court, and thus in effect his council, to determine what laws of England should extend where Maryland law was silent, and he reasserted his right to veto any laws to which he had not personally assented.

Other conflicts arose from this attempt to revise the laws and fueled later grievances. The lower house was eager to amend the oath of fidelity to include a reservation of allegiance to the crown, but no agreement could be reached with the upper house. The latter was willing to amend the Act for Deserted Plantations, of which the lower house had complained as early as 1674, but only if the burgesses could devise a means to ensure payment of proprietary quitrents. The act, which allowed the proprietor to regrant lands if more than three years of rent were in arrears, remained unchanged. Finally, the lower house wanted to soften the act of 1649 that established penalties for sedition against the proprietor. Under this act, two leaders of the incipient rebellion of 1676 had been executed and George Godfrey and Josias Fendall had been punished in 1681. Lord Baltimore was willing only that the judges should confine their sentencing

---

napolis, 1765) does not list the Act for Repeal as disallowed. Perhaps he concluded that Lord Baltimore's dissent to part of it in 1681 (*Md. Archives*, VII, 188) implied consent to the rest. Joseph H. Smith follows Bacon in stating that at the end of the proprietary period Maryland courts were to apply English law without discretion ("Foundations of Law in Maryland," 98). However, no sense can be made of the debates of 1684 by this interpretation. Kammen, "Causes of the Maryland Revolution," 301–2, mistakenly supposes that all eighteen acts of 1678 were vetoed. He also supposes that the acts that prohibited sale or embezzlement of His Lordship's "ordinance" referred to copies of the charter and laws and infers therefrom efforts of the proprietor and his council to keep the people ignorant of the contents of these documents.

[56] Acts 1684, c. 6, *Md. Archives*, XIII, 123–26.

to one or two of the punishments listed. Nothing was done.[57]

The sessions of the 1680's also saw efforts of the lower house to increase recognition of its claim to the privileges of the House of Commons. It invoked the right to judge the qualifications of its own members in resisting the upper house's efforts to unseat Coode in 1681. It fought, although unsuccessfully, for the speaker's writ of election, and after the election of 1682 the speaker's petition for "freedom of Speech in their house and Other their Antient Priviledges" was by the proprietor "allowed them as formerly had been" in accordance with traditions of Parliament. In that same session the lower house refused to receive messengers from the upper house until they removed their swords.[58] The last proprietary assembly before the coup of 1689 spent days wrangling over privilege. The new president of the council, William Joseph, demanded that the burgesses take the oath of fidelity to the proprietor, which they refused on the ground that no such oath was ever demanded of the House of Commons. Joseph at first charged that their refusal implied rebellion but was in the end reduced to a stratagem to obtain the oath. He prorogued the assembly for two days. During the interim the burgesses took the oath, but as individuals, not as members of the lower house. During the same session the lower house showed unmistakably that it was not under the control of the upper house. It refused to attend the upper house on command, claiming that only the proprietor or his representative sitting there could call them. The upper house had to insist that "his Lordship . . . is always present in his Upper house of Assembly."[59]

[57] *Ibid.*, 31, 33–35, 38, 39, 48, 49, 61, 77, 80, 82 (quotation). Criminal proceedings of 1676–77 for the Provincial Court are lost, but we know that Pate and Davis were hanged (V, 143; *Cal. S. P., Col., 1677–80*, no. 12). For the trials of Fendall, Coode, and Godfrey, see *Md. Archives*, V, 312–34.

[58] *Md. Archives*, VII, 135–39, 335, 414.

[59] *Ibid.*, XIII, 153–63, 159 (quotation). Kammen, "Causes of the Maryland Revolution," 305–6, offers other examples. For a general survey of the development of parliamentary privilege in the colonies, see Mary

Nearly all these controversies, legal and constitutional, showed the concern of the burgesses to maintain what they saw as their rights as Englishmen in the face of an old-fashioned charter and a proprietor determined to retain the prerogatives therein granted. An act to establish election procedures seemed the surest guarantee that the right to free elections would be preserved. A determined pursuit of parliamentary privilege was necessary to establish lower-house independence. A limitation on the time allowed for proprietary veto strengthened the legislative position of the assembly and the force of its acts. The anxiety to extend all of English law with modification only by act of assembly was also rooted in a fear of proprietary power. Attitudes on this last subject were to suffer change during the period of royal government.

These disputes in the assembly reflected some of the major concerns of landowners or merchants who had attained wealth and status sufficient for seeking and winning election.[60] They had the fears and discontents of a group in power, determined to improve its position. The attitudes of less well-to-do men are harder to discover, but the two attempted rebellions of these years shed some light on their concerns. The first was in August–September 1676, and following the execution of its leaders a "Complaint from Heaven with a Huy and Crye and a petition out of Virginia and Maryland" was addressed to the crown and Parliament. This bitter document, which eventually reached the Lords of Trade, tells that "a great many of us came in servants to others," clear suggestion of support for the protest from settlers of low economic status. High taxes—"Within this two years, the fourth parts of poore peoples livelyhood"—were a recurring theme. Yet the frontier remained unprotected, the levies being

---

Pattison Clarke, *Parliamentary Privilege in the American Colonies* (New Haven, 1943).

[60] Menard's chart "Major Office Holders" (see n. 17) demonstrates for three counties the relationships of wealth in land and personality to membership in the assembly.

"onely to maintaine my Lord and his Champions in their prince-ship." Many issues surfaced here that were later to arise in the assembly: the limitation of delegates, the exercise of veto many years after passage of acts, the oath of fidelity without allegiance reserved to the crown, the severe punishments for sedition against the proprietor. Also mentioned were Lord Baltimore's refusal to accept an act that allowed peaceful possession of land for five years to constitute ownership. The act had aimed to correct a serious evil, for ignorance and losses of records had left title in doubt for lands taken up or purchased in good faith; but the act would also, in effect, have allowed squatters to acquire land for nothing.

The most insistent theme, besides complaint of high taxes, was anti-Catholicism. Lord Baltimore was accused of discouraging Protestant churches, giving power mostly to Catholics and rela-tives, even conspiring with the French and Northern Indians to destroy the Maryland Protestants. The "Complaint from Heaven" begged that the crown appoint a Protestant gover-nor, send troops to guard the frontier, and establish Protestant churches.[61]

This anti-Catholic feeling had found expression earlier in the colony's history in Protestant-led rebellions against proprietary authority in 1645–1647 and in 1660.[62] Anti-Catholic rumbles evidently also accompanied the agitations of 1681. Perhaps the supposed ringleaders did not intend armed revolt, but observers in Virginia believed that discontent was strong, and Lord Balti-more assured his critics in London that rebellion, Bacon-style, had been afoot. Those arrested this time were men of status and substance: former governor Josias Fendall (leader of the mal-contents of 1660), Captain George Godfrey, Delegate John Coode. Depositions taken at their trials reflect the same under-

---

[61] *Md. Archives,* V, 134–52; 140, 143, 144 (quotations); Sparks, *Causes of the Maryland Revolution,* 69–73; Acts 1663, c. 7, *Md. Archives,* I, 787–89.

[62] *Colonial Period,* II, 308–9, 322–23.

current of anti-Catholic fear that characterized the "Complaint" of 1677, a fear that these men must have hoped to inflame if they indeed had planned rebellion.[63]

Behind this fear may have been a growing sense of discomfort at the failure of most Protestant communities to maintain churches. An unintended consequence of toleration had been the forming of few congregations other than those established by denominations which had found asylum in Maryland, the Roman Catholics and the Quakers. In 1689 these groups included less than 30 per cent of the population.[64] The majority of settlers were not churchgoers, and second- and third-generation Marylanders had never lived with the religious routines that were taken for granted in England, regardless of specific beliefs. In 1676 there were only three Anglican churches in the colony, and reports of dissolute life and recommendations for the establishment of the Church of England were reaching the Anglican Bishop of London and the Lords of Trade. Lord Baltimore successfully withstood pressures for such action. He claimed that the population "doe consist of Presbiterians, Independents, Anabaptists and Quakers, those of the Church of England as well as those of the Romish being the fewest"; these dissenting groups

[63] *Md. Archives*, V, 312–34; *Cal. S. P., Col., 1681–85*, nos. 180, 184, 185, 195, 260, 275, 319, 391.

[64] There are no reliable figures. In 1700 Commissary Thomas Bray set the number at 10 per cent of the population and Quakers alone at about 8 per cent. He may, however, have underestimated the number of Roman Catholics, for in 1708 there were at least 2,974 Roman Catholics and in 1710 the total population was given as 42,741 persons, making Catholics alone about 7 per cent of the total. Thus Bray's figure for Roman Catholics and Quakers combined probably should have been at least 15 per cent. The proportion was undoubtedly higher in 1689, however. Supposing there were about 6,500 Catholics and Quakers in 1708 and that their numbers had not dwindled since 1689, they would have constituted 26 per cent of the 25,000 people estimated as inhabitants of Maryland in 1688. See *Md. Archives*, XX, 81; XXV, 358–59; Evarts B. Greene and Virginia D. Harrington, *American Population before the Federal Census of 1790* (New York, 1932), 3; H. C. Thompson, *Thomas Bray* (London, 1954), 50.

were not likely to vote taxes to support the Anglican church. In 1678 the Lords of Trade recommended a plan for public support of a Protestant, not just Anglican, ministry, but not surprisingly Lord Baltimore did nothing.[65]

Nevertheless, Lord Baltimore's Protestant supporters were aware of an unmet need. William Stevens, an Anglican member of the council, wrote to Presbyterian leaders in Northern Ireland to request ministers for the growing number of Presbyterians in Somerset, and in consequence Francis Makemie arrived in 1683 to begin his missionary work in the colonies. Michael and Mary Taney of Calvert County, vigorous supporters of the proprietor in 1689, petitioned James II and the Archbishop of Canterbury for help in maintaining "an Orthodox Divine at Calvert Towne," lest neglect be "the utter ruine of many poore Souls."[66] This concern had not produced much result, however. Most Maryland planters had failed to give voluntarily. In 1689 there were probably no more than six Anglican and three Presbyterian ministers in Maryland, not all with settled congregations.[67]

[65] *Md. Archives*, V, 130–32, 133 (quotation); *Cal. S. P., Col., 1675–76*, no. 1005; *1677–80*, nos. 348, 349. On Dec. 22, 1690, John Coode told English officials that "of all the persuasions there the Church of England have had the least encouragement and respect" (*Md. Archives*, VIII, 225).

[66] *Old Somerset*, 214–15; Tanner mss., Bodleian Library, Oxford University, ff. 137 (quotation), 138, 139.

[67] Nelson Waite Rightmyer, *Maryland's Established Church* (Lebanon, Pa., 1956), 17–20, 135–50, 161–71, 192, 198, 207, 216; *Md. Archives*, XX, 106–11. During the 1650's and 1670's two Presbyterian ministers served a Presbyterian congregation in Charles County, but after 1679 there was none until 1704. Three Presbyterian ministers settled in Somerset County after 1683. Since there were also three Quaker meetings there by 1689, Somerset emerges as the county best supplied with active Protestant congregations. Quakers had meetings in Kent, Talbot, Anne Arundel, and Calvert counties. A community of Labadists had settled in Cecil County. Roman Catholics were concentrated in St. Mary's and Charles counties. *Old Somerset*, 85–111, 118, 215, 221, 222–23, 226–32, 236–37, 528n–529n; J. William McIlvain, *Early Presbyterianism in Maryland*, Notes Supplementary to the Johns Hopkins University Studies in History and Political Science, series VII, nos. 5–6 (Baltimore, 1890), 7–13;

This gap in the accustomed institutional framework of society may well have contributed to the unrest expressed in the disturbances of 1676 and 1681 and the final overthrow of proprietary government in 1689. Newcomers had to make severe adjustments to a new life. There were no villages, no commons to help support the poor, no ancient local customs to guide human relations. Sufficient churches and ministers would have filled a need.

The economic pinch of the 1680's affected all groups but hit the poorest especially hard and must have contributed to their uneasiness. Men who had finished servitude were finding it more difficult than earlier to obtain credit for stocking a plantation. Those who were leasing land or sharecropping could not easily accumulate capital toward taking up a land grant or purchasing land. Small land-owning planters faced rising costs for English manufactures at the same time that income was falling. Opportunity for men who started without capital must have noticeably diminished.[68]

Proprietary land policy, furthermore, must have been a source of anxiety to all landowners, or would-be landowners, rich as

---

Phebe R. Jacobson, *Quaker Records in Maryland*, Hall of Records Commission Publication no. 14 (Annapolis, 1966), introduction; J. Reaney Kelly, *Quakers in the Founding of Anne Arundel County* (Baltimore, 1963); Kenneth L. Carroll, "Maryland Quakers in the Seventeenth Century," *MHM*, XLVII (1952), 297–313; Bartlett B. James, *The Labadist Colony in Maryland*, Johns Hopkins University Studies in Historical and Political Science, series XVII, no. 6 (Baltimore, 1899); Thomas Hughes, *History of the Society of Jesus in North America, Colonial and Federal*, 4 vols. (London, 1907–17), text, vols. I and II.

[68] Russell R. Menard, "From Servant to Freeholder: Status Mobility and Property Accumulation in Seventeenth-Century Maryland," *William and Mary Quarterly*, 3rd ser., XXX (1973), 37–64. Unpublished research of Menard indicates that the 1670's saw an upswing in the tobacco economy, but that the 1680's were a time of depression. Jacob Price has suggested that this decade began a period of stagnation which lasted well into the eighteenth century. "The Economic Growth of the Chesapeake and the European Market," *Journal of Economic History*, XXIV, no. 4 (1964), 496–511.

well as poor. In 1683 Lord Baltimore abandoned the headright system whereby he granted rights to fifty acres of land for every person transported to his colony. Instead each demandant was to pay caution money of 100 pounds of tobacco—raised in 1684 to 120 pounds—for the right to each fifty acres. The proprietor explained that his purpose was to end speculation in rights to land. Newcomers or shipowners who had brought cargoes of servants had been selling the rights, which were then resold at dear rates. For the same reason he ended his policy of granting fifty-acre rights to men who had finished their servitude. The cost of the change to settlers was minimal, since the caution money was a small portion of the total cost of taking up a grant of land. On the other hand, this radical change from a policy established fifty years before was dramatic proof of the proprietary power over the livelihood of every settler.[69]

Proprietary power to reclaim escheated land was an additional source of friction. In the early 1670's Cecil Calvert established procedures to determine escheats through inquisitions by juries of the neighborhood, but there were complaints that lands were regranted before these legal steps had been finished. It was to be of importance that three revolutionary leaders, John Coode, Kenelm Cheseldyne, and Nehemiah Blackiston, all sons-in-law of Thomas Gerard, had suffered from Gerard's failure to establish his rights to 1,000 acres of "Snow Hill Manor" in the face of Lord Baltimore's rights of escheat.[70]

There was also dissatisfaction over fees. Both rich and poor suffered from the centralized system of probate, which required

[69] *Md. Archives*, XVII, 142–43, 239–41; *Cal. S. P., Col., 1681–85*, no. 1070; Kammen, "Causes of the Maryland Revolution," 310.

[70] John Kilty, *The Landholders Assistant and Land-Office Guide* . . . (Baltimore, 1808), 177–86; *Md. Archives*, VIII, 102, 215, 219; Kammen, "Causes of the Maryland Revolution," 322. The rebels complained that the proprietor claimed as escheat land given as bequests to Protestant churches, presumably by men without heirs. No example has been found, but this charge, like others, was probably based upon at least one instance.

either that administrators make expensive journeys to St. Mary's City or pay double fees for a special local commission to grant the proper authorizations and pass accounts. Proprietary creation, furthermore, of new fee-collecting officers could seem an unfair burden. One of these, His Lordship's attorney in the county (later called the clerk of the indictments), was to provide improvements in law enforcement, but he had no English counterpart. His existence without authorization by act of assembly was the subject of complaint when the rebels of 1689 came to justify their coup.[71]

Of all the causes of anxiety, however, whether felt by humble leaseholder or large landowner, the proprietors' policy of appointing Roman Catholics and close relatives to provincial offices was perhaps the most critical. Despite repeated claims to the contrary, this policy was evident. During the volatile years from 1666 to 1689 twenty-seven men sat on the Maryland Council (see Table 1). At least fourteen of that number were professed Roman Catholics; there were only eight known Protestants, while the religious affiliation of five councillors remains uncertain. A total of fifteen, including twelve Catholics and three Protestants, were related by blood or marriage to the immediate proprietary family. These same gentlemen, individually or in small groups, comprised the colony's judiciary above the county level, held most of the highest militia posts, and controlled the land council and other primary patronage positions. An "outsider" of means thus experienced a double frustration: He could not rise to such office himself, and he found men perhaps hostile and at best indifferent to his particular interests making the most important judicial and administrative decisions. Rich or poor, large numbers of settlers paid fees—court fees, port fees, fees for transactions in land or probate—that not only enriched this small group but kept it tied closely to the proprietary interest.

[71] Hartsook and Skordas, *Land Office and Prerogative Court Records*, 88; *Md. Archives*, VIII, 219; "County Government," text, 283–85.

Table 1. Proprietary councillors, 1666–1689

Councillor	Years on Council	Religion	Relations	County
Philip Calvert	1656–1682	Catholic	Brother of 2nd Lord Baltimore	St. Mary's
Baker Brooke	1658–1678/79	Catholic	Married to niece of 2nd Lord Baltimore	Calvert
Edward Lloyd	1658–1668	Protestant	Carried over from Puritan government	Anne Arundel
Henry Coursey	1660–1670 1676–1684	Protestant	Appointed by close friend, Philip Calvert	Talbot
Jerome White	1662–1670	Catholic(?)		St. Mary's
William Evans	1664–1668/69	Catholic		St. Mary's
Thomas Trueman	1665–1676 1683–1685/86	Protestant		Calvert
Richard Boughton*	1666–1667	Protestant		Charles
William Calvert	1669–1682	Catholic	Nephew of 2nd Lord Baltimore	St. Mary's
Samuel Chew	1669–1676/77	Protestant		Anne Arundel
William Talbot	1670–73	Catholic	Nephew of 2nd Lord Baltimore	St. Mary's

Table 1. (continued)

Councillor	Years on Council	Religion	Relations	County
Edward Fitzherbert	1670/71–1673	Catholic(?)		St. Mary's
Jesse Wharton	1672–1676	Catholic	Married to stepdaughter of 3rd Lord Baltimore	Charles
Thomas Taylor	1673–1688/89	Protestant		Anne Arundel
Thomas Notley	1676–1679	Protestant convert(?)		St. Mary's
Benjamin Rozer	1677–1681	Protestant; wife Catholic	Married to stepdaughter of 3rd Lord Baltimore	Charles
Vincent Lowe	1679–1689	Catholic	Brother-in-law of 3rd Lord Baltimore	Talbot
Henry Darnall	1679–1689	Catholic	Cousin of 3rd Lord Baltimore by marriage	Calvert
William Stevens	1679–1687	Protestant		Somerset
William Digges	1679/80–1689	Protestant; wife Catholic	Married to stepdaughter of 3rd Lord Baltimore	St. Mary's
George Talbot	1679/80–1684	Catholic	Cousin of 3rd Lord Baltimore	Cecil
William Burgess	1682–1686/87	Protestant	Daughter married to stepson of 3rd Lord Baltimore	Anne Arundel

Table 1. (continued)

Councillor	Years on Council	Religion	Relations	County
Edward Pye	1683–1689	Catholic	Married to stepdaughter of 3rd Lord Baltimore	Charles
John Darnall	1683–1684	Catholic	Brother of Henry Darnall	Calvert
Nicholas Sewall	1683–1689	Catholic	Stepson of 3rd Lord Baltimore	St. Mary's
Clement Hill	1685–1689	Catholic	Brother-in-law of Henry Darnall	St. Mary's
William Joseph	1688–1689	Catholic	Appointed president of Council from England	St. Mary's

*Boughton sat briefly on the council by virtue of his one-year tenure as secretary of Maryland, a post which brought automatic status as a councillor. Others who first gained access to the council through this office included Philip Calvert, William Calvert, William Talbot, John Darnall, and Nicholas Sewall.

The interlocking offices and relationships its members enjoyed made redress of injustice by any one officer or group difficult or impossible to obtain—or so it seemed, at least. Such conditions could arouse hysterical fears of popish plots and the enslavement of free Englishmen.[72]

Complaints of religious favoritism filtered back to England from neighboring Virginia officials as well as disgruntled Maryland settlers. These reports had become especially numerous by 1681, and accompanied by the unsuccessful revolt in the colony that year, they provoked the Lords of Trade to upbraid Lord Baltimore. The days of complete freedom without interference from Whitehall were ending. Disturbed "that there is partiallity and favour shewed on all occasions towards those of the Popish Religion to the discouragement of his Majestie's Protestant Subjects," the Lords admonished Baltimore "to cause the same if true to be speedily redressed," and to express his trust and confidence in the Protestants by placing the colony's arms and ammunition in their safekeeping.[73]

The proprietor hastened to defend himself by forwarding to the Lords a complete list of the council members and the militia colonels with the religion of each individual specified. In a spirit of vindication, he noted that four of the current eight councillors were Protestants and that nine of the twelve militia commanders were likewise non-Catholics.[74] As an additional endorsement of his policies, he enlisted the testimony of twenty-five high-ranking Protestants who dispatched a declaration to England denying the charges of discrimination against non-Catholics. They stressed the eminence of many Protestants and discussed in detail the officers whom Baltimore had more briefly mentioned.[75]

[72] *HLP* contains a revealing discussion of officers and their fees.
[73] *Cal. S. P., Col., 1681–85*, nos. 184, 260, 275; *Md. Archives*, V, 300–301 (quotation); Kammen, "Causes of the Maryland Revolution," 296.
[74] *Md. Archives*, V, 309–10; 348–50; *Cal. S. P., Col., 1681–85*, no. 349.
[75] *Md. Archives*, V, 353–55.

The casual Whitehall official might have been satisfied by these vindications and by Baltimore's commissioning of a Protestant, William Burgess, to join the council on October 12, 1682. What in both instances the proprietor and his faithful adherents failed to make clear, however, and which was well known in the colony, were the ties of family and friendship overshadowing religious allegiances. William Digges, one of the four Protestant councillors in 1681, was married to Baltimore's stepdaughter, and his promotion to the council had followed that marriage. A second, Henry Coursey, had been for many years the special friend and assistant of Philip Calvert, half-brother of Cecilius, the Second Lord Baltimore; Philip had first appointed him during a brief tenure as chief executive of the colony in 1660. The other two non-Catholics, William Stevens and Thomas Taylor, had gained admission to the council as rewards for exceptional services rendered the proprietor. Stevens was a major figure in the successful settlement of the lower Eastern Shore, which preserved Baltimore's claims in that region against encroachment from Virginia. Taylor, during his tenure as speaker of the lower house, was instrumental in obtaining the export duty of two shillings per hogshead of tobacco. Burgess, supposedly appointed as an indication of Baltimore's fairness to Protestants, had recently become the father-in-law of Baltimore's favored stepson, Nicholas Sewall, who joined him on the council the following year. Burgess had been active in county politics for more than thirty years, and for at least fifteen years he had been perhaps the most influential Protestant of Anne Arundel county; yet he was denied a council seat until the fateful marriage that committed him to the proprietary interest. At sixty years of age, he was considerably older than most men appointed during the proprietary period. Burgess was the last Protestant to become a councillor before the 1689 revolution; five more Catholics were appointed in the intervening period, four of whom were related to Lord Baltimore.[76]

[76] *Ibid.*, XVII, 118, 131; LXIX, xi; Sparks, *Causes of the Maryland*

When the proprietor sailed for England in 1684 to defend his boundary claims and charter, he left political power firmly concentrated in his council, commissioning them as deputy governors under his minor son, Leonard. Otherwise, the post of acting chief executive might have been expected to fall to Taylor, the senior member of the council in years of service, and a Protestant. In fact, Baltimore actually promoted his Catholic cousin, George Talbot, to the number-one place on the commission, a move he quickly regretted.[77] Henry Coursey, his patron Philip Calvert being dead, was removed from the council, and Baltimore later expressed considerable anger from England over the council's continued kindnesses to Coursey.[78]

As the troubles of the 1680's mounted, primary power descended correspondingly on the favored few. Henry Darnall, Baltimore's Catholic cousin by marriage, Sewall, and Digges became a ruling triumvirate among the deputy governors. Their presence was required for any significant action, and they alone held the authority to appoint men to certain positions. Individually, they controlled the land office, the secretary's office, the collection of the proprietor's revenue, and the keeping and use of the provincial seal, in addition to numerous special judicial functions.[79] The importance of the remaining Protestants on the council continued to decline. Thomas Trueman, probably a Protestant and not a relative, had died by early 1686. After Burgess died in 1686 and Stevens in 1687/88, Taylor represented in 1688 the only Protestant councillor not related to the proprietor, and he left the colony to return to England in February of 1688/89.[80]

Revolution, 40, 70; *HLP,* 95–96, 118, 125; *Old Somerset,* 326–29. Similar considerations had been prominent in the appointments of other Protestants earlier.

[77] *Md. Archives,* XVII, 247–50, 252–53.

[78] *Ibid.,* 252–53; VIII, 15. Coursey had continued to sit when the council functioned as the upper house of assembly.

[79] *HLP, passim; Md. Archives,* XVII, 426–37.

[80] Wills 4, ff. 165, 242, 296; *Md. Archives,* VIII, 66; the 1688 commission is on 42.

While the proprietor himself had been resident in Maryland, he had effectively countered any real thrusts against his authority. However, the system of divided leadership devised when circumstances forced his return to England in 1684 proved unable to govern cooperatively. Had Philip or William Calvert, the proprietor's uncle and cousin respectively, been still alive, they might have been able to exercise control, but both had died the previous year. The proprietor had hardly sailed before a catastrophe undermined public confidence in the deputy officials. The president of the council, George Talbot, murdered Christopher Rousby, the king's collector, and Talbot's successful escape and months of hiding raised suspicions that the deputy governors were conniving to prevent his capture.[81] Maladministration of various kinds followed: Militia officers impressed supplies, bypassing the county pressmasters; the attorney general had men bound over to appear at the Provincial Court without showing the cause for appearance; the secretary doubled his fees for land grants and ordered the naval officers to collect other fees in his name not legally authorized. The assembly of 1688 complained of all these acts but received little satisfaction.[82] When Charles Calvert himself was in Maryland he could control his officers and dismiss them if necessary, but the deputy governors were powerless to discipline each other, supposing in fact any thought it desirable. The rebels later could complain with plausibility that plural officeholding made redress impossible through ordinary channels.

Lord Baltimore's ultimate effort to restore stability and unified authority in Maryland with the appointment of William Joseph, a Catholic sent in 1688 to be president of the council, proved a disaster. Joseph, an unwelcome stranger, opened his first assembly in October 1688 with the espousal of divine right and proprietary privilege. Days went by in quarrels over his insistence that the delegates take the oath of fidelity to Lord Bal-

[81] Sparks, *Causes of the Maryland Revolution*, 96–97.
[82] *Md. Archives*, XIII, 171–73, 203–4.

timore. Once he had crossed this hurdle, he forced through an act to make the birthday of James II's Catholic heir a day to "be sett a part & kept holy." Only hostility and suspicion could result.[83]

Joseph's first assembly was his last. The passions and aftermath of England's Glorious Revolution soon merged with this local background of discontent to arm a small band of shrewd and ambitious colonists with the weapons necessary to ignite their own successful "Protestant Revolution."

[83] *Ibid.*, 148–63, 184, 185, 209; Acts 1688, c. 1, 210; Sparks, *Causes of the Maryland Revolution*, 98.

CHAPTER II

The "Risinge in Armes," March–September 1689

The heated assembly session of 1688 left considerable hard feelings and discontent among many of the burgesses. Several of them formed the nucleus of leadership during the upheaval which terminated Lord Baltimore's government the following year.

That revolt sounded its first rumblings in March of 1688/89 and owed its inspiration not only to local differences but also to the news of developments abroad. The revolution of 1688 in England and its subsequent effect on the alignment of European powers were much felt in the New World. First rumors and then official reports crossed the Atlantic telling of the overthrow of James II, the accession of William and Mary, and the outbreak of war between Protestant England and Catholic France. Although it was April of 1689 before definitive word reached the colonies, Maryland and her neighbors had been acting and reacting on the basis of incomplete and unofficial news for weeks before.[1]

The Maryland council, "takeing into Consideration the present Juncture of Affaires in England and the likelyhood that now is of warrs," decided to call in the public arms for repairs on January 19. The deputy governors reported their action in a

---

[1] The Virginia council officially proclaimed the new monarchs William and Mary on April 26 (*Executive Journals of Va. Council*, I, 106). On April 1, William Fitzhugh wrote in a letter of "this sudden turn of times in England" (*Fitzhugh*, 250).

letter that same day to Lord Baltimore and their intention to redistribute the repaired arms "into such hands as shall faithfully serve the King your Lordsp and the Country." They alluded to the news of "those troubles with you in England," a clear reference to William of Orange's invasion. This knowledge doubtless had prompted the recall of arms as well as the interception of two private addresses to the crown which the council now forwarded to the proprietor.[2]

It was not hard for men already distrustful and suspicious to read the most sinister motives into these actions by a government that was overwhelmingly Catholic. Other shrewd colonists sensed in the recall of arms an excellent issue with which they could undermine the proprietary authority. Joining with similarly discontented individuals across the Potomac River in Virgina, these men circulated rumors that the papist councillors of Maryland were conspiring with Seneca Indians to kill all the Protestants. Henry Darnall and Edward Pye of the council were particularly cited, as was William Boarman, a prominent Catholic in St. Mary's County. These three men had reputedly told the Indians "they must make haste and kill the Protestants before the shippes come in For after the shippes come the protestants would kill all the papists."[3]

Both the spreading and the acceptance of these rumors were concentrated in the lower Western Shore counties of St. Mary's, Charles, and Calvert, where Maryland's Catholic population was

[2] *Md. Archives*, VIII, 56–57, 62–65, 67. It was later charged that news of William of Orange's landing in England and his "glorious undertakeinge" had reached Maryland before the assembly adjourned December 8, and that the deputy governors "tooke all imaginary Care to Keep the County Ignorant of" this news which precipitated the calling in of arms ("Mariland's Grevances," 403–4). It seems unlikely that more than rumors of an impending invasion could have reached Maryland by December 8.

[3] *Md. Archives*, VIII, 77–78. For detailed secondary accounts of these episodes, see Raphael Semmes, *Captains and Mariners of Early Maryland* (Baltimore, 1937), 644–51, and Bernard C. Steiner, "The Protestant Revolution in Maryland," *Annual Report of the American Historical Association for the Year 1897* (Washington, D.C., 1898), 281–98.

most numerous, and in the Virginia counties of Stafford and
Westmoreland, where many Catholics with close ties to Maryland resided.[4] In both colonies this hostility centered in fiercely
anti-Catholic quarters and was greatly fostered by the activities
of three current or former Anglican ministers. It is no mere co-
incidence that Virginia's "mini" revolt was led by Parson John
Waugh, while John Coode, a former cleric, and John Turling,
one of Maryland's few Anglican ministers, were in the forefront
of the Maryland disturbance.[5] With their encouragement, planters in the two colonies passed along the unsubstantiated rumors
of a Catholic conspiracy. Nine thousand French and Indians had
allegedly landed in Maryland and had already murdered one
family, according to one report; another account increased the
number of invading Indians to 10,000 and had them building
fortifications at the head of the Patuxent River.[6] Still another
rumor recounted the council's promise to supply arms and boats
so that Choptico Indians could battle Protestants on the Eastern
Shore.[7]

The Virginia authorities moved rapidly to halt these "false
and Extravagant reports." They apprehended the primary culprits in that colony for questioning, while the councillors resident in the Northern Neck decisively exercised their authority
and regained control of events. The rumors had originated in an
observation of Indians on an annual hunting expedition south
of the Potomac. A planter, Burr Harrison, had circulated reports
he claimed to have received from one of the Indians that
Pye and other Maryland Catholics were devising a conspiracy.
Waugh had employed these reports in sermons which directed
the emotions of his parishioners against local Catholics. The

[4] For example, see *Fitzhugh*, 251 and *passim*.
[5] See Fairfax Harrison's description of "Parson Waugh's Tumult" in
Landmarks of Old Prince William, 2 vols. (Richmond, 1924), I, 127–42.
[6] *Ibid.*, 130.
[7] *Md. Archives*, VIII, 224.

councillors' investigation found no evidence to support the fears engendered by the rumors.[8]

The Virginia councillors were Protestant and commanded the respect of the colonists, but not so in Maryland. Here the very men who bore the responsibility for quieting the uproar were viewed with grave suspicion. Darnall and Pye were the commanders of the militia in their respective counties, and any use of military support on their part was suspect. The only Protestant on the Maryland council was Colonel William Digges, although he was also related by marriage to the proprietor. It was to him that several of the colonists now turned. Colonel Henry Jowles of Calvert county, a burgess and second in command of the militia under Darnall, appealed to Digges on March 24. "We are all over the Country in a great uproar and Tumult and know not who to apply ourselves too, in whome wee can confidently repose any Trust unless it be your honr whome wee doe all believe to be better principled than to betray the country to the Comon Enemy." Jowles repeated the rumors of Indian fortifications and solicited Digges' advice. The letter can be interpreted as a veiled invitation for the councillor to join forces with the malcontents.[9]

Digges disregarded the invitation, if invitation it was. His allegiance was clearly with the council and with the authorities in Virginia, where he had a large plantation. During the next two weeks, the Maryland council met almost daily in a hurried effort to dispel the growing fears. They undoubtedly recalled that a similar Catholic-Indian "threat" had precipitated the attempted overthrow of the government in 1681. They dispatched investigators and organized special patrols to scour the frontier and reassure the settlers. This action had the desired effect, for the search turned up nothing to validate the rumors. Families that had recently bound together in larger numbers for self-

[8] *Executive Journals of Va. Council*, I, 104; *Fitzhugh*, 251.
[9] *Md. Archives*, VIII, 70–71.

defense now returned to their individual homes, satisfied that they had been misled by "a groundless and imaginary plot." Leading figures in the three counties, many of whom had been active in the circulation of the rumors, were now enlisted to squelch them. Sixteen men, led by Jowles, signed a statement on March 27 that they had "made an Exact scrutiny and Examinacon into all circumstances of this pretended design, and have found it to be nothing but a slevelesse fear and imaginacon fomented by the Artifice of some ill minded persons who are studious and ready to take all occasions of raising a disturbance for their own private and malitious interest."[10]

Six men also accompanied Pye to interrogate the emperor of the Piscataway Indians, who testified that there had been no conspiracy or plot. He attributed the origins of the rumors to a runaway and untrustworthy Indian.[11] Virginia authorities attempted to arraign the Indian and thereby discover who had prompted his spreading of the rumors, but the Indian was killed before he could be taken into custody. Nicholas Spencer, Virginia's secretary, placed the blame for the murder on the same "notorious persons" who had instigated the trouble.[12]

Finally, the Maryland council authorized a thorough search of the area at the mouth of the Patuxent River. Contrary to the rumors, it was void of Indians, French, or papists.[13]

Only three months later, similar rumors circulated once again at the instigation of some of the same men who had been active in both spreading and dispelling accounts of the supposed conspiracy in March. By the summer, however, there was a stronger reason for the population as a whole to accept the anti-Catholic charges, which the leaders of the revolt may or may not have

[10] *Ibid.*, 70–85, 86–87. Both of the above quotations come from the March 27 statement.

[11] *Ibid.*, 90–91.

[12] Spencer to Blathwayt, April 27, 1689, Blathwayt Papers, XVI, Research Library, Colonial Williamsburg, Inc.

[13] *Md. Archives*, VIII, 94.

believed themselves. The council itself had now supplied more potent ammunition than a "groundless and imaginary plot."

The spring fleet had brought official news of the victory of William and Mary and their accession to the English throne. Virginia had proclaimed the new monarchs on April 26 and then had ordered special ceremonies in each county on May 23 to commemorate the event.[14] In other colonies, incumbent governments either made similar proclamations or faced serious opposition. Francis Nicholson's hesitancy in New York precipitated a revolt led by Jacob Leisler, whose revolutionary government promptly proclaimed William and Mary on June 22, 1689. It appears that Marylanders first learned of the New York developments a few days after their own revolt was underway. Leisler himself was well known in Maryland through past and current business ventures with both the government and individual colonists.[15]

Lord Baltimore's colonists were becoming increasingly uneasy over the continued absence of a proclamation from William Joseph, president of the council, and their uneasiness was threatening once again to spread into Virginia. The Marylanders were "rageingly earnest" to recognize the new monarchs, according to Nicholas Spencer's report from Virginia. Some people believed the councillors were deliberately concealing the order of proclamation in their continued support of James II. Spencer feared a rebellion would ensue and "unhinge the whole Constitution of that Government." His fears were prophetic.[16]

There was probably some truth in assertions that the council was inclined to favor James II over the new Protestant rulers, and it is probable that there were indiscreet expressions of these

[14] *Executive Journals of Va. Council*, I, 106–7.

[15] "Mariland's Grevances," 406–7; Michael G. Hall *et al.*, *The Glorious Revolution in America* (Chapel Hill, 1964), 83–140, covers Leisler's Rebellion. For Leisler's previous connections with Maryland, see *Md. Archives*, XV, 262–63; VII, 255; LXVIII, xxii–xxiii.

[16] Spencer to Blathwayt, June 10, 1689, *Md. Archives*, VIII, 112.

opinions.[17] It is less likely, however, that the councillors were withholding the order of proclamation; indeed, it is doubtful that they ever received one. Lord Baltimore later explained to English officials that his messenger bearing the order had died at Plymouth. Baltimore claimed to have dispatched a duplicate dated February 27, 1688/89, but no trace of that document has survived.[18]

Joseph continued to display a lack of leadership during the troubled spring months. He had decided to prorogue the scheduled April session of the assembly against the demands of the burgesses. This move had prevented the only opportunity for an orderly discussion and treatment of the rising opposition. Only the prospect of open discussion in the assembly and the possibility of some positive legal action had forestalled greater trouble in March. Sometime during the disturbance over the Indian rumors, Henry Jowles had marched to St. Mary's City "with about 150 men of Calvert County with such Armes and amunition as they could gett." These men had returned home only after receiving custody of their county's arms, which had earlier been called in for repairs, and after obtaining assurances of governmental action when the assembly convened. Now the assembly would not meet until the last Tuesday in October and the opportunity for an orderly airing of issues was lost. At the April meeting of the Provincial Court, the deputy governors had "Indavoured to clear themselves, but to so little purpose the people was worse satisfied than before."[19]

[17] See, for example, Henry Darnall's prayer for James II's "happy restoration without bloodshed," in a letter to Joseph, March 28, 1689, *ibid.*, 88; Deposition of James Forat, Oct. 4, 1689, *Cal. S. P., Col., 1689–1692*, no. 469; and the comments of Abington sent to New York in "Mariland's Grevances," 404.

[18] *Cal. S. P., Col., 1689–92*, nos. 394, 422. Charles M. Andrews has written skeptically of Baltimore's claim: "There is nothing to show that the duplicate was actually sent, or if sent was received, or if received was ever acted on" (*Colonial Period*, II, 372).

[19] *Md. Archives*, VIII, 69; "Mariland's Grevances," 405 (quotation).

In July, John Coode, the perennial malcontent, seized the initiative in the absence of provincial leadership. Over the past decade, this erstwhile minister–planter–military figure had replaced Josias Fendall as Baltimore's most persistent opponent. Born in England in 1648, Coode had taken orders there for the Anglican priesthood, a calling for which he was distinctly unsuited by temperament. He had abandoned the ministry for more profitable and adventurous undertakings shortly after he came to Maryland. In 1674, two years after his name first appears in the colonial records, Coode had married Susanna Slye, a wealthy widow fifteen years older than he. She was the daughter of Thomas Gerard, a prosperous Catholic whose stormy career encompassed numerous alliances and battles with the Calverts. Through this marriage, Coode had become a fairly large landholder in St. Mary's County, and for a brief period he had enjoyed the special favor of the proprietor. Baltimore's patronage had brought Coode a militia commission and a seat on the county bench, with election to the assembly following soon thereafter. Events which remain largely unknown, however, had sharply altered relations between Coode and the proprietor by 1681, when Coode had participated in the abortive uprising. Baltimore had then stripped Coode of his appointive offices and had fought for his expulsion from the assembly. In 1688, Coode was once again elected to the assembly, probably a sign of rising Protestant discontent in St. Mary's County, which had always been a Catholic and proprietary stronghold. In recent years, Coode had prophesied that the Catholics would be deposed, and after the revolution itself he boasted that he had brought it about for personal revenge.[20]

For his initial support, Coode depended primarily on relatives and neighbors who shared his deep-seated opposition to the proprietary circle. His three main cohorts were Nehemiah Blakis-

[20] For documentation and further details on Coode and the other three men discussed immediately below, see their biographies, pp. 236ff.

ton, Kenelm Cheseldyne, and Henry Jowles. Both Blakiston and Cheseldyne, who had migrated to Maryland in 1668 and 1669 respectively, had also married daughters of Thomas Gerard. Blakiston was the younger son of John Blakiston, a former member of Parliament and mayor of Newcastle. Nehemiah had become an active lawyer in Maryland and, after a series of minor royal appointments, had received a warrant as collector of the king's customs for the Potomac and Wicomico rivers in 1685. In that capacity he clashed frequently with the council. Blakiston had charged the council with obstructing his duties, and the council had accused him of dishonesty in collections.

Cheseldyne was the second son of an Anglican minister who was the vicar of Blaxham in Lincoln County. After the death of his father, Cheseldyne migrated to Maryland and continued the practice of law he had entered in England. Baltimore had rewarded his ability with an appointment as attorney general in 1676, but had replaced him in 1681 with a new favorite. Since that time, Cheseldyne had become a leading voice of opposition in the lower house, where he had presided as speaker since 1686.

Henry Jowles was the son of John Jowles of Surrey, Esq. He studied at Oxford and Gray's Inn before sailing for the Chesapeake sometime prior to 1672. Soon after his arrival he had acquired sizable landholdings in the usual manner for these men, a profitable marriage. Appointments as a militia officer, justice, and sheriff followed soon thereafter, more patronage than was typical for the rebels as a whole. By the early 1680's, however, Jowles's upward mobility had stalled, short of positions on the powerful provincial level of government. He, too, turned his talents to the assembly, to which he was elected in 1685.

A common pattern emerges from these four profiles, a pattern which will also be characteristic of a majority of the colonists who would soon lend their support and leadership in establishing a new government. These men were usually sons of English gentry who had migrated to Maryland after the Restoration in anticipation of a social and economic position in the New World which they could not expect to attain in England. They generally acquired such a position, but not the political power that would normally accompany it.[21]

Five other colonists participated actively in the initial stages of the revolt. They were all non-Catholics and residents of the lower Western Shore. Humphrey Warren, the most substantial member of this second group, was a generation removed from the immigrant pattern. He was born in 1655, about the time his father, the second son of a London merchant, was migrating to Maryland and settling in Charles County. The father became a justice, militia colonel, and burgess before his death in 1671; Humphrey Warren in 1689 sat on the county bench, held a militia captaincy, and he had served a brief tenure as county coroner.[22]

Ninian Beale, at age 64, was the oldest of the group. A Scotch Presbyterian, he had served as a coronet in the Scottish army and was among those resisting Oliver Cromwell. He was transported as a political prisoner and indentured servant first to Barbados and then to Maryland. In 1669 Beale began a long career of land speculation: surveying land on the frontier, selling it, and putting the proceeds into more land. By 1689, he had patented 11,377 acres, of which he still possessed at least 4,263 acres. He utilized his military experience as a lieutenant under Coode in 1676 and later as a captain of the rangers on the western fringes of settlement, and by 1689 had become a major of the militia.[23]

John Turling was a practicing minister, the only Anglican officiating in Calvert County and one of the few Protestant clergymen in the colony. During the disturbances in 1681, Tur-

[21] This understanding of the Maryland political and social scene owes much to Bernard Bailyn's suggestive essay, "Politics and Social Structure in Virginia," in James Morton Smith, ed., *Seventeenth-Century America: Essays in Colonial History* (Chapel Hill, 1959), 90–115.

[22] Harry Wright Newman, *Charles County Gentry* (Washington, D.C., 1940), 284–92.

[23] See his biography, pp. 234–35.

ling had been brought before the council for spreading rumors that Lord Baltimore was arming the Indians. He had again circulated such reports in March of 1689.[24]

Completing this group of early rebel leaders were Richard Clouds and John Cambell. Clouds, a "laborer" of St. Mary's City, had recently married the widow of John Goldsmith, a substantial landowner. Clouds was indicted and then acquitted in 1684/85 on the charge of obstructing the laying out of lots for the towns established by a recent act of the assembly. Cambell had arrived in Maryland some time in the early 1650's as an indentured servant. He enjoyed moderate success as a planter in the next two decades and had acquired at least 250 acres by 1689. Cambell had probably served with Coode in the St. Mary's militia. He was a captain from 1681 until his promotion to major in early 1689.[25]

These men had probably been nursing the idea of overthrowing the government for some time, and had hoped to launch the rebellion during the late winter. Early in 1689, according to one contemporary chronicler of the revolution, Cheseldyne had received a letter from Gerard Slye in London which sought to dissuade him from carrying out at that time "the design which they had against the Papists," and had provided several reasons why the incumbent regime would not easily fall. The letter had suppposedly been read by William Digges, one of the deputy governors.[26] Slye was the stepson of John Coode. A former jus-

[24] Ch. Ct. and Land Rec., P no. 1, 208; Percy G. Skirven, *The First Parishes of the Province of Maryland* (Baltimore, 1923), 126, 129, 134; *Md. Archives*, XV, 386, 393.

[25] On Clouds, Prov. Ct. Judg., TG, ff. 20–21; I&A 23, f. 113; Wills 4, f. 15. For Cambell, see his biography, pp. 241–42.

[26] Paul Bertrand to Bishop of London, Sept. 12, 1689, *Md. Archives*, VIII, 116. Digges had personally told Bertrand of the letter. Bertrand, a Frenchman, was a minister who had been recommended to Lord Baltimore by the Bishop of London in 1685. In April 1686, Bertrand arrived in Maryland with instructions from the proprietor that the council furnish him with a plantation, a Negro, and a horse (V, 461). He was naturalized by an act of the assembly in 1686 (XIII, 144). See also Nelson

tice, militia officer, and sheriff of St. Mary's County, he had
moved to England in 1681. He now operated out of London as
a merchant, and over the past decade he had been active in opposing Lord Baltimore and spreading rumors about the proprietary government among English officials.[27]

Despite Slye's admonitions, the plan went into operation in
midsummer. On July 16, the council received news that Coode
"was raising men up Potowmack." It quickly dispatched an
agent to investigate the report. Coode seized the agent as a spy
and continued to gather forces in Charles, Calvert, and St. Mary's
counties, while the council now desperately sought to deploy
its own defenses. Colonel Digges and eighty to a hundred men
stationed themselves at the state house in St. Mary's City and
the council ordered all other militia officers to raise their companies in defense.[28]

Meanwhile, Coode enlisted more and more "recruits" on his
march toward the capital. The council now intensified its efforts
to dissuade the rank and file from their intended attack. It focused its appeals particularly upon Henry Jowles, probably the
most widely respected of the rebels. Clutching for some solution, the deputy governors offered to make him the "Generall
of all the forces in the Province." After a slight hesitation, Jowles
declined and rejoined Coode on his march. The council then
announced its willingness to extend a general proclamation of
pardon upon condition of the laying down of arms. This, too,
was declined by the growing number of marchers. The rebel
leaders had now successfully convinced a majority in the area
that a Catholic plot truly existed. These colonists had deter-
minedly joined in arms to preserve the country from the Indians
and the papists and to proclaim the new king and queen.[29]

Waite Rightmyer, *Maryland's Established Church* (Lebanon, Pa., 1956),
161.

[27] *Md. Archives*, V, 296–97, 299–300, 421–24; XV, 66, 99, 228, 255, 272,
326; XVII, 29, 44.

[28] *Ibid.*, VIII, 155–56, 147–48.

[29] *Ibid.*, 118–19, 156–57.

On July 25, the rebels issued their "Declaration of the reason and motive for the present appearing in arms of His Majestys Protestant Subjects in the Province of Maryland." In order "to undeceive those that may have a sinister account of our proceedings," Coode and his colleagues summarized their complaints against Lord Baltimore. Heavy emphasis fell on the lack of sufficient allegiance to the English crown, prejudice against the Anglican church and its adherents, and arbitrary abuses of the powers granted in the proprietary charter. The latter category included the grievances disputed for the past decade in the assembly: the calling of two instead of four delegates per county, proprietary disallowance of acts of assembly, the unilateral suspension by proprietary proclamation of the penalties of the acts for towns, the heavy penalties for sedition against the proprietor, excessive and illegal fees, and illegal impressments of men and goods.

The declaration restated the threatened "loss of our lives, libertys and Estates" through the papist machinations with the French and Indians. The rebels denied any designs of their own or any intent to deal violently with anyone who cooperated with them. The new monarchs had been proclaimed in "all the other branches of their Majestys Dominions in this part of the world"; the authors of the declaration wished merely by their armed uprising "to preserve, vindicate and assert the Sovereign Dominion and right of King William and Queen Mary to this Province; to defend the Protestant Religion among us and to protect and shelter the Inhabitants from all manner of violence, oppression and destruction that is plotted and deseigned against them."[30]

The declaration had a persuasive effect among the colonists in that area. The eighty or more men under Digges at the state

---

[30] *Ibid.*, 101–7; see also Charles M. Andrews, ed., *Narratives of the Insurrections, 1675–1690* (New York, 1915), 305–14. The declaration was printed a few weeks after it first appeared, and it is the earliest known colonial publication with a Maryland imprint (304).

house now refused to obey his orders or to oppose Coode. Their action forced Digges to surrender on July 27; not a single shot had been fired.[31]

Sewall and Darnall were no more successful in their efforts to raise a troop of men from the area along the Patuxent. The officers of the militia were willing to support the council, but the general populace "were possessed with a belief that Cood rose only to preserve the Country from the Indians and Papists and to proclaim the King and Queen and would doe them noe harm." The two councillors were able to enlist only 160 men in their cause.[32]

As the two sides approached the final confrontation, a debate arose over the legitimacy of the revolutionary cause, a debate which would continue until there was a royal settlement. The rebels made their case with the declaration: Papist machinations had created an emergency that required displacement of the proprietary government in order to preserve the province for Their Majesties. Captain Richard Smith of Calvert County gave vivid expression to the position of Lord Baltimore's Protestant supporters as he tried to persuade his soldiers to follow him on the proprietary side. According to a report later sent to England, "Smith's men said they were willing to march with him upon any other occasion, but not to fight for the papists against themselves." Smith had then "alledged they mistook the case it was not religion but the settled peace, Government and Lawes of the Land, that he then endeavoured to preserve, from the Encroachment of such as had no legal pretence to it, many said we doubt not they have power from England to justifie their proceedings. . . . Smith answered if they have any power from the King of England, we are all obliged to stand by them, you may be sure they have none, for if they could produce any such thing, need not to take up armes, for I am confident all Maryland will not

---

[31] *Md. Archives*, VIII, 116, 156.
[32] *Ibid.*, 156.

afford one man to oppose the King's authority."[33] Both sides accepted the crown as the source of all legitimate exercise of power. The problem revolved around Lord Baltimore's position. Had he forfeited his position as the legitimate agent of the crown? Coode and his men said yes, hence the emergency that required their "appearance in armes." The proprietor's men said no, that only orders from the crown could remove Lord Baltimore's government.

Proprietary forces gathered at Mattapany. The opposition, now numbering more than 700, procured cannon from a London ship and laid siege to the plantation garrison.[34] The proprietary cause was obviously hopeless at this point. Significant resistance would have resulted in much fruitless loss of life. Consequently, again without bloodshed, the council signed articles of surrender and vacated Mattapany on August 1. The articles were quite brief: The defeated were promised safe-conduct to their homes and "free and full enjoyment of yours & theirs just rights and priviledges equall with the rest of their Majesties Subjects according to the Laws of England and this Province." Only one statement foretold what was to come; henceforth no papist would occupy any office, civil or military, "as by their Majesties Proclamation and the Laws of England."[35]

Two days later, the victorious "most loyall Protestant Subjects Inhabitants of the Province of Maryland" addressed King William and Queen Mary with congratulations on the outcome of the English Revolution and an explanation of their own en-

---

[33] *Ibid.*, 148.

[34] According to the narrative of Henry Darnall, Captain William Burnham lent the cannon. Darnall had angered several ship captains by refusing to clear ships in the name of Their Majesties (*ibid.*, 157, 178).

[35] *Ibid.*, 107–8. The articles were presented by Coode, Jowles, Cheseldyne, Turling, Cambell, Beale, and Warren, and, in turn, were signed by Joseph, Darnall, Sewall, Pye, and Hill. See also "Mariland's Grevances," 406. Apparently this bar did not extend to attorneys willing to take the oaths of allegiance and supremacy, for Charles Carroll was allowed a legal practice until the arrival of the royal governor. See *Md. Archives*, VIII, 522–23.

deavors in Maryland. "Stirred up by the overruling hand of Divine Providence in opening our eyes to discern our Duty. Wee have undertaken and hope in a short time to compleate throughout this Province the publick and general acknowledgement of Your Majesty's undoubted right thereunto, as well as other your Dominions and Territories, having for the purpose taken up arms in your Majesties Names, and without the expence of one drop of blood blessed be God rescued the Government from the hands of your Enemies and shall [p]reserve the same in such secure manner as wee can for Your Majesties Service, until such time as in your princely Wisdom you shall deign to make settlement thereof upon such person and in such manner and form as your Majesties shall seem meet and convenient." Meanwhile, the petitioners implored a speedy establishment of a Protestant government for the colony. This declaration was sent to England in two ships that sailed about August 5.[36]

The deputy governors and their supporters had surrendered upon promise of safe passage to their homes and protection of their rights as citizens. It was important to the rebels, however, that these men not be allowed to send letters or to take passage on the ships then preparing to sail for England. The ship captains evidently accepted Coode's authority, for they surrendered to him letters given them by the Catholics and refused passage to members of the deposed council. Captain Richard Smith of Calvert County, who had joined the garrison at Mattapany, was even briefly put in custody until the ships sailed to prevent his intended departure. The rebels released him immediately thereafter.[37]

[36] *Md. Archives*, VIII, 108–110. One copy of this "Address of the Protestant Inhabitants of Maryland to the King and Queen," dated August 3, 1689, was entrusted to Captain William Johnson of the ship *Content*, and another to Captain William Burnham of the ship *Constant*. Apparently both ships were taken by the French (110, 124, 151, 170, 178). The copy eventually received by the English officials in late December was a printed document, probably the second item printed in the colony (CO5/718/I).

[37] *Md. Archives*, VIII, 148, 153–54, 157.

Deputy governors Henry Darnall and Nicholas Sewall escaped northward "to Pennsylvania to endeavour to get a passage," but the ships had already departed that area. They learned there of the overthrow of the Dominion of New England. The two men then returned to Maryland and "stayd in Ann Arrundell County (who never had joyned with Cood nor his party.)" In the succeeding weeks, they went into other northern counties and to the Eastern Shore in efforts to retain the allegiance of colonists in those areas not involved in the initial stages of the rebellion. Darnall eventually obtained passage to England with Captain Thomas Everard of the ship *Thomas and Susanna*, which left Maryland on September 26.[38]

The other deposed councillors bided their time for several weeks. At some point in October, William Joseph and Sewall fled to northern Virginia where they sought refuge on a plantation owned by their fellow councilman William Digges. By late November, the rebels had put guards over Catholic councillors Clement Hill and Edward Pye. Coode identified them at that time as the "two onely in custody." They had allegedly been devising a plan to escape northward with three priests on a small brigantine.[39] Significantly, these arrests did not come for some weeks after the surrender, and then not until the councillors were attempting to stir up opposition against the new government or to escape the colony. In August, both sides must have been hoping some word from England would soon arrive to settle the legitimacy of Lord Baltimore's government one way or the other. Meanwhile, bloodshed or significant disorder could only weaken the position of either side. Still, the situation could not remain static. During these initial days, the uprising had been

[38] *Ibid.*, 157. See also "Mariland's Grevances," 406–7; Jacob Leisler to Assembly of Maryland, Sept. 29, 1689, in *DHNY*, II, 19–20; and Deposition of James Forat, Oct. 4, 1689, *Cal. S. P., Col., 1689–92*, no. 469. With the delay of news from England, Coode later feared that Darnall had intercepted his letters to the crown being carried by the same ship (*Md. Archives*, VIII, 178).

[39] *Md. Archives*, VIII, 127; Coode to Leisler, Nov. 26, 1689, *DHNY*, II, 26; "Mariland's Grevances," 408.

restricted to the lower counties of the Western Shore, and to maintain their position the Associators would need backing from the leadership of other areas.

Affairs assumed a different complexion and a greater geographical impact when Coode called in mid-August for the election of an assembly to consist of four delegates from each county and two burgesses from St. Mary's City. He was thereby asserting the legitimacy of a new rebel government and seeking to extend its control throughout the colony. The summoning of four delegates was a deliberate maneuver to dramatize the opposition to Baltimore's summoning of only two men in recent years. Coode issued the call in Their Majesties' names. It accompanied a proclamation that all officers "not being Papists or haveing beene in actual armes nor any ways declared against their Majestie's service, honour and dignity should continue in their places."[40]

Opposition to this move rapidly crystallized. It was one thing to approve the Glorious Revolution in England and support or acquiesce in the dispossession of a Catholic council, but it was quite another matter to assume authority and to run a government. To a people much embued with the concept of the legitimate derivation of power, there was little basis for Coode's summoning of an assembly. What would that assembly do? By what power would it act? Only those men actively championing the overthrow of the proprietary government welcomed this development. At least one sheriff refused to execute the order to hold an election. Michael Taney of Calvert County, whose commission derived from Lord Baltimore, regarded himself as "discharged of my Office" by the surrender of the council. Many other freeholders of the county preferred to delay any election until the arrival of a "Lawfull power from England." Sixty-eight residents of Calvert County forthrightly expressed this conviction in a petition to the crown signed on election day, August 20. It contained the reasons for their refusal to partici-

[40] *Md. Archives*, VIII, 119.

pate. All of the signers were Protestants who looked forward to a non-Catholic government appointed by the crown, but they were not enthusiastic about a self-appointed Protestant government. It was their belief that "in a short time wee shall have some Person come from England with a full and lawfull authority and Comission to govern this Province & most assuredly he will then call an Assembly which we doubt not will be in October next at farthest time enough to perfect and settle the Affaires of this Province." There was no need for precipitate action or any harm to anyone in the meantime.[41]

According to several accounts, these doubts were shared by freeholders of other counties. Nevertheless, elections did proceed in all but Anne Arundel, the most populous county in the province. That Quaker stronghold emphatically rejected the call for an election and temporarily withstood a later demand from the assembly itself for immediate compliance. At least four sources loyal to Lord Baltimore reported a poor turnout elsewhere— "some few people here, out of each County only, sideing and making part with them"—and one asserted that the election "was in most Countyes awed by their souldiers."[42]

However, these accounts specifically mention only two such forced elections. One was in Calvert County. Protestants there threatened to be as recalcitrant as those of Anne Arundel. Sheriff Taney refused to officiate and leading freeholders boycotted the election and signed the petition already described. Henry Jowles was neither willing to wait nor to allow a proprietary appointee to foil him. He rode about the county announcing the forthcoming election, normally the duty of the sheriff. After rounding up the voters, most of whom were his own soldiers, and treating them to drinks, Jowles conducted a poll. Not surprisingly, all four of the elected delegates were currently rebel

---

[41] *Ibid.*, 120, 148, 110–11.

[42] *Ibid.*, 120, 122 (quotation), 125 (quotation), 159, 235–36; Arthur E. Karinen, "Maryland Population: 1631–1730," *MHM*, LIV (1959), 365–407.

officers—Jowles himself, Major Ninian Beale, Captain Henry Mitchell, and Ensign James Keech.[43]

The second instance was on the Eastern Shore in Talbot County, next largest in population after Anne Arundel. Here, some proprietary adherents staged a strong opposition initially. Coode's disciples took the precaution of seizing the arms of Colonel Peter Sayer and Madam Philemon Lloyd, the chief Catholics of the area, and then succeded in conducting the election.[44] Nothing is known for certain about the elections in other areas of the colony, or how many freeholders in fact participated.

The first session of the Associators' Convention, as this assembly would be called, convened on August 22. Thirty-two of a potential forty-two members were in attendance for fourteen days. They were joined on the last day, September 4, by four latecomers, the delegates from Somerset County.[45]

A profile of these thirty-six men, and five others who are known to have sat at subsequent sessions, is revealing (see Table 2).[46] The membership consisted primarily of active participants and supporters of the revolution, but there were some moderates who were more circumspect in their attitudes toward the events of the preceding six weeks. Like the initial leaders of the revolt, the Associators were overwhelmingly men who had migrated to the colony roughly ten to thirty years before 1689. Only three native Marylanders, Gilbert Clarke, John Courts, and William Sharpe, sat in the convention, although three other delegates, John Stone, John Brooke, and Hans Hanson, had arrived

[43] *Md. Archives*, VIII, 117, 120, 154.

[44] *Ibid.*, 158–59.

[45] *Ibid.*, 117; XIII, 231–47. Anne Arundel had no representation at this session, and Cecil County had only two delegates present (VIII, 160). Thirty-five delegates signed an address to the crown on September 4, 1689; presumably Charles James of Cecil County had left St. Mary's City before the last day of the session (CO 5/719/I, no. 1).

[46] Full sketches are provided in the Biographies. Only two Cecil County delegates have been identified, and it is quite likely only two were elected. Cecil was the most recently established county.

Table 2. Delegates to the Associators' Convention, 1689–1692

Delegates, by county	Arrived in Maryland	Served as county justice	Served in militia	Served as sheriff	Sat in assembly	Profession
St. Mary's County						
Kenelm Cheseldyne (1640–1708)	1669	1686–			1676–82; 1686–	Attorney
John Coode (1648–1708/09)	1672	by 1677–81	Capt., 1676–81		1676–82 1688–	Planter
Nehemiah Blakiston (–1693)	1668					Attorney; customs collector
John Cambell (–1695/96)	by 1653		Capt., 1681–89 Major, 1689–			Planter
Robert Mason* (1653–1700/01)	1677					Merchant
St. Mary's City						
Gilbert Clarke (c. 1654–1700)	Native					Planter
William Blanckenstein (1660–)	1678					Planter; factor
Kent						
William Harris (c. 1644–1712)	by 1674	1686–			1686–	Attorney; planter

Table 2. (continued)

Delegates, by county	Arrived in Maryland	Served as county justice	Served in militia	Served as sheriff	Sat in assembly	Profession
Kent (continued)						
Michael Miller (c. 1644–1699)	1670	1680–83		1678	1686–	Attorney; planter
Hans Hanson (c. 1647–1703/04)	1655	1685–		1680–82		Planter; miller
Thomas Davis	?					
Anne Arundel						
Thomas Tench (–1708)	by 1684	1685–				Merchant
William Hopkins (–1702)	by 1658					Planter
Nicholas Gassaway (1634–1691/92)	1650	1679–	Capt., 1679–85; Major, 1685–			Merchant; planter
Nicholas Greenberry (1627–1697)	1674	1686–	Capt., 1686–			Planter
Calvert						
Henry Jowles (c. 1640–1700)	by 1672	by 1679–81	Major, 1676–79; Col., 1679–	1681–83	1686–	Planter
Ninian Beale (c. 1625–1717)	1655	1685–	Lt., 1668–78; Capt., 1678–89; Major, 1689			Planter; surveyor
Henry Mitchell (–1701)	by 1658					Planter

Table 2. (continued)

Delegates, by county	Arrived in Maryland	Served as county justice	Served in militia	Served as sheriff	Sat in assembly	Profession
Calvert (continued)						
James Keech (c. 1651–1708)	by 1671		Ensign, 1689			Planter
Charles						
John Stone (1648–1697)	1649	1670–			1678–82 1686–	Merchant; planter
Henry Hawkins (–1699)	1666	1680–			1688–	Planter; tanner
John Addison (–1705)	by 1674	1687–				Merchant; planter
John Courts (1655/56–1702/03)	Native	1685–				Planter
Baltimore						
John Thomas (–1717/18)	by 1680					Planter; carpenter
Thomas Staley (–1700)	?					Planter
Thomas Thurston (c. 1622–1693)	1663				1686–	Trader; cordwainer
Christopher Gist (–1690/91)	by 1679					Planter

Table 2. (continued)

Delegates, by county	Arrived in Maryland	Served as county justice	Served in militia	Served as sheriff	Sat in assembly	Profession
Talbot						
John Edmundson (–1697)	by 1658				1676–82 1686–	Merchant
George Robotham (–1698)	by 1669	1681–			1681–82 1686–	Merchant; planter
William Sharpe (1655–1699)	Native	Refused oath, 1685				Merchant; planter
Robert Smith (–1706/07)	by 1677					Attorney
Dorchester						
John Brooke (–1693)	1654	1671–74 1676–			1681–82 1682–84 1686–	Chirurgeon
Henry Trippe (1632–1698)	1663	1669–71 1674–76 1681–85 1687–	Capt., 1676–		1671–75 1681–82	Planter
Charles Hutchins (–1700)	1672	1674–				Planter; carpenter
Thomas Cooke (–1692/93)	1683					Merchant; attorney

Table 2. (continued)

Delegates, by county	Arrived in Maryland	Served as county justice	Served in militia	Served as sheriff	Sat in assembly	Profession
Somerset						
Francis Jenkins (c. 1650–1710)	1671	1676–83	Capt., 1687–	1683–88		Merchant; planter
David Browne (–1697)	by 1670	1672–73	Capt., 1679/80–			Merchant
Robert King (–1696)	1666	1687–				Merchant
Samuel Hopkins (–1711/12)	1680	1687–				Planter; factor
Cecil[†]						
Charles James (–1698)	1661			1676		Merchant; planter
Edward Jones (–1697)	by 1661	1685–87 1688–			(?) 1686–	Planter

Note: Open date in service columns means the individual was holding the office in July 1689.

* Elected in 1690 as a replacement for Coode or Cheseldyne, who were in England, or possibly for Clarke (St. Mary's City), who had been appointed sheriff of Charles County in the ordinance of September 4, 1689.

[†] Only two delegates for Cecil County have been identified.

as children. With the further exception of two men whose origins remain uncertain, the other thirty-three Associators had first entered the colony as adults.

The majority of these adult immigrants had arrived with some capital at their disposal. Like Coode, Cheseldyne, Blakiston, and Jowles, they were generally sons of well-to-do Englishmen, for whom America seemed to hold brighter prospects than did the Old World. The establishment of trade connections apparently accounts for the migration of such men as John Addison and David Browne, while others like Michael Miller and Robert Smith undoubtedly expected to employ their education and legal knowledge to profitable advantage. The easy availability of land, at much lower prices than in England, drew still others. In contrast to these men, a small number of Associators came from more humble origins. Eight had their way paid by other individuals.

The prevailing pattern among all these men was to contract an advantageous marriage shortly after arrival in the colony. Evidence suggests that only seven of the Associators immigrated with wives. The others soon wed established widows or the unmarried daughters of prosperous colonists. With the advantages of such unions and their own resources, the future Associators had quickly achieved economic success.

Economic and social prosperity did not guarantee political power, however, at least not at the provincial level. Indeed, ten Associators had apparently held no office whatever of profit or power, a situation the convention would soon partly remedy. Three more had held only minor positions—ensign of the militia, deputy sheriff, county attorney. Nehemiah Blakiston also held no proprietary offices, but as a royal collector of customs he did occupy a significant position.

More typical were those twenty-six Associators who had been or currently were a justice, burgess, sheriff, or militia officer. Twenty-two had officiated as justice of the peace, but this preferment had come for ten of them only after Lord Baltimore's return to England in 1684, and the last commissions prior to the revolution had not included the names of former justices Michael Miller and John Coode. Thirteen of the Associators had previously represented their counties in the assembly, but six had first sat in the heated sessions of the last proprietary assembly. Their election and the return of Coode and Cheseldyne had been an indication of the growing discontent in the colony among Protestant leaders or would-be leaders. Nine men had served as militia officers, but only Henry Jowles served above the rank of major. Only four Associators had been sheriff, the most powerful of the local appointive offices. Two of these men, Michael Miller and Charles James, had been dismissed for misconduct, and only Francis Jenkins had actually held the office of sheriff since 1683. Consequently, although a majority of the Associators had served in some office of responsibility, very few of them had enjoyed proprietary patronage beyond the position of justice or had much confidence of receiving such favors in the future. They perhaps saw an opportunity for such advancement through the revolution.

Some Protestants clearly had resisted the apparent opportunity presented by the events of July and August. They had declined to stand for election. Many had even refused to vote, and they would later oppose the Associators. In contrast to the rebels, these opponents appear more likely to have been longer residents of the colony or to have immigrated as servants. For example, of twenty-eight local officeholders definitely identified as Protestants and opponents of the revolution, all but one were in Maryland prior to 1660, twelve were second-generation colonists, and five others had probably entered the colony as servants. Their reservations about the convention perhaps arose from a greater confidence in awaiting their turn for promotion, a stronger tradition of loyalty to Lord Baltimore, or more uneasiness over an illegitimate assumption of government.[47]

[47] See Table 4. The table shows twenty-nine, but one officer not appointed was Councillor William Digges. The term "second-generation" is

Such hesitancy clearly was not characteristic, however, of the vast majority of men who now gathered in St. Mary's City to serve as Protestant Associators. After posting a prohibition on the presence of any Catholics in St. Mary's City during the session, the convention turned its attention to the state of the colony. The rebel leaders first publicly divested to the convention "that supream power which they usurped att first," but in fact, they seem to have maintained a considerable control and direction of the proceedings. Unfortunately, no journal of the convention survives and what little we know about its work comes from the few documents it produced—letters, proclamations, and an ordinance—and from an account sent to Lord Baltimore by Peter Sayer, a Catholic of Talbot County.

A nucleus of seven men—all from St. Mary's, Calvert, and Charles counties—appears to have dominated session business. Coode apparently was acknowledged as the primary military figure, and Cheseldyne presided over the assembly as its speaker. Blakiston and Jowles cooperated closely, and major support came as well from John Addison, John Courts, and Gilbert Clarke, who had all been active in spreading and later denying the March rumors. Blakiston, Jowles, Clarke, "and one or two more" provided the membership for a "Committee of Secrecy," instructed to investigate and report on the alleged conspiracy.[48] Coode, Cheseldyne, Jowles, Clarke, Addison, and Courts became a committee empowered to "allot, lay and assess" the public taxes after the convention had adjourned.[49] Individually, these figures fared very well in the new set of judicial, military, and administrative commissions which the convention issued before

---

used here to include both those who were born in Maryland and those who immigrated as very young children. Russell Menard's "Politics and Social Structure in Seventeenth-Century Maryland" (ms, 1973), charts time of arrival, first appointment to office, longevity in office, and social origins for all Maryland colonists who were justices, sheriffs, burgesses, and councillors, 1634–1692.

[48] *Md. Archives*, VIII, 159–61; XIII, 240.
[49] *Ibid.*, 247.

adjourning. Coode became commander in chief of the militia as well as naval officer for the Potomac River and a quorum justice of St. Mary's County. Blakiston now sat as a quorum justice and served as militia captain and coroner of St. Mary's County. He remained royal collector for the Potomac. Clarke became the new sheriff of Charles County, despite an earlier conviction for perjury, while Addison and Courts added militia commissions to their recently acquired judgeships. Cheseldyne and Jowles now were to preside over their respective county courts; the former continued as recorder of St. Mary's City, the latter as a colonel of the militia.[50]

Since the revolt ostensibly had been necessary to preserve Maryland Protestants from a conspiracy of Roman Catholic officials cooperating with an invading force of the French and the Northern Indians, the convention had to take some action to investigate the threat. A report from a Talbot County delegation to local Indians on the Eastern Shore indicated that they were "very civill and kind, and desire nothing but peace and quietness."[51] The Northern Indians were less easy to find. The convention ordered Jacob Young, an Indian trader and interpreter, to report for instructions on negotiating with these Indians. Interestingly, Young had been impeached by the lower house in 1682 for impeding peace negotiations with the Northern Indians while acting as interpreter. However, the complaint had originated with Lord Baltimore and the evidence against Young had come primarily from members of the council.[52]

[50] *Ibid.*, 241–47. Six of these seven accumulated other offices in the next two years. A justice of the quorum was one whose presence was necessary before the court of which he was a member could transact most business.

[51] *Ibid.*, 231.

[52] Young had married a Susquehannock woman. The upper house had found him guilty and had demanded bond in £1,000 with four sureties for good behavior and his personal appearance before succeeding assemblies. In the end, three sureties, all Cecil County men, had been accepted (*ibid.*, VII, 370–372, 386–92, 472–73, 475–76, 477, 479, 480, 485, 500; XIII, 234–35).

Young's orders now indicated that he was to take instructions from Coode or Blakiston, if the convention should adjourn before he could appear. Whether Young ever came is unknown, but the Committee of Secrecy reported on the last day of the convention in a fashion calculated to keep alive fears of popish plots and Indian invasion. The committee unequivocally stated that "the late popish Governors have contrived, conspired and designed by several villanous practices and machinations to betray their Majestie's Protestant Subjects of this Province to the French, Northern and other Indians . . . the verity of the above particulars are to be further proved by other numerous Circumstances and evidences that are now in custody of the said Committee for their Majestie's service." There is no record, however, that the committee ever produced that evidence, if indeed any existed.[53]

Coode and his comrades-in-arms faced far more critical issues. There were three pressing and immediate problems: They needed to gain colonywide support and allegiance for the de facto government; they required recognition and endorsement from royal authorities in England; and they desired to establish their legitimacy in the eyes of neighboring colonies. For the time being, a "Letter to Adjacent Colonies" satisfied the third objective.[54] The other two goals were of greater concern and required closer attention.

[53] *Ibid.*, XIII, 240; VIII, 159–60. One apparent attempt to document the charges, albeit not very convincing, was the deposition of Matthew Tennison of St. Mary's County about testimony from the Choptico Indians (224). Evidently the flight of Darnall and Sewall to Pennsylvania (for the purpose of finding passage to England) was also considered evidence (157, 160–61). The copy of the committee's report in the Public Record Office carries the following handwritten memorandum: "Notwithstanding the country have often desired a proofe of the accusations this Committee charged upon some of the Lord Proprietaryes Deputyes yet the same could never be obtained or was any wayes made appear" (CO5/718/I).

[54] *Md. Archives*, XIII, 233–34. The Associators were in frequent contact with New York by September and had an agent there (VIII, 123). See also Leisler to Gov. of Boston, Sept. 25, 1689, *DHNY*, II 19.

The delegates had agreed by August 25 on an address to the crown which endorsed the account of grievances drawn up in July. The convention now joined in asking "such a deliverance to your suffering people, whereby for the future our religion, rights and Lyberties may be secured, under a Protestant Government by your Majestyes gracious direction especially to be appointed." The Associators promised to maintain their present loyalty and vindication of the crown "against all manner of attempts and opposition whatsoever" while awaiting "your Majestyes pleasure herein." The declaration was printed upon order of the convention. It was to be sent to the crown by the next available ship, which in fact did not sail until the end of September. As soon as possible, petitions signed by the freemen of the counties were to follow.[55]

The obtaining of colonywide support for these measures was the most critical problem. The leaders knew that there was great anxiety among the general population and disapproval on the part of many former proprietary officeholders. The Associators needed to contain the opposition without taking steps that would alienate the undecided.

The convention was first of all anxious to obtain delegates from Anne Arundel County so that the petitions to the crown would include endorsement from all ten counties. The delegates dispatched a letter to Richard Johns, a highly respected Quaker of that county. They sought to allay the fears of widespread imprisonment or seizure of property and through Johns's influence to conduct an election.[56] No cooperation was forthcoming. On September 2, two days before adjournment, the Associators finally resorted to a proclamation denouncing Richard Hill, their foremost opponent in the county. This document attempted to counter some of the rumors about the personal motivation of

---

[55] *Md. Archives*, XIII, 231–32 (quotation); VIII, 123, 127, 151. A printed "true copy of the originall" reached England December 31; the document, so endorsed, is in CO 5/718/I.

[56] *Md. Archives*, XIII, 235–36.

the rebels and the nature of their proposed rule of the colony. The proclamation did not call for Hill's arrest, possibly because the convention could not have accomplished this, but it decreed that henceforth any opponent of the Associators would be considered a rebel and traitor to the crown.[57]

The convention took stronger steps against opposition leaders in Calvert County, for here the Associators had strength. On August 25, they ordered the arrest of Sheriff Michael Taney, Clerk of Court Cecilius Butler, and militia captain Richard Smith, all of whom had actively opposed holding the election. Taney and Smith were Protestants. They came before the assembly for questioning on September 3. The Associators futilely demanded an acknowledgment of their power, but the prisoners persisted in saying they would obey that power "lawfully descended from the Crown of England." The convention did not really wish to keep imprisoned Protestants of such standing and tried to release all three men on bonds for good behavior. The three refused to sign such bonds, however, "for that we knew they would make anything they pleased breach of good behaviour," including statements that the Associators' revolution was illegal. Evidently, various members of the convention pleaded with the three to reconsider, but they were willing only to sign a bond to appear before an authority specifically authorized by the crown. As late as September 26, at least Smith and Taney were still in custody.[58]

It is significant that these appear to have been the only political arrests of Protestants for ten months after the coup. The Associators were probably careful to make note of those men whose allegiance was in doubt. Once the government was secure, it could consider moving against them.[59] For the moment, how-

---

[57] *Ibid.*, 237–38.

[58] *Ibid.*, VIII, 120–21 (quotation), 125, 149 (quotation), 155. Smith's wife Barbara sailed for England with Henry Darnall on September 26 to present her husband's case to royal officials (154, 155).

[59] It did so move, once royal approval arrived. See pp. 112–16 below.

ever, it needed to maintain order without bloodshed in a situation at best uneasy. The leadership wanted nothing that could undermine the theory by which their actions were justified: that the Protestants had acted to secure Maryland for Their Majesties and that a temporary "settlement of all affairs military and civill" was being made by a convention which represented the whole body of "dutyful & loyal Subjects."[60]

Such a settlement would require caution, and the temporary government now organized by the convention reflected remarkable restraint. The new arrangements were outlined in an ordinance passed September 4, the last day of this first session of the convention.[61] One of the most notable features of this ordinance was its omission of all provincial offices and any centralized power. The deputy governors were deposed, but no one was appointed to fill their roles or carry on the functions of the central offices of the government. John Coode had urged the creation of an executive committee that could act for the convention after its adjournment, but the delegates were unwilling. Peter Sayer, in his account to Lord Baltimore, doubtless correctly described the motives of some as the wish "to be all alike in power." But others must have feared any appearance of seizing more power than was absolutely necessary to maintain public order until word arrived from the crown.[62]

---

[60] *Md. Archives*, XIII, 232, 241. There are some second-hand accusations of imprisonment, but there is no evidence to confirm them, and the absence of mention of them in the well-documented charges against the Associators leads one to treat them suspectly. See, *Cal. S. P., Col., 1689–92*, no. 632, which quotes a letter from Maryland that twenty Protestants were imprisoned as traitors. The president of the Virginia council reported to the Lords of Trade on March 11, 1689/90, that the Associators had "imprisoned divers papists" (no. 787). Coode claimed no harm had come to Protestants in his letter to the Earl of Shrewsbury, March 24, 1689/90 (*Md. Archives*, VII, 172), and he remarked on another occasion that only two men were in custody, presumably Pye and Hill. See Coode to Leisler, Nov. 26, 1689, *DHNY*, II, 26.

[61] *Md. Archives*, XIII, 241–47.

[62] *Ibid.*, VIII, 160–63 (161, quotation).

Not only was there no attempt at this point to seize powerful and lucrative offices, there is little evidence in the ordinance of retaliation against those who had been slow in enlisting behind the new government. The Associators needed all the support they could get, and they attempted no immediate large-scale transfer of political power in making local appointments. The main dismissals were confined to St. Mary's and Calvert counties, Catholic areas where the revolution centered. More than half of the removals, twelve of twenty-three, occurred in these two counties. In Calvert, the Associators replaced five justices, of whom at least three were Catholic; in St. Mary's, seven justices, at least four of whom were Catholic, lost their posts, and seven newcomers replaced them. Since the sheriffs and clerks (at least one a Catholic) were also changed, these counties had essentially new administrations. In the other eight, however, out of eighty-four judicial appointments, there were only eleven dismissals, although a higher percentage of the administrators—two sheriffs and three clerks—were replaced.[63] The religious affiliations of some of these men are unknown, but in all the counties only six men among those removed have been positively identified as Protestants. Like Richard Hill, all no doubt had made unmistakably clear their opinion that the overthrow of the government was "Rebellion in the highest degree."[64]

In allowing many other Protestants to remain in office, the Associators evidently hoped these prominent men would eventually support the new regime. In at least seventeen instances,

[63] See Appendix B, Tables B-1 and B-4.

[64] *Md. Archives*, VIII, 196. The other five Protestants were George Wells of Baltimore, James Murphy of Talbot, both of whom were active in their opposition (134, 225); John Sollers of Anne Arundel, probably the John Sollers who by November of 1689 was signing the anti-Associator petition from Calvert County (132), but who made his peace sufficiently to be sitting on the Calvert bench by May 10, 1692 (472); Major Thomas Taylor of Dorchester, who disappeared from the public scene but did not die until 1708 (Wills 12, f. 113a); and Michael Taney of Calvert, discussed above, pp. 63–64.

the convention obviously overlooked the strenuous doubts if not open resistance of some officeholders. For example, the ordinance retained Edward Dorsey as a major in Anne Arundel and even promoted him to a quorum justice; yet Dorsey proved as active, if not as intemperate, as Hill in opposing the new government. George Lingan and Richard Ladd had both signed the petition in Calvert against holding an election, but both were reappointed as justices, although neither appears to have served and Ladd lost his militia command. On the other hand, in some instances the offer of participation in the new regime may have been a successful strategy. John Griggs and Thomas Tasker had joined Lingan and Ladd in signing the Calvert petition, but after their reappointments to the bench, they served and both signed a petition in November which enthusiastically endorsed the Associators' activities.[65]

Sensible caution dictated a different strategy in militia appointments. Care was taken to replace officers whose loyalty to the proprietor was well known, even though some of these men retained their judicial posts. The Associators could not afford to continue disaffected men in positions of command with access to troops, arms, and ammunition. Eight colonels out of ten were dismissed, for most had been members of the council or closely connected to the proprietary circle. In the lower ranks of major and captain, at least fourteen more also lost their commands. Of the fifty men appointed by the convention's ordinance, only fourteen are known for certain to have held similar commissions at the outbreak of the revolution, although eight more were probably also then serving. By contrast, twenty-five appointments went to men not known to have held commissions previously. Five more

[65] Appendix B, Table B-2; *Md. Archives*, VIII, 110, 144–45, 213, 374–75; Test. Pro. 16, ff. 3, 8, 17, 23, 25, 29, 44. Test. Pro. 16 is a record of the probate proceedings of Calvert County from January, 1689/90 to June 21, 1692. For the seventeen individuals, see Carr and Jordan, "Service of Civil and Military Officers, July 1689–September 1692," the columns for men appointed and refusals to serve (table on file at the Hall of Records, Annapolis).

of those appointed had been captains in the past but were probably civilians at the time of the rebellion. There may have been about a 56 per cent change in militia appointments as opposed to 23 per cent in civil appointments.[66] Nevertheless, just as the Associators did not appropriate the powers and patronage of the council, they did not appoint many to the vacant ranks of colonel (eight) and major (four). Only two of each were created.[67]

It is also true, of course, that most members of the Associators' Convention received measurable boosts to their own careers. Six delegates became justices for the first time, while seven others received promotions to the quorum. First militia commissions or promotions went to eleven Associators, and ten assumed appointments they had not held before as sheriff, coroner, or naval officer. Only five of the thirty-six men present at the convention were not named to any office; of these, at least three were Quakers, who had conscientious objection to militia service and to the settlement of disputes in the secular courts.[68] On the whole,

[66] See Appendix B, Table B-6, and Carr and Jordan, "Service of Civil and Military Officers." Eleven of the new officers had been justice or sheriff in July 1689 and one was then a county surveyor. Thus 61 per cent of the militia officers appointed (36) had held *some* office before the overthrow, a fact which must have diluted somewhat the impact of the change.

[67] Captains John Coode and Humphrey Warren became colonels; Captains Henry Trippe and James Smallwood became majors. Coode had led the coup, and Warren was the ranking militia officer in Charles County; his allegiance was above question. Trippe's promotion was a natural rise. Smallwood, a trader with the Indians, had been a frequent proprietary agent in Indian affairs until his complicity in Captain George Godfrey's plot to free Fendall in 1681. Smallwood rarely appears in the records thereafter until 1689 (*Md. Archives*, XV, 56, 232, 353, 402, 404, 409; XVII, 92, 94). See also Arthur L. Keith, "Smallwood Family of Charles County," *MHM*, XXII (1927), 139–86; Keith's article contains some factual errors, however.

[68] Those not receiving appointments were Thomas Davis, Thomas Thurston, John Edmundson, William Sharpe, Robert Smith and Thomas Cooke. William Blanckenstein's only appointment was as alderman of St. Mary's City. Thurston, Sharpe, and Edmundson were Quakers; however, Thurston had accepted a militia commission by 1692, and Edmundson

however, the appointments represented considerable political sagacity; the convention filled only essential offices, and it rewarded active supporters of the new regime without supplanting men whose support would be necessary if the peace were to be maintained.

The ordinance of September 4, 1689, also contained provisions "for the present settlement of this Province." It continued all temporary laws "as by law they ought as if this present Generall Convention has never happened." It also continued all actions and process pending in the Pronvicial Court "Until their Majesties further pleasure be knowne in relation to this Province." After appointing the justices, sheriffs, clerks, coroners, and militia officers for each county, it authorized them to be sworn in Their Majesties' names in open court and to execute their authorities and trusts "as have been formerly accustomed . . . or as such Officers ought and are bound to doe by the lawes of England or the lawes of this Province." All actions and process at that moment undetermined in the county courts were to be proceeded upon and no errors in the proceedings were to "be sufficient to reverse any Judgement." The only extension of county court jurisdiction came in the area of testamentary business, which had been the province of the now suspended Prerogative Court, in itself a focus of grievance. The county courts were empowered to take probate of wills and grant letters of administration and were required to keep such records with those of the court. The militia officers were authorized to train their men "as . . . formerly accustomed" and "to suppress all homebred insurrections or foreigne invasions against their Majesties Crowne and Dignity and the safety and welfare of the Inhabitants."[69]

Nowhere in the ordinance was there mention of a central au-

---

sat on the reconstituted Provincial Court in 1691. Smith had a lucrative law practice. Cooke was also an attorney and kept an ordinary. Davis remains a mystery. See their biographies for details.

[69] *Md. Archives*, XIII, 245–47.

thority. John Coode was named commander in chief of the militia, but he had no defined powers outside of St. Mary's County. There was no mention, for example, of who was to determine if a "homebred insurrection" was afoot. "Coode & his adherents now have no more power out of their County than have we cashiered Officers," observed Peter Sayer.[70] Thus from September 4, 1689, until the second session of the Associators' Convention in April, complete responsibility for keeping order rested on the local justices and the local militia. It was to be a testing period to prove their stability and effectiveness.

[70] *Ibid.*, VIII, 161.

CHAPTER III

"The Unsettled State of our Present Constitution," September 1689–May 1690

When the convention adjourned September 4, no blood had yet been shed—an important psychological advantage to the Associators. To that time, at least, the resistance of those Protestants who opposed the new government was apparently too scattered and unorganized to challenge seriously the position of the revolutionary leaders, precarious though that was until they could obtain royal approval of their proceedings. Some opponents claimed that many would voice objections were they not under threat of reprisals,[1] but there is little to show that most people wanted anything but a definite settlement of the government by the crown one way or another. The province rested uneasy, expecting direction from England with the arrival of every ship.[2]

[1] "Some few people here, out of each County only, sideing and making part with them, soe that they might with ease have been subdued; but that for a handful of people to take armes one against another & other reasons which induces us rather to suffer that with patience which could not be prevented but by making the case worse; for as hitherto noe blood hath been spilt altho' we are in great fear and terror that it will not end without" (Richard Hill to Lord Baltimore, Sept. 20, 1689, *Md. Archives*, VIII, 122). See also 185, 192–93.

[2] "We live in dayly hopes of the forward ships but more especially some order from the Crowne of England to setle and compose our present distractions; here is a small Ketch or Packet boat that have brought letters for this Government and private letters alsoe but all is kept husht and some private letters I have seen that have bin opened before they

Although Coode and the group from the southern counties who had dominated the convention had not obtained creation of an executive committee, they obviously retained a potential for exercising power, especially within their own counties. Men who withheld approval of the coup complained of surveillance; "It is difficult to send or receive any leter for feare of its being opened," wrote Richard Johns of Anne Arundel to a London merchant.[3] Coode sometime in September even ordered the muster of the St. Mary's County militia for a march into Anne Arundel County, but the march seems not to have taken place. Possibly the return there of Darnall and Sewall from Pennsylvania had inspired the move, but cooler counsel evidently prevailed. Most of the ousted councillors from St. Mary's, Calvert, and Charles counties found it wise to leave Maryland. Clement Hill and Edward Pye, who remained, were under house arrest.[4]

There was no central authority, but circumstances occasionally necessitated that someone be spokesman for the province. For example, a royal packet, the *Crane*, arrived about mid-September with news of the outbreak of war with France and orders to prepare defenses. It was Coode as "Commander in Cheife of His Majesty's forces in this Province by the order and appointment of the representative body of the whole Province," writing from "His Majesty's Garrison at Mattapany in Maryland," who acknowledged receipt of the orders. As the fall progressed, it was Coode who kept in touch with the English authorities and corresponded with neighboring colonies. Within the province itself, Coode and Cheseldyne were the individuals

---

came to the owners hands. . . . I'le add that I am confident the least scrip of order or Commande from King William would be gladly received and readily acknowledged with a general submission from the Freeholders of the Province God grant it may come quickly" (Richard Johns to Samuel Groome, Sept. 27, 1689, *ibid.*, VIII, 126).

[3] *Ibid.*

[4] *Ibid.*, 121. Vincent Lowe of Talbot may have remained in the colony. He was active in Talbot County by September 1690. (Talb. Test. Pro., 1689–92, Sept. 16, 1690).

to whom anxious men turned in seeking authority to deal with local problems.[5]

Nevertheless, maintaining order was the responsibility of the county governments empowered by the convention ordinance. The rebel leaders would lose their most powerful argument should they be obliged to use force against a fellow Protestant, and they lacked authorization to call anyone to account, except insofar as they were themselves local government officials. The local magistrates would have to keep the peace and maintain necessary public services. If they were unwilling to act, or if their powers were insufficient to the task, or if they could not command the respect required for successful exercise of authority, disorders would be likely.

The regularly scheduled autumn court sessions of the ten counties provided the new regime with its first major test. Proceedings remain for only four counties during the period from September through November, but these records provide some indication of the problems faced by what amounted to ten separate governments.

The September courts were undoubtedly the scene of many local debates and very little regular business. At least one, Talbot County Court, openly met, four strong, in the name of the proprietor. Two Cecil County justices, including one of the quorum, adjourned to November without any recorded proceedings or any indication that they recognized either Lord Baltimore or the new monarchs as the source of their authority. Courts in Somerset and Charles counties met in Their Majesties' names, but the former court was without a sheriff and the latter without a clerk. The Somerset justices ordered process to issue in the names of William and Mary, but they postponed officially qualifying as justices, presumably because the appointed sheriff, William Whittington, had not appeared. Six of the ten appointed justices of Charles County and the sheriff took "the usual oath," except that it, too, was in the name of William and Mary. Neither court

5 *Md. Archives*, VIII, 123, 127–28, 151–52, 162–64, 168–73, 177–80.

undertook any business of importance. The September court probably met in the other six counties, if only to keep the necessary governmental machinery operative; no accounts suggest otherwise. A failure to meet and adjourn would have terminated every criminal and civil procedure, and only an act of assembly could then reinstitute them.[6]

At least abbreviated sessions were likewise held during the November court days in these four counties, and it is clear that except in Cecil the revolutionary party had taken control. In Talbot County little was recorded, but the court met in Their Majesties' names for at least two days with two additional justices and a new clerk. Some testamentary business was transacted and deeds were acknowledged in open court, but a petition to the crown was probably the main subject of discussion.[7]

Surviving records from Cecil County contain more information but shed less light on proceedings. Four justices convened on November 12 and, in the clerk's words, "for reasons knowing to themselves" adjourned without action.[8] Casparus Herman, a justice reappointed by the convention who refused to sit during these months, furnished testimony in 1692 which hints at what the county records do not disclose. He accused James Frisby, a former member of the assembly and a strong proprietary man, of persuading several justices and the sheriff to ignore the ordinance and to hold court in Lord Baltimore's name.[9] How far the court went in this defiance is uncertain, for the book containing

[6] Talb. Land Rec., NN no. 6, f. 315; Cecil Judg., 1683–92, f. 82; Ch. Ct. and Land Rec., P no. 1, f. 185; Som. Jud. Rec., 1689–90, f. 2. For the consequences of failing to meet and adjourn, see C. Ashley Ellefson, "The County Courts and Provincial Court of Maryland, 1733–1763" (Ph.D. diss., University of Maryland, 1963), 255–56.

[7] Talb. Land Rec., NN no. 6, f. 315; KK no. 5, f. 245a; Talb. Test. Pro., 1689–92, Nov. 21, 1689.

[8] Cecil Judg., 1683–92, f. 82. In November, a release dated 1687 was recorded.

[9] *Md. Archives*, XIII, 318–19. Herman, the son of the prosperous German immigrant Augustine Herman, was himself accused of treason and papism in 1689, and he did not subscribe his oaths as a justice until August 11, 1691 (*Cal. S. P., Col., 1689–92*, no. 632; Cecil Judg., 1683–92,

all the criminal proceedings has not survived. Nothing in the civil record indicates that the four justices who appeared took oaths in the names of William and Mary, nor does it show they sat for the proprietor or attempted more than to maintain the existence of the court by meeting and adjourning. It is intriguing that one of the four, Edward Jones, was later accused of having opposed the revolution, yet he was a Cecil delegate in attendance at the August–September convention and was appointed to its interim committee in April 1690.[10] More certain opposition came from nineteen Cecil residents, including four justices who refused to sit. These men signed a petition to Their Majesties on November 18 asking for a restoration of Lord Baltimore's government. Their leader, St. Leger Codd, was apparently very active in stirring up opposition, for an accusation of some undetermined nature was "proved against him" at the second session of the Associators' Convention in April 1690.[11] If Cecil County was a persistent center of support for Lord Baltimore, it was also isolated, thinly populated, and only a minimal threat to the peace of the province. Excepting Anne Arundel County, opposition was not so extensive in any other area of the colony.[12]

The November court presented a special problem for the still unsworn justices of Somerset. Their sheriff, William Whittington, had refused to serve. With no legal or functioning provincial government from which to seek help, the justices had petitioned Coode and Cheseldyne after the September court; the suggestion returned that they appoint one of the coroners as sheriff. On October 29, the justices ordered Whittington to

---

f. 114). See also Rev. Charles Payson Mallory, "Ancient Families of Bohemia Manor," *Papers of the Historical Society of Delaware*, VII (Wilmington, Del., 1888), 11–23.

[10] *Md. Archives*, VIII, 196, 199; XIII, 364, 68; Cecil Judg., 1683–92, ff. 82–84.

[11] *Md. Archives*, VIII, 134–35; XIII, 359–60.

[12] Lord Baltimore's efforts to encourage settlement in Cecil County areas disputed with the Penns may account in part for his support there. See George Johnston, *History of Cecil County Maryland* . . . (Elkton, Md., 1881), 11; *Md. Archives*, XVII, 230–36, 239–40.

appear before them the following Tuesday, as he was the only person who "impeads their proceedings." Whittington pleaded illness and stayed away, but he sent a letter to the court explaining his conduct. His statement represents the concern with legitimate derivation of authority which led others to refuse to cooperate with the Associators. He indicated he had proclaimed Their Majesties and would prefer to serve the crown, but that he had taken an oath to Lord Baltimore which bound him until the crown dissented to Lord Baltimore's government. He observed that a packet had arrived from England which ought to contain news of royal pleasure, but that its contents had been kept secret. Whittington's suggested solution resembled the procedure actually adopted in Cecil County: Let the undersheriff call the court, which could then adjourn.[13]

On November 5, the justices met preparatory to the regular court session scheduled for the next week. Following Coode's advice, they appointed as sheriff William Brereton, one of their own number and also a coroner. The justices, sheriff, clerk, and clerk's deputy (selected by the clerk and approved by the justices) all subscribed to the oaths of office slightly amended to fit the new circumstances.[14] Only two of the fourteen men appointed to the court failed to qualify.[15]

[13] Som. Jud. Rec., 1689–90, ff. 3, 5–7. Richard Smith, Jr., of Calvert County stated a similar position when called before the convention (*Md. Archives*, VIII, 149–51). A "packet" had indeed arrived, but since it had left England in June, it contained nothing of relevance to the issue at dispute. See also Richard Johns's comment in n. 2, above. Coode discussed the royal letter "signifying war with France" in his letter to Jacob Leisler, Nov. 26, 1689, *DHNY*, II, 25–26. This was probably the letter Secretary of State Shrewsbury wrote on April 15, 1689 (CO5/723/I, f. 115).

[14] Som. Jud. Rec., 1687–89, f. 3; 1689–90, f. 7. The main change eliminated all references to the proprietor and the commission by which the justices were ordinarily authorized to act, and added a reference to the Laws of England. From September 4 until the arrival of Governor Copley in 1692, the justices' authority rested upon convention ordinance, not a commission. For discussion of the commission, see "County Government," text, 127–43.

[15] Som. Jud. Rec., 1689–90, ff. 7–8. Roger Woolford appeared but

The normal court session commenced on November 12. The justices appointed a clerk of indictments and two other attorneys were sworn. A grand jury made several presentments for thefts, sabbath-breaking, bastardy, and adultery—the usual assortment of offenses. The court appointed constables for the year and issued orders for the construction of a bridge. It ran through the civil docket, continuing most of the cases and taking final action in six where no contest was involved. On the second and last day of the court, the grand jury asked the justices to concur in an address to the crown which they and "many others that attended the Court" then signed and ordered "sent over the bay, in order to be presented to their Majesties."[16]

In Charles County the obstacle to orderly proceedings was the clerk, Richard Boughton, an old proprietary hand who refused to issue process or make entries in the names of William and Mary. At the regular November session of court, which began November 12, the justices appointed a new clerk; then they adjourned until November 26, apparently for lack of the court records. On that appointed day, Boughton appeared in the sheriff's custody and refused to acknowledge the authority of the justices. The court ordered that he remain in custody until the records were delivered; the sheriff was to demand the key for the trunk containing the records, and to break open the trunk should Boughton not surrender the key. The sheriff, clerk, and deputy clerk were all empowered to search any houses

---

asked time to consider; he did not appear again until he took the oaths and sat on August 11, 1691 (1690–91, f. 149). Thomas Newbold was specifically noted as absent on November 5, 1689; he did not appear thereafter until June 1690. However, he did sign the county address which was circulated and signed during the November 1689 court and which asked the crown for a Protestant government (*Md. Archives*, VIII, 139–40).

[16] Som. Jud. Rec., 1689–90, ff. 8–19; the quotation is on f. 19. For the text, see *Md. Archives*, VIII, 139–40 (incorrectly dated November 28); CO5/718/II (dated November 13). Attendance at the court must have been very large, for there are 242 signatures.

where records might be concealed, and the sheriff was authorized to break any locks if necessary. This procedure finally produced the essential records. Boughton was released from custody at the next court after a six-week imprisonment.[17]

The session beginning November 26 was the first in Charles
County to attempt regular business, and seven of the ten men
named in the September ordinance were now participating.[18]
Sheriff Gilbert Clarke empaneled a grand jury which made two
presentments, one for bastardy and the other for suspected murder. No attorneys had been sworn, however, and there is no
indication that the clerk called over a civil docket. The court
dispatched some servant business and laid the county levy. This
was an act of some importance, for it meant that taxes continued
to be collected to pay for poor relief.[19]

Proceedings in the other six counties probably followed one
or another of the patterns described for these four. Many courts
may have postponed as much business as possible. Nevertheless,
law and order and essential services must have been maintained
or complaints would have reached the outside world.

By the November court sessions, both revolutionary adherents
and proprietary stalwarts had been able to draw up petitions
and systematically to rally supporters for their respective posi-

[17] Ch. Ct. and Land Rec., P no. 1, ff. 185–88 From February 1665/6
to December 1667, Boughton was secretary of Maryland. Since that time,
he had been clerk in Anne Arundel and Charles counties (*HLP*, 126,
147, 149, 150).

[18] Capt. William Barton, absent in September, appeared and qualified.
The three noncooperating justices were John Stone, chief judge of the
court, Henry Hawkins, and William Hatton. All but Hatton appeared
as soon as royal approval came in the late spring of 1690 (*Md. Archives*,
XIII, 243; Ch. Ct. and Land Rec., P no. 1, ff. 185, 186, 188, 191; R no. 1,
ff. 2, 27). Hatton finally took the oaths of allegiance to Their Majesties
but not the oath of justice (P no. 1, ff. 185 *et seq.*; R no. 1, ff. 1–92, 93,
165–66).

[19] Ch. Ct. and Land Rec., P no. 1, ff. 185–88. Until this session, the
court's only business had been the issuing of three orders concerning
servants.

tions. Such petitions and addresses to the crown appear to have circulated in each county and most must have been signed during the November court. A total of nine addresses from eight counties have survived, six of them favorable to the recent revolution. The Associators expected and may have received sympathetic endorsements from all ten counties. When Coode dispatched six petitions to England on December 17, he promised others from the remaining counties for which the ship could not wait.[20]

The Associators were obviously anxious to enter these addresses as evidence of local support in their strategy to gain royal approval. Coode knew that proprietary spokesmen had already departed for England to represent their side of the uprising. They would later assert that signatures had been forged on the petitions favorable to the rebels, a charge which Coode and Cheseldyne labeled a "notorious falsehood."[21]

Petitions denouncing the overthrow of government and proclaiming confidence in Lord Baltimore have survived from Cecil, Baltimore, and Calvert counties. They protested against the motives of the rebels and decried the "Illiterate Persons and persons of evil life & conversation" who were made justices and militia officers; the clear desire of these men, in the words of the Cecil

---

[20] Coode's accompanying letter had originally mentioned five petitions, but this had been struck out and "six" inserted (Coode to Your Lordships, Dec. 17, 1689, CO5/718/I). These petitions, from Charles, Somerset, Kent, Talbot, Calvert, and St. Mary's counties, are in CO5/718/II, and are reproduced in *Md. Archives*, VIII, 135–47, with some slight errors. Only two are dated, Somerset (Nov. 13) and Kent (Nov. 28); the latter was probably the sixth and last to arrive. Five of them contain a total of 543 signatures or marks. The Kent petition does not bear individual names, but is endorsed by the statement "Justices and Grand Jury."

[21] "Petition of Loyal Protestant Subjects," undated, *Md. Archives*, VIII, 212–13; "Answer of Coode and Cheseldyne to Petition," undated, 206–7.

petition, was "that the Lord Baltemore may be restored and sent back again unto this his former Government."[22]

All nine addresses were signed by Protestants and contained assurances of loyalty to William and Mary. The two strongest statements for the proprietor came from the frontier counties of Baltimore and Cecil, a fact that may be related to the Calvert policy of encouraging settlement in those areas to protect the boundaries of the Maryland grant. Only Calvert County produced two petitions, with the pro-Baltimore supporters outnumbering the Associators' sympathizers 108 to 19.[23]

The uneasiness and latent hostility evident in these petitions mounted with the continued delay of news from England. Some outbreak of direct conflict or violence seemed unavoidable in this atmosphere of increased tension. Such a confrontation came in early January and provided the Associators with a new grievance by which they could sustain the fires of anti-Catholic prejudice and consolidate their wavering support.

Nicholas Sewall, Baltimore's stepson and a deposed deputy governor, had secretly returned from his Virginia refuge on December 28 to obtain some needed provisions on his Maryland plantation. Sewall was traveling in a small vessel which he anchored in one of the area's many creeks. News of his presence reached John Payne, a newly appointed militia captain and a

[22] The three original petitions, only one of which bears a date (Cecil—Nov. 18, 1689, is written on the outside) are also found in CO5/718/II and printed in *Md. Archives*, VIII, 129–32, and 134–37; quotations are on 136 and 135. These petitions bear the signature or marks of 153 Protestants.

[23] Interestingly, Thomas Collier signed both petitions. Thomas Tasker and Edward Batson, who had signed the August 20 petition refusing to elect burgesses, were now among those endorsing the new government. Tasker refused, however, to sit on the Charles County grand jury this same November and was fined (Ch. Ct. and Land Rec., P no. 1, f. 186). Tasker had been made a captain of the militia for Calvert County in the September ordinance. His position is very confusing.

collector of customs for the Patuxent River.[24] Payne, accompanied by men in two armed boats, went after Sewall, and the fateful encounter came on the moonlit night of January 3. Sewall was apparently not present, but his men opposed Payne's intentions to board the ketch. In the ensuing struggle and confusion, guns fired and Payne was killed. Sewall and his men fled back to Virginia.

Whether Payne had been acting legitimately as customs collector in trying to inspect the vessel's cargo or was forcing entry as an officer of the Associators' militia to arrest Sewall was widely debated at once and at the murder trial fifteen months later. Coode had diligently but unsuccessfully sought to bring several of the ousted proprietary officials into custody since September. He now seized this opportunity to proclaim the news of a "barbarous murder" committed on a royal official by papists. Only five years before, a proprietary councillor had murdered Christopher Rousby, another customs collector. With the memory of that event renewed in the minds of Marylanders, it may not have been too difficult to convince them of the guilt of Sewall and the men aboard the ketch that evening.[25]

Although the incident in all likelihood forestalled any open resistance in Maryland to the Associators and prevented any substantial defections in the absence of royal communication, it also represented the first bloodshed and posed in acute fashion the problems created by the absence of central authority. For who

[24] *HLP*, 179; *Md. Archives*, VIII, 148.

[25] Coode to Secretary of State, Jan. 10, Feb. 18, and March 24, 1689/90, CO5/718/II; *Md. Archives*, VIII, 169–70, 170–73. For the fullest secondary account of the murder and ensuing developments, see Bernard C. Steiner, "The Protestant Revolution in Maryland," *Annual Report of the American Historical Association for the Year 1897* (Washington, D.C., 1898), 323–24, 345–51. Steiner is mistaken, however, in his assertion that Sewall was never tried. The presentment and trial came at the September session of the Provincial Court in 1692; Sewall was found innocent (Prov. Ct. Judg., DSC, f. 46). The trial of others charged with the murder came in April of 1691 and is described below, pp. 140–45.

could require the Virginia government to return the suspects, and what tribunal had jurisdiction to try them? Coode informed the English authorities of the incident and wrote repeatedly to Nathaniel Bacon, president of the Virginia council, to request the arrest and return of the accused. The Virginia council issued warrants for the men who had been aboard the ketch at the moment of the murder, but not for Sewall. Nor would Bacon return any of the men to Maryland. Indeed, eventually a Virginia court allowed them to go free on "Recognizance with good Security to keep the peace" until the English authorities should command other action.[26]

This was not the first time that the Virginia authorities had proved uncooperative, nor would it be the last. Jacob Leisler's rebel government in New York had responded enthusiastically to the convention's "Letter to Adjacent Colonies,"[27] but Virginia had remained aloof. In November Coode had written to ask that Joseph, Sewall, "one Woodcock," and two priests be arrested as fugitives and kept in custody for return to Maryland, but he had received no reply. Nor, as the winter progressed, did Nathaniel Bacon and his colleagues prove willing to participate in the exchange of exaggerated reports and rumors of Catholic, French, and Indian conspiracies. They also declined to lend assistance at New York, despite the requests of Leisler and Coode. Their convenient excuse was that they could "proceed to nothing till the arrivall of their Gouvernor." Their suspicions of the revolutionary governments found expression in their actions if not their words.[28]

Coode was most anxious both to remedy his ineffectiveness in intercolonial relations and to eliminate other internal prob-

---

[26] *Md. Archives*, VIII, 163–65, 166–71, 176–77; "Account of General Court held at James City, Virginia, Apr. 29, 1690," CO5/713/I, no. 8.

[27] The correspondence between the two colonies may be followed in *DHNY*, II, 19–20, 25–26, 32–33, 42–44, 101–3, 117–18, 126–27, 140, 206–9, 211–12, 225–27, 248–50.

[28] *Md. Archives*, VIII, 127–28, 152, 163; *DHNY*, II, 140.

lems arising from the lack of an authorized central government. When the convention reconvened in St. Mary's City on April 1, 1690, the need for an interim committee was a major item on the agenda. Undoubtedly the leaders recited their problems of the past few months as they pressed again for the creation of a "Grand Council." In addition to their lack of power in dealing with Virginia, they could recount troublesome local issues. Somerset County, for example, had sought advice on two occasions; without clearly defined channels of authority, the local officers had appealed to both Coode and Cheseldyne. In the first instance, it was to solicit suggestions for dealing with a recalcitrant sheriff. Then, in January, the justices had sent their new sheriff to St. Mary's to "Mr. Cheseldyne or to those in present Authority" to relate the "insolencies" of some local Indians, to obtain ammunition, and to "receive a particular answer" to a special letter. The letter indicated the court's discomfort as it attempted to maintain the routine of local order and its concern about the existence somewhere of a "present authority." "We have lately understood of some transactions happened in your parts and likewise of Mr. Pains untimely End, as also that a Proclamacon was Issued out after some persons inhabiting in our parts, which said Proclamacon we have not yet received. Here is many disaffected persons here which absolutely denyes this present power. . . ." Among the disaffected was William Whittington, who had read publicly at Snow Hill Town three letters from Baltimore's former councillors which said the proprietor's charter had been confirmed by the crown. There were also rumors Cheseldyne now regretted his part "in this Revolution of government."[29]

The concern for greater direction probably existed in other counties as well; certainly, a desire to exercise greater direction existed among Coode and his immediate cohorts. In their necessary cautiousness heretofore, they had been most careful not to

[29] Som. Jud. Rec., 1689–90, f. 41.

intrude overtly in county issues but to leave their resolution to local leaders. The one exception had been Coode's instructions to the militia officers of each county, in accordance with a royal command, "to make all necessary preparation of defence" for the war with France.[30]

The arguments in favor of some centralized authority now proved persuasive. Someone or some group had to represent Maryland with authority in correspondence with England and neighboring colonies; some one must be armed with authority to demand the return of fugitives; someone must be given power at least to advise county governments. The convention therefore appointed two delegates from each county to serve as a "Grand Committee of Twenty"; it also appointed Coode, as commander in chief of the armed forces, to preside over this committee which would advise and assist him in governing between sessions of the convention. This body was to receive messages "relating to the publick" and to "issue such fitt and necessary orders and Instructions as shall be requisite and convenient for the Publick comodietie upon all emergency of affaires" until the next convention or until "other lawfull Power" intervened. Any seven or more people could act, and in the event of a tie, Coode was to have the "casting vote."[31]

The appointments to the Grand Committee reflected the growing consolidation of power in the tightly knit core of original rebel leaders and their earliest followers. Cheseldyne, Blakiston, Jowles, and Beale all obtained seats, as did men who had proven their dependability, like George Robotham and John Edmundson, who led the insurgent victory in Talbot County. Appointments went to John Addison and John Courts, whose enthusiasm for the revolution surpassed that of the more experienced and more cautious Charles County delegates John Stone and Henry Hawkins. With the exception of Stone, Hawkins,

[30] See *Md. Archives,* VIII, 123–24. The letter containing this command had left England in June.

[31] *Ibid.,* 199.

and Thomas Thurston of Baltimore County, all Associators with prior assembly experience received appointment: William Harris and Michael Miller from Kent; John Brooke and Henry Trippe of Dorchester; Edward Jones of Cecil; Edmundson, Robotham, Jowles, and Cheseldyne. None of these nine had offered any opposition to the revolution; indeed, so far as the records exist, they indicate that these men were willing to lend significant assistance to the overthrow of Baltimore's government.

The action of the convention in appointing this body also resolved, at least temporarily, the question of supremacy of power which had earlier plagued the rebel leadership and would bother them again. Who was foremost in authority? It is clear that in the initial days of the revolution, the proprietary council had viewed Jowles as a key member of the coalition and had concentrated its efforts on wooing him away with a proffered appointment as "General of all the forces in the Province." After the coup, however, Darnall described Jowles as "Chief of their party next to Cood," and Jowles's signature was second to Coode's on such important documents as the articles of surrender and "The Declaration of the reason and motive for the present appearing in arms."[32] Most observers conceded Coode was the military leader, and his continued claims to leadership rested upon his military position. As "Commander in Chiefe of His Majesty's forces," he acted as the colony's spokesman in letters to England and other colonies, although nothing in the ordinance of September 4 suggests that this title conferred on him any provincewide power.[33]

It is not clear, however, that other Marylanders accepted Coode's claim to pre-eminence. The Somerset justices, for example, had appealed both to Coode and to Cheseldyne "or to those in present Authority."[34] Cheseldyne, as speaker of the lower house since 1686 and holder of that same position in the

---

[32] *Ibid.*, 156, 101–7, 107–8.
[33] *Ibid.*, 123, 127–28, 151–52, 163–65, 168–73, 177–79.
[34] Som. Jud. Rec., 1689–90, f. 41.

Associators' Convention, undoubtedly drew the respect of many people as the most "legitimate" person of authority above the county level. Nonetheless, the action of the convention in April in placing Coode over the committee rendered the "Commander in Chiefe" the foremost in authority. But as many were all too conscious, it was still an authority without royal sanction.

"The unsettled state of our present constitution not having any orders from England or knowing their Majestys pleasure relating to this province" occupied the minds of the delegates to the second convention in April.[35] They apprehensively awaited the impending arrival of the spring fleet and hopefully the crown's blessing. Meanwhile, they continued to mark time as far as possible. Some business could not be postponed. There had to be sufficient magistrates and militia officers, and those appointed in September who had refused to accept their offices and perform their duties, or who had resisted the new government in other ways, had to be replaced. Nevertheless, the convention's actions, in the absence of news of royal sanction, was limited. The offenders were simply not renamed in the new ordinance that apparently now issued.[36] This ordinance probably specified that officers take the oaths of allegiance and supremacy, since these oaths soon appear in the county records for the first time.[37] It furthermore required sheriffs to give bond for the proper performance of their duties, a procedure neglected in the September ordinance.[38]

It is likely that the convention declined to reappoint at least sixteen of the original 105 justices, presumably because of their continued open—though yet peaceful—resistance to the rebels and their defense of Lord Baltimore.[39] Nineteen new justices

[35] Coode to Leisler, May 19, 1690, *DHNY*, II, 140.

[36] The April ordinance has not survived; conclusions about it are drawn from the county records that indicate the presence of new officers and new procedures after this convention.

[37] See Ch. Ct. and Land Rec., R no. 1, f. 27 (Aug. 1690).

[38] *Ibid.*, ff. 1–2.

[39] Sixteen men refused service. See Appendix B, Table B-2, and Carr

can be identified in county records as taking their places on the bench between April and the next convention in September; they were presumably all appointed in April.[40] It is also reasonable to assume the convention confirmed the earlier appointment of William Brereton by the Somerset justices to replace William Whittington as sheriff, and probably the substitution of Abel Brown for Henry Hanslap as sheriff of Anne Arundel. Fewer changes were required in militia appointments, since far greater care had been exercised in selecting those officers in September. Still, four of the fifty appointed at that time had refused to support the new government and were probably replaced.[41] It is certain that some new appointments and promotions occurred, such as the rapid rise of Charles Hutchins of Dorchester to the rank of colonel.[42]

The Associators temporized on all other business. Coode did present the urgent appeals of New York for fifty or one hundred men to join in a campaign to prevent Indian "incursions" from Canada. The delegates considered the request and "unanimously voted speedy aid and assistance against that common tyrannicall Enemy," but they hesitated over "the way and manner of soe doing & the measures therein to be taken for the more effectuall doing thereof." A select committee further studied the matter but could come to "noe determinate resolucon." Coode

---

and Jordan, "Service of Civil and Military Officers, July 1689–September 1692," table on file at Hall of Records, Annapolis.

[40] See Appendix B, Table B-5.

[41] Edward Dorsey and Henry Hanslap of Anne Arundel, John Hynson of Kent, and probably Walter Smith of Calvert. See Carr and Jordan, "Service of Civil and Military Officers." Of fifty officers appointed, service is proved for thirty-seven and is probable for four more. It is undetermined for five. See Appendix B, Table B-6.

[42] Dor. Land Rec., O no. 4½, f. 195. Hutchins did not receive a militia appointment in September, and the first reference to his colonelcy was in August 1690. He was a member of the Grand Committee of Twenty. Three men in Somerset County (David Browne, Robert King, and John King) received either a promotion or a new appointment (Som. Jud. Rec., 1689–90, ff. 63, 111, 147, 156).

reported to Leisler the great difficulty in raising men and apportioning expenses while Maryland remained in her unsettled state. At a meeting of the Grand Committee in May, however, he gained sufficient support for sending agents to New York to consult with Leisler on the best means for assisting him given the present circumstances.[43]

The English fleet had anchored in the Chesapeake Bay by mid-May, and it had brought Virginia's new lieutenant governor, Francis Nicholson. Coode wrote Nicholson on May 19 to congratulate him on his safe arrival and to make an "early tender of my due servince and respects." More importantly, Coode wanted information on "any comands you may have from his Majesty to remit to this province."[44] More than a week passed with no answer. On May 28, Coode dispatched a more anxious and hurried note to Nicholson in which he begged an answer to his earlier request.[45]

An answer was not forthcoming until June 6, when Nicholson wrote "to those that for the time being take care to execute the Laws etc. in the Province of Maryland." His letter suggested both sarcasm and suspicion. Nicholson inquired to whom he should address his letters and requested the names of those "preserving the peace, administering the Laws." These calculated efforts to put Coode in his place reflected both Nicholson's previous unpleasant experiences with Leisler's rebellion in New York and conversations with the Virginia council since his arrival. At several points he indicated he would act only after "I can rightly and fully be informed . . . from such persons as

[43] Leisler to Coode, Mar. 4, 1689/90; Cheseldyne to Leisler, Apr. 3, 1690; and Coode to Leisler, May 19, 1690 (*DHNY*, II, 101–3, 117–18, 140). In early 1692, the Privy Council voted to allot £250 from the public revenues of Maryland to assist New York in her defense against the French and Indians (*Md. Archives*, VIII, 290).

[44] *Md. Archives*, VIII, 179–80. Coode also could not resist including some of his resentments against the Virginia council for protecting papists and murderers.

[45] *Ibid.*, 180.

are lawfully authorized by their Majesties." With regard to the charges against the exiled Marylanders, he demanded evidence of their misdoings, for "the writing soe in a letter without proofe can be noe accusation of any man." Without mention of royal news, Nicholson in a businesslike manner instructed his correspondents on the proper procedures for having the ships gather at Point Comfort to sail home in a fleet, by royal order.[46]

Coode's certain displeasure at such treatment was surely tempered for the moment by the long awaited letter from the crown which had been separately forwarded by Nicholson on May 30.[47] The king's letter, dated February 1, 1689/90, contained his request that the Associators "continue in our name your care in the administration of the Government and preservation of the peace and properties of our Subjects, according to the Laws and usage of that our Province untill upon a full examination of all matters and hearing of what shall be represented to us on behalf of the Proprietor and his Right. We shall have taken such finall resolution and given such directions for a lasting settlement as shall most conduce to our service and to the security and satisfaction of our subjects." The king instructed them to "take especiall care that the severall Acts of trade and Navigation be duley observed" and "to suffer the Proprietor or his agents to collect the Revenues arising there." Only that part of the revenue normally applied to the administration of the government could be employed by the Associators.[48]

The relief of the colony at the arrival of royal sanction for its temporary government and the anxiety which had accompanied the long delay is evident in the proceedings of the county courts. These had continued to reflect both the strengths and weaknesses of the interim government. The peace had been kept,

[46] *Ibid.*, 186–88.

[47] *Ibid.*, 193. Nicholson had been entrusted in England with the letter for delivery to Maryland (169).

[48] *Ibid.*, 167–68.

but magistrates had not always forced unwilling residents to recognize the new regime.

In Somerset County, for example, a generally stable area, the
murder of Payne combined with rumors from Virginia that Lord
Baltimore was to be reinstated in his province created unrest
which was apparent at the January court. It conducted normal
business, but less than usual. The court impaneled two juries,
although five jurymen failed to appear and substitutes had to be
found. It heard criminal and a few civil cases, one with a jury.
It also laid the county levy but must have reduced the items to
be paid at this time to a minimum, because the charge per poll
was only eighteen pounds of tobacco.[49] In addition, it considered complaints about the "insolencies" of some Indians and appointed representatives to discover the grievances and to have
the Indians present their complaints at court. Ominous, however, was the undersheriff's report that Matthew Scarborough
had refused service of a writ on the ground that "he denyed the
power now in being." William Whittington had also been among
"many disaffected persons here which absolutely denyes this
present power dayle." Whittington was particularly upsetting
some people with his statements that Lord Baltimore was returning to Maryland to reassume full control of the colony and that
Cheseldyne now regretted his participation in the overthrow of
the proprietary government and would "rather have given five
hundred pounds then been concerned in this Revolution of government." The court dispatched the sheriff to St. Mary's with
a letter reporting Whittington's agitations and the rumors of
Cheseldyne's defections.[50]

[49] Som. Jud. Rec., 1689–90, ff. 28–40, 41 (levy). The levy itself is not
written into the record, but it may have covered only eight months. The
Associators proudly boasted in 1689 that they had laid the lowest provincial levy in years; it probably did not exceed twenty-five pounds of
tobacco per poll (*Md. Archives*, XIII, 238; VIII, 228).
[50] Som. Jud. Rec., 1689–90, ff. 28, 40, 41. *Old Somerset*, 339–52, con-

The Somerset magistrates kept control of the situation, however. What reassurances Sheriff William Brereton may have brought back from St. Mary's are not recorded in the March proceedings, but the business of the court appears to have returned to normal. There were a large number of civil cases, and several were tried by jury. Scarborough, presented and tried for his contempt, even issued an apology.[51]

Greater uneasiness, and therefore greater caution and less activity, were characteristic of Charles County Court during the same period. The grand juries of November and March made presentments and indictments against only eleven people, as compared to twenty-five presentments in Somerset. The court disposed of only one of these eleven, a presentment for bastardy.[52] There is nothing to indicate the court appointed a clerk of indictments who could have prosecuted in a formal trial. Five men, including Major John Wheeler, a justice at the outbreak of the revolution, appeared on summons at the January court, where witnesses accused them of failing to assist in an arrest; all were bound to good behavior. A grand jury indicted them in March, but they were not tried until the following September.[53]

The Charles court conducted almost no civil business, although the lack of sheriff's returns and clerk's dockets make the extent of its inactivity uncertain. No attorneys appear to have been sworn before January when John Skipper was admitted to practice; proceedings recorded for two entirely routine civil cases indicate that George Plater was also considered an attorney of the court. The March court awaited these two men in order to conduct pending business and eventually fined them for their nonappearance, which necessitated adjournment of the court. It

---

tains a very well documented account of activities in the county from August of 1689 to the arrival of the royal letter.

[51] Som. Jud. Rec., 1689–90, ff. 46–86.
[52] Ch. Ct. and Land Rec., P no. 1, ff. 186–87, 191–92.
[53] *Ibid.*, ff. 190, 188–89; R no. 1, ff. 44–46. A jury found them innocent.

is impossible to determine whether they failed to appear as a matter of discretion in the increasingly uneasy situation or for nonpolitical reasons. The justices, however, may have been under some pressure to re-establish proceedings at law, for the court had made no civil determinations since the previous June.[54]

Throughout these months, the justices conducted some essentially administrative functions, such as inspecting the indentures of servants, licensing an ordinary, and laying the county levy.[55] Evidently they appointed constables, for one refused to serve.[56] In all respects, however, the court was far less active than that of Somerset County, where the proceedings from September through March fill eighty-six pages in contrast to thirteen pages for Charles County.

Two seemingly minor items suggest the attitude brought by the Charles County justices to their problem. They bound over a murder suspect to the Provincial Court, and they rejected a petition for a reversal of judgment on the validity of an indenture, telling the aggrieved party to take out a writ of error.[57] Both actions represented a refusal to expand in any way the previous jurisdiction of the court and an assumption that the normal routine of government would soon be re-established. Relief is evident in the pages that record the proceedings of the June court in 1690, the court which met just after the receipt of royal approval of the revolution. Ten justices appeared and were sworn, after which they admitted four attorneys to practice. Eighteen pages record the first civil determinations in the

---

[54] *Ibid.*, P no. 1, ff. 190–91, 195. The last previously recorded judgments were in June 1689 (ff. 171–74).

[55] *Ibid.*, ff. 185, 187, 188, 194–95, 196. As in Somerset, the levy seems unusually small at 29,803 pounds of tobacco; the levy for the preceding year was 61, 428 pounds (ff. 33, 187).

[56] Robert Thompson (*ibid.*, f. 190). Since he signed the prorevolutionary address from the county, his refusal may not have had any political overtones.

[57] Ch. Ct. and Land Rec., P no. 1, ff. 191, 194. A writ of error assumed the existence of both the chancellor and the Provincial Court.

county in a year. The legal basis of the court was no longer in question.[58]

Anne Arundel County, which had refused to send delegates to the first session of the convention, might logically be expected to have maintained the greatest resistance to the rebels. Although the court proceedings of that county are destroyed, the land records provide a glimmering of what may have happened there in these nine months.[59] The exact events of the fall, after the county refused to elect delegates to the convention, remain unknown. Presumably Coode's threatened march into Anne Arundel with the militia did not occur. The available evidence suggests that local leaders concentrated on keeping the people quiet and maintaining regular procedures until orders arrived from England. Until June of 1690, most of the county deeds were written without reference either to Lord Baltimore or to the king and queen, and acknowledgments not made in open court were made before two justices not designated as authorized by the proprietor or the crown. How this procedure was managed may well have depended upon the wishes of parties to the various conveyances, for it was the security of their property which was at stake.[60]

[58] *Ibid.*, R no. 1, ff. 1–2, 7–25.

[59] A fire destroyed all records of Anne Arundel County in 1704, and special arrangements were made for rerecording deeds from existing instruments (Acts 1705, c. 1, *Md. Archives*, XXVI, 507–9). The rerecordings in five volumes are not in chronological order and are incomplete.

[60] On September 11, Henry Constable and Thomas Knighton took an acknowledgment of a conveyance without reference to the proprietor or Their Majesties; the clerk recorded that they acted according to the act of assembly, but did not designate them justices (AA Land Rec., IH no. 1, f. 91). Knighton's name does not appear again. He was in England in November 1690 protesting the actions of the new government (*Md. Archives*, VIII, 213). The next deed, dated December 4, 1689, was recorded in the proprietor's name and acknowledged before Nicholas Gassaway and Nicholas Greenberry "of his Lordships Justices of the Peace" (AA Land Rec., IH no. 2, ff. 50–54). Only two days later, however, another deed, not recorded in any name, was sealed and delivered before Gassaway and Constable without mention of their status as jus-

The first deed made out in Their Majesties' names and acknowledged before Their Majesties' justices bears the date June 23, 1690.[61] It is possible, therefore, that from September or November until June the Anne Arundel court met without being sworn in the name of Baltimore or the crown. However the matter was managed, it is clear the county leaders made an effort to maintain the regular function of government.

Delegates may have attended the convention in April when Nicholas Gassaway and Nicholas Greenberry were appointed as Anne Arundel representatives on the interim committee; with other of its members they signed an address to the crown on July 11. From this time on, at least, the local court must have been held in the name of the crown.[62]

Royal confirmation probably brought to Cecil County its first court held in Their Majesties' names and possibly the first court to conduct any proceedings since the overturn of the proprietary government. Criminal proceedings for the 1680's and 1690's

---

tices (IH no. 1, ff. 298–302). In January, Greenberry and Constable acted as justices, but again not in anyone's name (f. 29). Other deeds for these months similarly handled are in IH no. 2, ff. 144–46, IH no. 3, ff. 120–23.

[61] AA Land Rec., IH no. 2, ff. 248–51. Two more deeds, made out in Baltimore's name, were dated as late as July 3, 1690, and signed by John Brown, mariner of London. He may have been the John Browne, master of a London ship, about whom the council complained to the crown in July 1692 for his "notorious false Reports Lyes, and Suggestions to stir up the People of this Province to a thro [thorough] Dislike of the Government" (IH no. 2, ff. 69–74, 201–5; *Md. Archives*, VIII, 333).

[62] *Md. Archives*, VIII, 196. Henry Hanslap, appointed sheriff by the Convention, served until February 1689/90, when he either refused to continue or was dismissed; see AA Land Rec., IH no. 1, ff. 29, 91; IH no. 2, f. 146. Thereafter he took alienation fines for Lord Baltimore and by July 1692 he did so with the title of His Lordship's Subcollector (*ibid.*, ff. 164, 205; IH no. 1, ff. 34, 302). He should be listed as one who opposed the provisional government. Abel Brown served as sheriff from February 1690; he was called "late high sheriff" in May of 1692 and by June 8, 1692, was a justice (*Md. Archives*, VIII, 324; XIII, 266–67). Henry Bonner served as clerk throughout the period (see the above references in the land records).

are lost, but the book of civil proceedings shows that, from November until June, the court simply adjourned from session to
session, without reference to authorization. The only activity
shown for the whole period is an attachment granted in January.[63] Conceivably, criminal and administrative business continued, but it was probably kept to a minimum. If all activity
was suspended, the impotent poor must have been fed and housed
by informal arrangement to be compensated when times were
more orderly; and magistrates must have been willing to exercise
their peace-keeping powers at least to the extent of binding over
offenders to appear before the court, once it had proper authorization.[64] However local affairs were managed, the convention
made no drastic changes on the bench; in April it reappointed
all the Cecil justices except St. Leger Codd and Gideon Gundry.[65] The action, to be sure, may have reflected more despera-
tion than confidence in the Cecil justices. Even in June, after
the arrival of the royal letter, there was agitation to recognize
Lord Baltimore, apparently on the grounds that approval of the
power in being meant approval of men still sworn to uphold
Lord Baltimore's authority.[66] A court sworn in the names of
Their Majesties was at last convened, however, and in August it
began routine business.[67]

Court proceedings for these crucial months have not survived
from any of the remaining counties, but fragmentary records
show that courts met, and they provide no evidence of serious
disorders.[68] Had there been any significant conflict, it surely

[63] Cecil Judg., 1683–92, ff. 82–84.

[64] For a discussion of the peace-keeping powers of single magistrates,
see "County Government," text, 98–113.

[65] Proceedings of the June court show that Charles James and Edward
Blay replaced Codd and Gundry (Cecil Judg., 1683–92, f. 84).

[66] See pp. 124–27 below.

[67] Cecil Judg., 1683–92, ff. 85a–87b. The cases on the docket of June
1689 had been continued until court was again in operation; see ff. 82a,
85a, 88a.

[68] Some testamentary proceedings survive for Calvert County for the

would have been mentioned in the correspondence, addresses, and other papers that document the negotiations in England among the contending parties. These accounts complain of the arrests at the beginning of the revolution and of others, to be discussed, immediately after the arrival of the king's letter, and they charge that Protestants loyal to the crown were discharged from office and threatened for failure to support the Associators. There are no assertions, however, that the machinery of government had fallen apart, nor details of any other significant conflict or disruption of local governmental processes.[69]

Until May 30, 1690, the debate in Maryland seems to have revolved around the problem of legitimacy. Since the Catholic minority was silent, there is little suggestion that many questioned or regretted the changes in England,[70] but a number continued to question the legal right of Maryland Protestants to take comparable action against Lord Baltimore,[71] at least so long

---

period beginning in January 1689/90; they indicate which justices sat. See Test. Pro. 16, ff. 1–50. A few testamentary papers were recorded in Dorchester County at the January and March courts, proving that courts did convene there. Maj. Henry Trippe, Dr. John Brooke, and Mr. Jacob Lookerman sat in March (Dor. Land Rec., O no. 4½, ff. 1–6). Testamentary proceedings for Talbot begin in November 1689 and show that the courts sat at least on Nov. 21, Jan. 22, Feb. 18, March 18, and March 27. The justices sitting are not listed, but several are authorized to swear administrations (Talb. Test. Pro., 1689–92).

[69] See for instance the following accounts: James Heath's protest against Coode, June 19, 1690; Thomas Smithson to Bishop of London, June 30, 1690; Petition to the crown, Nov. 13, 1690, signed by eleven Maryland Protestants; *Md. Archives,* VIII, 188–90, 192–93, 212–13.

[70] On July 15, 1690, Richard Hill was accused of having said during the August court of 1689 that King William "could not give account how he could come by the Crowne of England by faire play, for he could claime noe Right neither by decent Law or Justice" (*Md. Archives,* VIII, 196). Simon Wilmer of Kent County was acquitted in September 1692 of calling King William a rebel on June 27, 1690 (Prov. Ct. Judg., DSC, f. 42). Edward Dorsey was accused of uttering on board ship "mutinous and seditious speeches" which may have reflected on William's claim to the throne, but the record is not specific (*Md. Archives,* VIII, 375).

[71] See the statements by Richard Smith, Jr., and Michael Taney, pre-

as he was a loyal English subject acting under a legal charter. The Associators had acted with extreme caution. Proven enemies of the new government, such as Richard Hill, were left at large, possibly on the understanding that they would offer no act of resistance but await a royal settlement.[72] There was no interference in local governmental affairs even after the establishment of the Grand Committee. In all correspondence with England and Virginia, Coode emphasized that he was spokesman for a convention elected by loyal Protestants, and though he spoke as commander in chief, he was careful not to leave the impression that Maryland was under military rule. Through the anxious winter, the leaders sought to avoid any action that might in the end be labeled illegal or even treasonable.

The chief responsibility for keeping order and thus ensuring success rested with the county courts. In part, their achievement was possible because those who might have led resistance preferred to avoid armed conflict that would certainly lead to bloodshed. Thus as long as the civil arm could keep the peace and prevent minor disorders from sparking greater ones, the military had no need to act. Undoubtedly the existence of a militia officered by men known to be loyal to the interim government strengthened the hand of the courts, especially in the seven counties where several justices or the sheriff also held militia commissions.[73] A cornerstone of the Associators' position, how-

---

pared while under arrest in September 1689 (*Md. Archives*, VIII, 119–21, 149–51) and Whittington's letter to the Somerset County Court (pp. 88–89 above).

[72] For Hill, see pp. 112–14 below.

[73] Civil officers appointed under the first ordinance who held military commissions were distributed as follows: St. Mary's, 4 of 9 justices; Calvert, 3 of 12 justices; Charles, 4 of 10 justices; Anne Arundel, 5 of 12 justices and the sheriff; Baltimore, 2 of 10 justices and the sheriff; Cecil, none of 11 justices and the sheriff; Kent, 2 of 9 justices; Talbot, 1 of 11 justices; Dorchester, 1 of 7 justices; Somerset, 4 of 14 justices. Total, 26 of 105 justices, 3 of 10 sheriffs. Of these 29, 2 justices and a sheriff refused to serve, and the response of one justice is unknown. Only 6 of the 25 who served were not holding their civil appointments at the out-

ever, lay in the fact that civil, not military, government prevailed; its ability to prevail, and to prevail without the supporting institutions of provincial government, was a product of far
more than militia support. The local justices felt a responsibility
to maintain the peace, and they were men of a caliber to command respect. The courts on which they served had a generation of development behind them. The proprietors themselves,
by allowing the development of a local magistracy trained to
the exercise of real power, had made a large contribution to the
success of the rebels who overthrew the proprietary establishment.

---

break of the revolution. See Carr and Jordan, "Service of Civil and
Military Officers July 1689–September 1692," table on file at the Hall of
Records. Insofar as the militia bolstered the civil government, then, it
did so largely with men who were already accepted figures of civil
authority.

CHAPTER IV

"Preservation of the Peace and Properties," May 1690–April 1692

With the arrival of the royal letter in late May of 1690, the Associators' government gained legal authorization from the crown to "continue in our name your care in the administration of the Government and preservation of the peace and properties of our Subjects." Nevertheless, the governmental order that prevailed in July 1689 had by no means been restored. For the next year Maryland continued to operate without courts above the county level and for the next two years without most of the normal provincial departments. The convention, made up of four delegates from each county elected by the freeholders, met at St. Mary's City twice a year, but as an executive, not a legislative, body. The Grand Committee could act in emergencies, but its powers were in no way equivalent to those of the council. Until the re-establishment of the Provincial Court in April of 1691, the main center of authority remained in the county courts. For the entire period before the arrival of a royal governor, the smooth operations of local government were necessary to the survival of an uneasy interregnum.

Nevertheless, the hand of Coode and the Grand Committee was now greatly strengthened. At last they possessed a temporary royal sanction, and they did not hesitate to employ it immediately in actions against those individuals who had been actively opposing them. The cautious treatment of the opposition since September surrendered on May 30 to a more vindictive spirit, and military power was probably used for the first time since the previous August.[1]

On May 31, "near forty men in armes in a most violent rage" attempted to arrest Richard Hill of Anne Arundel County, one of several men for whom warrants were issued.[2] Hill escaped his pursuers and hid in the wilderness until he could flee first to Virginia and then to England. The men ransacked his house and seized his ship in an attempt to prevent his escape by water. Their warrant contained no mention of any specific crime, according to three defenders of Hill, who himself claimed he had "neither spoken nor acted anything that can carry the least tincture of dishonor or loyaltie to their sacred Majesties nor ill becoming a loyall subject but indeed I have somewhat opposed their illegal and arbitrary proceedings."[3]

Hill's opposition, especially vocal just after the rebellion of the preceding summer, had occupied the attention of the Associators at their first session. That opposition probably contributed to Anne Arundel's slow acceptance of the new government, but no details remain on Hill's specific actions in the interim. True to his fashion, Coode's accusations against him in a letter to Nicholson on June 24 were vague and unsubstantiated; he wrote of "one Richard Hill fled lately into Virginia for treasonable words against their Majesties and for raising of men and being in actual arms here against the present Government since their Majesties Proclamation." Nicholson's earlier letter should have sufficiently warned Coode he would gain no assistance in such causes with-

[1] Although the ordinance passed in September had empowered militia officers to "suppress all homebred insurrections," there is no indication that military power was exercised. It is noteworthy that Somerset took no action against Whittington for his refusal to serve as sheriff, and Boughton was imprisoned in Charles in order to obtain the county records, not as a punishment for his refusal to serve as clerk. Neither court attempted to force the appearance of appointees who preferred not to cooperate. This was apparently the case elsewhere in the colony as well.

[2] *Md. Archives*, VIII, 181–82, 188–90.

[3] *Ibid.*, 181–82, 184–85.

out more specific evidence. The Grand Committee later informed Nicholson that the evidence to support all the charges would be "produced when he [Hill] shall be secured for Justice." The evidence consisted of a deposition sworne against Hill on July 15 by John Hammond, who related statements allegedly made by the accused at the August court in 1689 against the rebellion and his strong reluctance to recognize William and Mary.[4]

Other men were not so fortunate as Hill in escaping the authorities. James Heath, an agent of Lord Baltimore, complained on June 19 of the "Rifleing and Pillaging of Severall of the most eminent protestants Houses, the imprisoning of the persons of Same, and sending armed men in pursuit of others from place to place with warrants to ffetch them Dead or alive; thereby Driving them ffrom their Habitations." One of the "most eminent protestants" arrested was Thomas Smithson of Talbot County who described his imprisonment and that of others in an appeal to the Bishop of London.[5] Smithson's primary offense had apparently been the solicitation of signatures for petitions against the Associators which circulated in Kent and Talbot counties in early June. These documents denounced "the falsehood and unfaithfulness of John Coode and others his associates," described the false rumors that had been deliberately circulated by the rebels, and protested the removals from office of "severall of your Majesties good subjects of unquestionable Loyalty and affection to the Church of England who approved not of [Coode's] actions."[6]

---

[4] *Ibid.*, 191, 198–99, 196. The charges proved insufficient, and the English Privy Council released Hill from a bond for his good behavior on January 1, 1690/91 (CO5/723/II, ff. 210–11). Hill did not hold public office again until Nicholson's governorship of Maryland, when he became a burgess, naval officer, colonel of the militia, Provincial Court justice, and nominee for the council (*Md. Archives*, XX, 137, 160–61, 180; XXIII, 419).

[5] *Md. Archives*, VIII, 188–89, 192–93.

[6] *Ibid.*, 128–29, 132–34. The editor of the *Md. Archives* mistakenly dates these petitions in November 1689. Their reference to the king's proclamation and collaborating evidence from Smithson's letter more

A total of sixty-nine men signed the petitions, seventeen from Kent and fifty-two from Talbot. It is interesting that three of them had also signed the November petition from Talbot requesting a Protestant government; those three were Smithson, Michael Turbutt, and James Smith. All had been justices under the proprietor, had been reappointed by the Associators, and had sat as justices in the king's name from November at least through March. Smith and Turbutt had not sat thereafter, but Smithson had exercised his magistratical power to take a sworn deposition as late as May 1. He must therefore have been reappointed in April and removed, perhaps with Turbutt, by the committee in June. Smith was still sitting on June 17 and probably had made his peace with the Grand Committee.[7]

The petitions were probably sparked first by the attempted arrest of Hill and then by committee action in removing Smithson and others from the bench. At the very least, those who opposed Coode did not feel that the king's letter empowered the Associators to remove from office men who had been faithful in keeping order in Their Majesties' names. How many men were imprisoned is unknown. Their imprisonment must have lasted at least two weeks, for Heath wrote on June 19 and Smithson's letter was sent on June 30. All must have been released on bond soon afterward, however, for nothing more appears. The following January, furthermore, the Lords of Trade dismissed all grievances with the recommendation "that severall matters in difference be referred to the examination of the Governor that shall be sent thither by your Majesty's directions."[8] Neither the oppression suffered by the protesters nor their crimes against the crown seemed to demand the immediate attention of the English

---

correctly place them in June. There are four of these petitions in the English records, three from Talbot and one from Kent; the latter was originally drawn up for Talbot, but that county's name was scratched out and replaced by "Kent." The original petitions are in CO5/718/II.

[7] *Md. Archives,* XVII, 380; V, 565; Talb. Land Rec., KK no. 5, ff. 247a, 249b, 253, 256, *et seq.;* NN no. 6, f. 324.

[8] *Md. Archives,* VIII, 212–13, 229.

government. Nevertheless, these events must have impressed upon all inhabitants of Maryland the dangers of resistance.

After moving against the opposition, the Grand Committee turned its attention to two disturbing aspects of the royal letter: the instructions regarding the provincial revenues and the king's intentions to launch a complete investigation into the revolution and its causes. The Associators detected the frightening possibility that Baltimore might retain the colony. They were well aware that supporters of the proprietor were already in England presenting charges against them, and others were preparing to sail with the next fleet. These opponents were armed with petitions and accusations against the rebel leadership. The committee recognized the necessity of sending representatives to protect the incumbent government and to counter the arguments of Baltimore's witnesses. Accordingly, in July it appointed Coode, Cheseldyne, and Robert King of Somerset as "Agents and Deputies" to depart for England as soon as possible.[9]

The agents would carry a list of grievances to present to the crown. In main points these had changed little since the "Declaration" of July 25, 1689, or even the protest of 1677. They emphasized the constitutional conflicts of the preceding years and the proprietor's exercise of regal authority—"assumeing the royall stile dignity authority and prerogative," as one version of the grievances put it. The summoning of two instead of four delegates to the assembly, the proprietary veto, the proprietor's unilateral suspension of a law to which he had assented (the act for towns), and the severity of the sedition laws were all listed. There is a fascinating omission, however. No plot with the French is mentioned, it being clear by the summer of 1690 that the French invasion had been imaginary. Instead, the grievances accused the deputy governors of "Magnifying the present French

---

[9] *Ibid.*, 195–96. Six Marylanders and three traders had testified before English officials in January (162–63). Concern over such testimony is expressed in Coode to Secretary of State, May 14, 1690, and Committee to King, July 11, 1690 (178–79, 194).

designes," although several accusations implied that the council had attempted to procure the assistance of the Indians to prevent the establishment of government in Their Majesties' names. The anti-Catholic element was still present, of course. The grievances gave high priority to complaints that Catholics held the highest offices and that Catholic churches were encouraged whereas the Protestant clergy received no support. The failure to supply the public magazine from the two-shillings duty per hogshead was also revived as an issue.

To these central points often raised in the past were added new ones that concerned legal procedures. Proof of these accusations, whether sound or specious, could not be so easily found in events that were known to everyone, but it is probable that most charges were grounded on at least one incident of the past thirty years, and it is known that Coode took with him as evidence at least one volume of Provincial Court proceedings. Men not freeholders had sometimes sat on criminal juries; the council had heard causes cognizable only at common law; men accused had been forced to find high bail or had received sentences that imposed unreasonable fines; the proprietor had granted the proceeds from fines to judges in criminal cases before an accusation had been made, much less a conviction obtained; and he had endeavored to "obstruct Justice upon persons accused for supposed murders." The aims of these charges appear to have been to bolster the impression that under proprietary rule Maryland colonists were losing vital rights granted Englishmen by English law.

The offenses of the deputy governors were outlined in some detail. The complaints of the assembly of 1688 were all repeated. The deputy governors had ordered payment of the proprietor's quitrents in coin; the attorney general had commanded men to appear before the Provincial Court without stating the cause for appearance; when the commissary had refused local commissions for probate, administrators of estates had been obliged to make expensive journeys to St. Mary's City; the secretary had been exacting illegal fees; the naval officers and clerks of towns had been collecting three pence per hogshead for tobacco exported, against the explicit provisions of the acts for towns (but in compliance with an agreement between English merchants and Lord Baltimore); and militia officers had impressed provisions in time of peace. The injustice of requiring the oath of fidelity from the delegates in 1688 was emphasized by pointing out that it contained no reservation of allegiance to the crown.

The events of the months just before the coup were brought to bear in both frivolous and serious charges. These began with complaints that in order to have convicts to pardon in honor of the birth of the Prince of Wales the Provincial Court had ignored the defenses of the accused. The calling in of arms to repair in preparation for possible war with the French was presented as a ruse to disarm Protestants. The fact that several of the Associators—described as "unwary though well meaning Inhabitants"—had signed statements supporting the deputy governors after the early rumors of invasion had proved false was attributed to deceit and craft of a council endeavoring "to obscure and smother their aforesaid wicked purposes and maschinations," although these machinations were no longer clearly defined, there having been no invasion afoot. Undoubtedly during the days of uncertainty as to the outcome of the English revolution, Maryland Catholics had expressed hope that James II would prevail, possibly using, as charged, "scandalous resolute and treasonable Invectives against their Majesties . . . Threatening and menaceing the Protestants of this Province with death ruine and extirpation." The resistance of the proprietary forces against the coup was described as "Taking up Armes and publickly declaring against the proclayming their Majesties within this Province."

The final charges against the deputy governors were undoubtedly the most potent. First, as members of the Provincial Court, they had judged matters of fact "whereby severall have beene condemned and executed which in construction of Law is no less than murder." The criminal proceedings of the Provincial

Court for the years of the deputy governors' rule show no trials without jury, but this charge, if proved, undoubtedly would raise alarm. Finally, two of the deputy governors (in truth, only one) had actually murdered two of the royal collectors "and the same owned and Justified by them and their adherents." Here the direct interest of the crown was at stake and would surely compel attention.

It is interesting that the indictment of Lord Baltimore's government did not end here. It continued with a list of additional charges largely of an administrative nature. Most of these had first appeared—along with the standard accusations—in a justification of the coup sent to New York early in 1690, probably by Andrew Abington, then sheriff of Calvert County. They pointed out that the proprietor and his council had established new offices and set fees for them without act of assembly; that he had regranted escheated lands before inquisition to prove the lands escheatable; that the courts had fined absent men without giving them a day in court to answer (usually for administrative defaults, although the statement is not explicit); that the judges of probate charged double fees for granting local commissions for probate in the counties and did not keep the Prerogative Court at the appointed times; that offices of trust were sold to incompetent men at prices so high that these officers in turn were obliged to extort illegal fees and that incompetent or short-tenured clerks so appointed kept court records improperly; and finally that writs of error, in England becoming a matter of right, were in Maryland still granted or denied arbitrarily. Above all—and here the objections harked back to the protest of 1677 as well as to Abington's letter—redress of evils was impossible because plural officeholding and the close relationships among councillors meant that judges and offenders were related or even identical.

Though many of these accusations were petty in themselves, their cumulative effect was not. Lord Baltimore stood indicted not only of misuse of his charter rights but of judicial and administrative misgovernment from which redress in Maryland was impossible. These arguments undoubtedly had had an effect in Maryland. It remained to be seen how much weight they would carry when presented to distant English administrators.[10]

The agents would also carry to England the committee's position on the ticklish issue of provincial revenues. The Associators had been battling with Baltimore's agent James Heath for over a month. They conveniently interpreted the royal instructions regarding Baltimore's share of the revenue as nonretroactive; Heath, of course, was attempting to collect money for the entire period since August of 1689. On June 2, he had presented the committee with a list of four demands. They included delivery of all bills and bonds remaining in the Land Office or elsewhere; surrender of the proprietor's house at Mattapany and the plantation with an account of the disposal of its stock; an account of all shipping entered and cleared since August and the bills of exchange or money received for the duties; and, finally, delivery of all papers and materials relating to Baltimore's private estate.[11]

The committee considered the demands at its meeting June 18 in the Talbot courthouse. The location was probably calculated to bring the new central government more visibly before the people of Talbot, where recent opposition had been especially strong. The committee agreed to turn over all private papers and the Land Office material, except for lands for which no

[10] *Ibid.*, 215–20. For a comparison with other lists of grievances, see *ibid.*, 101–7 (Declaration of 1689); V, 134–49 (protest of 1677) and "Mariland's Grevances," 369–409 (Abington's list). Criminal proceedings of the Provincial Court 1673–82 and 1689 do not survive. The records Coode took to England may have been for these periods (*Md. Archives*, VIII, 262). "County Government," text, 254–55, discusses instances in which at the defendant's request trial for misdemeanor could be by the court rather than by jury, but no instances were recorded in the Provincial Court Proceedings 1682–88 (Prov. Ct. Judg., TG, *passim*). Chapter VI below assesses the validity of the accusations.

[11] *Md. Archives*, VIII, 182–83.

certificate had been returned and recorded. Heath was to make what use he would of the plantation, but the garrison at Mattapany would not be surrendered until so ordered by the crown.[12]

Heath could obtain no satisfaction concerning the revenue itself. He protested that Coode completely disregarded the royal instructions and would neither allow him an account of what had been collected nor permit him to collect anything from the ships currently in port. Heath was seeking the fourteen-pence-per-ton duty on ships trading to Maryland and at least half of the two shillings per hogshead collected on all exported tobacco.[13]

The Associators now contended that Baltimore had not devoted half of the two-shilling duty to support of the government, as the law required, and that such expenses had been met instead by "an equall Assessment upon the Inhabitants." They forwarded to the king's receiver general "the whole imposition excepting onely what is necessarily expended or reserved for Your Majesties and the Countrys immediate service."[14] The proprietor renewed his pleas in England for receipt of his rightful revenues, and nineteen months later Colonel Henry Darnall appeared before the Grand Committee with a duplicate of the Privy Council's order of February 26, 1690/91. It explicitly directed payment to Lord Baltimore of half of the two-shillings-per-hogshead tax and all of the fourteen-pence tonnage duty. The committee resolved to reimburse Baltimore for these revenues, and henceforth naval officers and collectors were not to clear vessels without a certificate from either Darnall or his agents.[15] Nevertheless, Baltimore's efforts to obtain his back rev-

[12] *Ibid.*, 183–84.

[13] *Ibid.*, 188–90. Newton D. Mereness, *Maryland as a Proprietary Province* (New York, 1901), 78–80, 89–90, describes the two taxes.

[14] *Md. Archives*, VIII, 193–96. The two duties for the year ending August 22, 1690, amounted to £2,690.7.3 (204–5).

[15] Som. Jud. Rec., 1690–92, f. 163. The Privy Council ruling is found in CO5/723/II, ff. 219–22.

enues extended well into the royal period, and the collection and distribution of the two imposts remained a divisive subject for many years.[16]

The Grand Committee convened for several days of business each month during the summer of 1690, and met somewhat less regularly thereafter. Attendance normally ranged from the requisite quorum of seven to ten or eleven present. The location apparently changed from session to session in convenience to the members and to bring this agency of the central government before as many people as possible.[17]

Members of the committee generally adhered strictly to the instructions of the convention and interpreted their powers quite narrowly. There is little evidence of any attempt to supervise the local courts. An order of September 5, 1690, did require the justices of each county to inspect all bonds and recognizances taken before them in court or otherwise for good behavior and keeping the peace. Those which had been broken were to be prosecuted and new bonds required.[18] Since the taking of security for good behavior was one of the most potent and most commonly employed devices for controlling troublemakers and disorderly persons, this order was a reminder to maintain a basic efficiency.[19] It was apparently the committee's only supervisory order concerning the courts. More informal supervision was

[16] See William Blathwayt's Journal, 1680–1717, I, 425–30, transcript in PRO-Treasury Papers, Library of Congress. Also *Md. Archives,* VIII, 211, 286, 295, 299, and "Royal Period," 68–70. With the arrival in Maryland of Nicholson and Edward Randolph, surveyor general of customs, collection of all trade duties and the honesty of Maryland collectors and naval officers became heated issues. "Royal Period," 98–104; Michael G. Hall, *Edward Randolph and the American Colonies,* (Chapel Hill, 1960), *passim;* Nicholson to Lords of Trade, Feb. 26, 1691/92, *Cal. S. P., Col., 1689–1692,* no. 2075.

[17] The committee itself has left no surviving journal of proceedings. Information about its activities must be culled from county court records and from its correspondence.

[18] Som. Jud. Rec., 1689–90, f. 192.

[19] See "County Government" text, pp. 99–100, 204, 273, 277–78.

quite possible, however, as each county bench included at least one and usually two members of the committee.[20]

Only two other orders from the committee to county officials have been found, both recorded in the Somerset proceedings. In March 1690/91, the clerk recorded a letter from Blakiston to Colonel David Browne. "It did pertaine to mustering of Soldiers in our County the well fixing of Arms, as also some injury done [by] Indians."[21] The third order was the committee's notification that Darnall or his agents were to receive the port duties belonging to Lord Baltimore and that certificates of clearance would go only to those ships that had paid these taxes.[22] Since the Somerset County records are exceptionally complete in the reporting of documents of all kinds, it seems probable that these three were the only general orders sent to the counties during the committee's two years of existence.

This group of pseudo-councillors was probably much more active as an agency with authority to cope with particular crises in individual counties. It was this body which had apparently moved against Hill, Smithson, and others after the arrival of the royal letter on May 30. More direct evidence confirms its intervention in the problems plaguing the still disrupted government of Cecil County.

The peculiar situation in Cecil actually predated the revolution. Maladministration and factionalism in this distant and newest of counties had provided frequent headaches for Lord Baltimore's government. As recently as the summer of 1688, Henry

[20] All twenty members were currently local justices except Michael Miller, Ninian Beale, and John Edmundson. Miller was clerk of Kent County, and Beale held a militia commission. Edmundson, a Quaker, is the only member for whom no proof exists of service at any time in the county government (*Md. Archives*, VIII, 199; XIII, 241–45; Cecil Judg., 1683–92, f. 84).

[21] Som. Jud. Rec., 1690–91, f. 63.

[22] *Ibid.*, f. 163. Darnall appointed William Whittington as his agent to collect these imposts and also the quitrents and other dues of the proprietor in Somerset County (f. 164).

Coursey had registered complaints of judicial misconduct with the council and had suggested improvements in the selection of justices. A new commission issued the following October had embodied most of his recommendations for changes in personnel. This careful selection of loyal proprietary men may help account for opposition to the Associators on the part of at least eight of the nine Cecil justices sitting at the time of the revolution.[23]

Even after the arrival of the royal letter, opposition to the Associators did not diminish in Cecil County. One of the justices, William Ward, later accused George Warner and Edward Jones of calling the June court in Lord Baltimore's name and denying the convention's authority. According to Ward, he "did in open Court sitting demand the Oath in their Majesties Name, which the said [Warner and Jones] utterly refuse to take."[24] The county records indicate that five justices swore the required oaths and that three more, including Jones and Warner, swore but reserved the last clause of the oath. William Dare refused any oath on the ground that the royal declaration continued him in office and that he need take no new oath until "lawfully called for he had been allready Sworne." His meaning is not clear, for it is unlikely he had taken the oath in Their Majesties' names after appointment in September. Perhaps he considered that the royal declaration continued whatever arrangements had existed under the Associators, even if they included the existence of a court still sworn in the name of Lord Baltimore. Three remaining men refused or delayed, and thus only five of twelve justices were fully qualified. These five fined the others "according to Act of Assembly" and sent an account of the proceedings to the Grand Committee.[25]

The committee devoted considerable attention to the situation

---

[23] *Md. Archives*, VIII, 32–34, 49; also V, 545–46. In September 1689 the Associators had continued in office all of the men named in the last proprietary commission.

[24] *Ibid.*, XIII, 364–65.

[25] Cecil Judg., 1683–92, ff. 84–85.

at its meeting on June 19. It determined that Charles James had been the spearhead of the effort to fine the foot-dragging justices and to report their opposition. James was himself a controversial figure. Twenty years earlier he had been impeached for gross misconduct while serving as sheriff, and the assembly had "disabled [him] to bear anie publick office."[26] Nonetheless, in September 1689 the Associators' Convention had appointed him a captain in the militia, and in April he had been named a member of the Grand Committee and a justice.[27]

James apparently was not present for the committee's deliberations on June 19. Jones was present, however, and undoubtedly his explanation of the Cecil situation proved convincing to the committee. It now rescinded James's appointment as a justice on account of his "severall misdemeanors" and "ordered that the severall fines unjustly laid at the last County Court" be remitted. The justices named in the last ordinance were to be sworn when the court next met.[28]

James was but temporarily rebuffed. Presumably he appealed personally to his colleagues on the committee when they met on August 7 and 8, reminding them no doubt of his early and fervent support for the revolution at a time when few were favoring the Associators in Cecil County. At any rate, the committee issued an order summoning the sheriff and three of the dissenting justices to inform the committee of the "late disturbance in Cecil County tending to the breach of the peace." Meanwhile, military and civil affairs were to remain as constituted by the last ordinance, "notwithstanding any Order."[29]

[26] *Md. Archives*, II, 480, 491, 496, 499. The charges included perjury, suborning others to perjury, and false imprisonment.

[27] James did not sign the convention's letter of September 4, 1689, to the crown; Jones is the only known delegate of Cecil County present at that first session of the convention, although James may have been absent only the last day.

[28] Cecil Judg., 1683–92, f. 84a; *Md. Archives*, VIII, 183–84.

[29] Cecil Judg., 1683–92, f. 93a. James was among those signing the order, while Jones appears not to have attended the two-day session (*Md. Archives*, VIII, 198–99).

The next Cecil court considered this order tantamount to re-instating James.[30] Of the three justices who had earlier refused to take the oath in full, only one is recorded as swearing again, but all three sat and presumably all three swore the oath. From among those who had refused to swear at all, only one came forth to serve. The records mention no proceedings against the others.[31]

The committee's intervention thus temporarily settled the court to the point that it could conduct civil proceedings for the first time in a year. The August, September, and November sessions caught up on a backlog of cases, although three attorneys refused the oaths of allegiance and supremacy and were suspended from practice. The peace and resumption of normal business was only temporary, however. Dissension reached new heights during the winter months, and the committee once again stepped in to resolve the differences. The exact problem and its resolution remain something of a mystery, but four new appointees took the oath of justices at the March court. Evidently the committee was seeking some solution by turning to new faces. Since the next meeting of the convention was only a month away, pressing reasons must have prompted the committee to assume appointive powers. It is interesting that the convention apparently did not entirely uphold the committee's actions, for two of the four new men do not appear again.[32] Presumably they failed to be included in the April ordinance. Circumstantial evidence suggests that the convention had decided by April to rely upon neither the Jones faction nor James, but to proceed with a new figure, Ebenezer Blakiston, a cousin or nephew of the president of the Grand Committee. Blakiston's close ties to the Associators were perhaps responsible for his being named a militia captain in September 1689 and his being

---

[30] Cecil Judg., 1683–92, f. 93a. However, James is not listed as sitting again until July 1691 (ff. 93a, 100a, 114a).

[31] *Ibid.*, ff. 84a, 88, 88a, 93a, 100a, 110a, 114a, 114b, 115a, 119a.

[32] *Ibid.*, ff. 84a–110a, especially 87; 110b, 114b *et seq.*

one of the new justices appointed by the committee in March. Now, in April, Blakiston became sheriff, replacing William Pearce.[33]

Even the new appointments did not resolve the problems. The court met and adjourned in June without conducting any civil or testamentary business. On July 28, a special meeting convened to swear in a new court named in a *dedimus potestatem* from the committee dated July 10, 1691. This order recognized James as the head of the court and implies that some justices named in April had since been suspended. As usual, the appointees were not all agreeable to the proceedings. One refused to swear until the next regular session of court, while another declined because his eyesight was failing. At the August court these two and others took their oaths, and the courts sat for three days.[34]

The court adjourned again in September after qualifying an undersheriff. Abbreviated sessions characterized the November, December, January, and March courts. Despite the efforts of convention and committee, completely routine and normal business could not be restored in Cecil before the advent of royal government.[35]

The episodes with Cecil County are the only explicit accounts of the committee's action to prevent a paralysis of local government or to make appointments. It may have appointed new sheriffs upon the deaths of Thomas Long of Baltimore and Andrew

[33] *Ibid.*, f. 114b; Christopher Johnston, "Blakistone Family," *MHM*, II (1907), 54–60. Blakiston's wife was also a half-sister of the Gerard wives of Coode, Cheseldyne, and Nehemiah Blakiston. His cruelty to his wife was so great that William Fitzhugh of Virginia, married to her sister, wrote unsuccessfully to the Maryland council in 1681 to arrange a separation (*Fitzhugh*, 97–98, 98n–99n, 100n). This scandal may have kept Blakiston out of office before 1689. Pearce was a dissident also, for he was not transfered to the bench.

[34] Cecil Judg., 1683–92, ff. 114a–115a.

[35] *Ibid.*, ff. 115–121. See also testamentary business recorded in *ibid.*, 1692–98, ff. 1–8.

Abington of Calvert,[36] and some militia appointments or promotions may have come originally from the committee.[37] As a rule, however, the convention, not the committee, exercised the appointive powers which ordinarily belonged to the governor and council.[38] Nor is there any other reference to a dedimus. The committee may have issued this one partly as a method of suspending some justices and partly to force others to qualify, but it was careful not to give the appearance of usurping the powers of the convention. The words of the dedimus, as paraphrased by the clerk, specified that those being sworn were "by Ordinance Appointed and not disabled by Law or Suspended by this Committee."[39]

Otherwise, the committee served those purposes for which it was created: to provide an authoritative agency to correspond with other colonies and with England and to conduct interim business, whether that business might be Indian affairs, the tobacco fleet, the return of exiled Marylanders, aid to New York, or regular reports to England.[40] Relations with Nicholson and the colony of Virginia even experienced a slight improvement once correspondence went through an authorized body.[41]

Fundamentally, the convention remained the primary execu-

---

[36] Long was dead by November 1691, and his replacement, John Hall, was in service in December (Balt. Ct. Pro., F no. 1, ff. 73, 104). Abington died by November 1691 also; his replacement was William Parker (*HLP*, 159; *Md. Archives*, VIII, 340–41).

[37] For example, Charles Hutchins of Dorchester and David Browne of Somerset are first referred to as "colonel" in August 1690, although it is possible the appointments were made the preceding April (Dor. Land Rec., O no. 4½, f. 195; Som. Jud. Rec., 1689–90, f. 147.

[38] See the appointments recorded in Ch. Ct. and Land Rec., R no. 1, ff. 1, 189, 275; Som. Jud. Rec., 1690–91, f. 180. After September 4, 1689, the local courts appointed their own clerks (f. 157; Ch. Ct. and Land Rec., P no. 1, f. 185; Dor. Land Rec., O no. 4½, f. 112.

[39] Cecil Judg., 1683–92, f. 114a.

[40] See, for example, letters to Virginia on Aug. 8 and Sept. 17, 1690 (*Md. Archives*, VIII, 198–99, 206–7); to England, July 11, 1690 (193–96); to New York, July 29, 1691 (*Cal. S. P., Col., 1689–1692*, nos. 1636, 1673).

[41] *Md. Archives*, VIII, 208–9.

tive authority of the provisional government insofar as there was one. The delegates convened in St. Mary's City twice annually, each August or September and each April, until the arrival of Governor Lionel Copley in April 1692. Sessions ranged from one day to two weeks.[42] It is impossible to determine the complete membership of the convention over the two-and-a-half-year perod. Elections subsequent to August, 1689, were held at least twice, and probably more often. Anne Arundel County's delegates apparently first sat in April of 1690.[43] Robert Mason, not an original delegate, was sitting in April of 1691. He had been elected either as a St. Mary's County replacement for Coode or Cheseldyne, both now in England, or as the representative from St. Mary's City in place of Gilbert Clarke, who had been appointed sheriff of Charles County at the first session.[44] Vacancies existed in other counties owing to appointment as sheriff, which traditionally required a delegate to surrender his seat, or to the death of a representative.[45]

A leadership struggle may have occurred with the departure of Coode and Cheseldyne, who had occupied the two most im-

[42] Aug. 22–Sept. 4, 1689; April 1(?)–3(?), 1690 (*DHNY*, II, 117–18 and *Md. Archives*, VIII, 172); Sept. 29–Oct. 6, 1690 (*ibid.*, 207 and Thomas Bacon, *Laws of Maryland with Proper Indexes* [Annapolis, 1765], note after laws of 1688); Apr. 15(?)–25, 1691 (*Md. Archives*, VIII, 248–50); Aug. ?–Sept. 10, 1691 (Ch. Ct. and Land Rec., R no. 1, f. 275); Apr. 9, 1692 (Bacon, *Laws of Md.*, note after laws of 1688.)

[43] See Table 2. Nicholas Gassaway and Nicholas Greenberry were named to the Grand Committee at that session. The first definite evidence for the attendance of William Hopkins and Thomas Tench is at the fourth session (*Md. Archives*, VIII, 250). No information on attendance is available for the third meeting.

[44] *Md. Archives*, VIII, 250. Mason was also appointed to the Provincial Court at this session, which would suggest he had been active for some time. It is probable that he had attended the third session and had also become a member of the committee in place of Cheseldyne.

[45] Christopher Gist of Baltimore had died by March 10, 1690/91 (Balt. Land Rec., RM no. 45, f. 331). Gassaway had died by Jan. 27, 1691/92 (I&A 11, f. 37½). Thomas Cooke of Dorchester became sheriff of his county after the fifth session (Dor. Land Rec., O no. 4½, ff. 108, 112).

portant offices in the Associators' government. The selection of these two men as agents to England remains an intriguing mystery. Perhaps they wished personally to defend their actions before the royal officials who would soon be making a crucial determination regarding the colony's future government. Or perhaps others were anxious to be rid of the two men. Bernard Steiner has suggested that Blakiston and Jowles were the real "brains" behind the rebel government, and therefore Coode and Cheseldyne, "who were in the way, were removed by being sent to England." Blakiston and Jowles do appear to have been shrewder individuals, less flamboyant or unstable than their fellow leaders. They may have preferred to remain in Maryland to keep command of the local situation, but such a theory does not account for the dispatch of supposedly "weaker" men to represent the colony in very critical matters in England. It seems more likely that the real struggle for power, if one occurred, came after the selection of the agents. By September 16, the committee had appointed Blakiston as the new president.[46] His election was clearly a personal victory over Jowles, whose signature had consistently come immediately after Coode's on all important documents of the rebel regime. Furthermore, Jowles had been recognized by the proprietary party as second only to Coode in importance, and he was now the ranking militia officer. It is impossible to determine the factors at play in Blakiston's selection. One possible explanation rests in his possession of a royal commission as customs collector, which might have conveyed greater legitimacy and authority upon him in the estimation of fellow Marylanders, neighboring governors, and royal officials. He may have bested Jowles in a display of power, but it would seem that Blakiston's power was not yet beyond challenge. The

[46] Bernard C. Steiner, "The Protestant Revolution in Maryland," *Annual Report of the American Historical Association for the Year 1897* (Washington, D.C., 1898), 334–35, 352. Blakiston announced his selection in a letter to Nicholson, Sept. 17, 1690 (*Md. Archives*, VIII, 206–7).

full convention which gathered in late September chose George Robotham as its speaker. By the following session in April of 1691, however, Blakiston was also occupying that post and he apparently encountered no other open resistance to his leadership. He continued to serve as the principal figure in the colony until the arrival of the royal governor a year later.[47]

As an executive body, the convention continued to issue ordinances, which included appointments to civil and military offices and set the conditions of officeholding. In the fall of 1690, it approved a proclamation, similar to ones previously issued by the governor, which forbade the exportation of Indian corn from the province until July 10, 1691.[48] It avoided taking legislative action. For example, the session of September 1690 rejected efforts of some members to repeal three acts of the assembly passed in 1688 "as not within the Cognizance of that House." It is also likely that the convention renewed treaties with the Seneca and Susquehanna Indians and treated other defense problems.[49]

The delegates acted to fill gaps created by the absence of central courts or administrative agencies. When George Newman of Charles County, for instance, refused to take the oaths of allegiance and supremacy, the local court ordered his appearance at the next convention to answer for his contempt.[50] Formerly, he might have been sent before the governor and council. In April 1690 the convention resolved that a widow be granted letters of administration by Somerset County Court on the estate

---

[47] Bacon, *Laws of Md.*, note after laws of 1688; *Md. Archives*, VIII, 250. Robotham did not sign the letter to the crown from the April session, nor did he take his seat on the Provincial Court which was meeting concurrently; therefore, he may not have been present to serve as speaker.

[48] Som. Jud. Rec., 1690–92, f. 33; *Md. Archives*, XV, 44, 194; XIII, 217–18, 220–23; Bacon, *Laws of Md.*, note after the laws of 1688. The acts of 1688 had attempted to encourage economic diversification.

[49] *Md. Archives*, VIII, 207.

[50] Ch. Ct. and Land Rec., R no. 1, ff. 46–47.

of her dead husband because former letters granted to another had been surreptitiously and illegally obtained.[51] Since the Prerogative Court had issued the first letters, the county court may not have felt free to set them aside on its own authority. The convention met too infrequently, however, to exercise much control over local administration. It did necessarily serve as a clearinghouse for any official materials, such as the accounts of imports and exports required by the Navigation Acts; after such documents had been examined and verified, the convention would order the seal of the province to be affixed.[52]

The convention's fourth session in April 1691 effected the last change in the structure of the interim government, this time in response to an order from the crown to provide for the trial of Payne's murderers. The Associators invoked this royal letter of April 26, 1690, as the basis for its re-establishing the Provincial Court. The court jurisdiction was similar to that "formerly used and accustomed" except for "matters relating to Titles of Land."[53] Therefore, during the last year of provisional government, a central court could provide an alternative tribunal for many causes, and review of county court decisions was again possible.[54]

In constituting the new court, the convention gave little heed to the Associators' earlier grievances about the concentration of offices in the hands of a few individuals. They had particularly complained of the overlapping membership of the proprietary

[51] Som. Jud. Rec., 1689–90, f. 88. Talbot court showed no such caution, however; see Talb. Test. Pro., 1689–92.

[52] Talb. Land Rec., NN no. 6, f. 317.

[53] *Md. Archives,* VIII, 243–45; the royal letter is on 175–76. Evidently it did not arrive in time for the September convention to act.

[54] Appeals were made. Those settled by the Provincial Court re-established by Governor Lionel Copley in 1692 are in Prov. Ct. Judg., DSC, ff. 125–76. Nehemiah Blakiston acted as chancellor and William Taylard as register in chancery, but this activity appears to have been confined to issuing of writs of error (Som. Jud. Rec., 1690–91, f. 149; Prov. Ct. Judg., DSC, f. 111).

council and the Provincial Court. The new court was in effect a slightly smaller version of the Grand Committee, the "acting" council. Blakiston was designated the chief justice, followed immediately in rank by Jowles. Seven of the nine other justices also sat as members of the committee: Robotham, Greenberry, Robert King, Dr. John Brooke, Gassaway, Edmundson, and John Addison. Only Thomas Tench and Robert Mason were newcomers, and both of them were members of the convention. It is very likely that Mason also had obtained a seat on the Grand Committee by this time. Tench's elevation was stalled for the time being, since fellow justices Gassaway and Greenberry were Anne Arundel's representatives on the committee. All but Edmundson had been appointed justices of their county courts in 1689.[55]

County autonomy ended with the establishment of a higher court, while the influence of the committee, so heavily represented on the court, must undoubtedly have grown remarkably. The local courts were still the mainstay of administration and were independent and strong enough to withstand what they might consider unwarranted intrusions from above. For example, they obstructed an attempt on the part of Attorney General George Plater to appoint clerks of indictments for each county.[56] Nevertheless, the existence of a court to which appeals could be

[55] *Md. Archives*, VIII, 242–44. The geographical representation on the court was as follows: Anne Arundel, three justices; St. Mary's and Talbot, two each; Calvert, Charles, Dorchester, and Somerset, one each.

[56] Plater, appointed attorney general to prosecute the Payne murder trial (*Md. Archives*, VIII, 247), commissioned clerks of indictments in the summer of 1691. Peter Dent produced his commission in Somerset County at the August court, but the justices postponed qualifying him, and in September the convention passed an ordinance that authorized the county courts to continue making the appointment. In November, the justices refused to honor Dent's commission. There is nothing in other county records to suggest Plater succeeded elsewhere (Som. Jud. Rec., 1690–91, f. 149; 1690–92, f. 133; Ch. Ct. and Land Rec., R no. 1, 235–74; Dor. Land Rec., O no. 4½, ff. 195–158 [paged backwards]). There are no criminal proceedings for Cecil County.

made, especially one manned by key members of the convention, was a vital change that gave local courts essentially their former position in the political structure.

Since May 30, 1690, the county courts and militia had operated with royal sanction. Despite some continuation of unsettled times, it appears that normal procedures characterized the business of these local instruments of government. Five of the ten counties have left at least partial records and provide our picture of local government from 1690 to 1692.[57]

The county justices continued to maintain order and services without need for militia intervention. There were occasional punishments for contempt of authority, but no more than are found in better-ordered times.[58] Lawbreakers were prosecuted and debts collected, although there is some evidence of legal actions being postponed because "the times were unsettled and troublesome."[59] The courts seemed to have functioned adequately in their only area of expanded jurisdiction: probate. Testamentary proceedings remain for eight counties, and all show that wills were probated according to standard form, letters of administration were issued, estates were appraised and inventories filed.[60] In three counties, a few administration accounts also

[57] Two are complete from June 1690 through March 1692: Ch. Ct. and Land Rec., R no. 1, ff. 1–412; Som. Jud. Rec., 1689–90, 1690–91, 1690–92. Cecil Judg., 1683–92, ff. 84–121a, contains only civil proceedings. Dor. Land Rec., O no. 4½, ff. 195–158 (reverse pagination), begins in August 1690 and continues through March 1692; unfortunately, there are no other Dorchester proceedings with which to compare these records before 1728. Balt. Ct. Pro., F no. 1, begins in November 1691. Calvert and Talbot counties have left only testamentary proceedings; see n. 60 below.

[58] For instance, Som. Jud. Rec., 1689–90, ff. 105, 107; 1690–91, ff. 1–2; Ch. Ct. and Land Rec., R no. 1, ff. 139, 163; Dor. Land Rec., O no. 4½, ff. 108, 123.

[59] Som. Jud. Rec., 1690–91, f. 75.

[60] Cecil Judg., 1692–98, ff. 1–24; Som. Jud. Rec., 1690–92, ff. 1–118; Ch. Ct. and Land Rec., Q no. 1; Test. Pro. 16, ff. 1–50 (Calvert); I&A 11, ff. 1–50 (Anne Arundel); Balt. Ct. Pro., F no. 1, ff. 1–185, *passim;* Dor. Land Rec., O no. 4½, ff. 1–6; Talb. Test. Pro., 1689–92.

passed, although the first ordinance, at least, did not specifically authorize final settlements.[61] In Charles County, the proceedings are far more elaborate than elsewhere, probably because the Charles lawyers possessed a higher degree of familiarity with English testamentary law and the procedures of the Prerogative Court in Maryland than did the attorneys of other county courts.[62]

In only one area of judicial administration does evidence remain of chronic uncertainty and continued indecision about the state of Maryland since the revolution. This occurs in records of land transfers. In Baltimore County from August 1689 through December 1690 only three, possibly four, deeds were executed. One of these, dated October 26, 1690, was in the name of the crown, but three mentioned both the crown and "the Right Honorable Charles Lord and Absolute Proprietor of the Province of Maryland." During the next fifteen months there were sixteen transfers. Four of these mentioned neither the crown nor the proprietor—an acceptable form that appeared both before and after the revolution—four mentioned both, and five were in the name of the crown alone. Not until the arrival of a royal governor does one find all entries being made in Their Majesties' names, when this form was used.[63]

[61] Talb. Test. Pro., 1689–92, Mar. 20, 1690/91; Nov. 17 and 20, 1691; Jan. 5, 1691/92; Ch. Ct. and Land Rec., Q no. 1, ff. 26, 32–33; Balt. Ct. Pro., F no. 1, f. 119; *Md. Archives*, XIII, 246.

[62] Ch. Ct. and Land Rec., Q no. 1, is devoted mostly to testamentary and orphan business for 1689–92. The proceedings include presentments of June court grand juries for waste, mistreatment of wards, and other matters regularly under the cognizance of the county courts, but they also include matters that would ordinarily have come before the Prerogative Court. See, for instance, the negotiations over the division of Robert Doyne's estate according to his nuncupative will, ff. 23–24, and the "Libell of William Barton" complaining of the sale by his father's administrator of Negroes belonging to the estate, ff. 21–22.

[63] Balt. Land Rec., RM no. HS, ff. 321, 324, 329, 333, 335, 338, 341, 345, 348, 349, 351, 353, 354; IR no. AM, ff. 68, 70, 77, 80, 83, 101, 107, 113; HW no. 2, ff. 239–40. There are earlier and later examples of the form that referred to no authority in RM no. HS, ff. 307, 353, 354; Ch. Ct.

Baltimore County was not unique in this respect. The Talbot County records reflect the same uneasiness and indecision. No deeds were written in Their Majesties' names until June 17, 1690, after the arrival of royal approval. Through the winter the issue had been avoided by using the form that made no mention of either authority. From June 1690 through the end of 1691, this remained the usual form, although occasionally there were transfers in the name of the crown. What is puzzling, however, is that beginning August 19, 1690, there are occasional deeds recorded in the name of the proprietor.[64] In all likelihood, here, as in Anne Arundel County, clerks recorded the transfers according to the wishes of the participating parties, whose property titles were at stake. What action, if any, the committee or convention may have taken in these transfers is unknown.

There is little evidence that local officers misused their power to maintain local order. The examples that are known appear to be no different either in number or in type from earlier or later periods. While Gilbert Clarke was sheriff of Charles County, he forced a prisoner, Richard Smith, Jr., to sign a bond for 7,500 pounds of tobacco, from which Governor Lionel Copley's first Provincial Court released him in 1692 because the signature came under duress. Thomas Pattison was convicted in the same court of overcharging fees while clerk of Dorchester County in April 1691. Both men had lost their posts.[65] Had misuse of power been

and Land Rec., R no. 1, ff. 230–31. This last was acknowledged in July 1689 before councillors Darnall and Digges, who must have found the form acceptable.

[64] Talb. Land Rec., KK no. 5, ff. 243–340b; NN no. 6, ff. 3–6 (rear). Through September 1689 transfers were in the proprietor's name (KK no. 5, ff. 243–52). Associator Robert Smith was party to one action in Baltimore's name and one in the name of Their Majesties, both acknowledged in the fall of 1690 (ff. 271, 274). Seven other deeds in the proprietor's name are ff. 262a–64a, 274a–78, 310a–13. In all other counties with extant records, deeds are in the name of the crown or without mention of crown or proprietor.

[65] Prov. Ct. Judg., DSC, ff. 150–52, 380–84; Ch. Ct. and Land Rec., R no. 1, f. 189; Dor. Land Rec., O no. 4½, f. 112. Overcharges by clerks

very serious or very widespread during the interregnum, one would expect to find more complaints, especially after the successful prosecution of these two cases.

Meanwhile, the county militia mustered and trained according to customary regulations.[66] All colonists could still appreciate the need for military training. Although there had been no serious conflict with the Indians since 1681, there were occasional scalpings, and Indian-White relations were uneasy.[67] After all, rumors of hostile Indians supporting a French invasion had helped arouse support for the Associators, and during the summer of 1690 there were new alarms.[68]

The use of soldiers in the period immediately following arrival of the royal letter, however, remains the only indication of open dependence on the militia for maintaining the power of the provisional government. The impression is strong, particularly after a close study of the county court records, that terrorism was kept to a minimum. The county courts had the strength to keep peace without it. Otherwise, more instances of summary court actions against troublemakers could be expected.

Indeed, prosecutions of any kind for defiance of the government are hard to find after May of 1690.[69] Henry Hewes of Charles County, without formal presentment or trial, received nine lashes at the September court of 1690 for raising "several false rumors & reports tending much to the disturbance of the peace and the quiet Government of this Province." In similar fashion six months later, Hugh Gardner received twenty lashes

---

were listed among the Associators' grievances. There are later examples of such offenses in "County Government," text, 410.

[66] Som. Jud. Rec., 1690–91, f. 63; Ch. Ct. and Land Rec., P no. 1, f. 190.

[67] For instance, on February 15, 1687/88, two Nanticokes had killed Richard Enock of Baltimore County and had dangerously wounded his wife and Francis Freeman (*Md. Archives*, VIII, 5).

[68] *Ibid.*, 155–57, 206.

[69] The new government had collected the arms and ammunition of most Catholics as a precaution and some arms were still being held as late as 1695 (*ibid.*, XX, 224).

for "abuses and affronts offered and done by him to Coll Humphrey Warren of their Majesties' Justices," an offense not necessarily politically inspired. No other summary actions of this nature appear in the Charles County records during the revolutionary period. The three men presented in March 1689/90 for refusing to assist the sheriff in an arrest were all acquitted in September. The following January Daniel Bateman, ordered before the court for refusing to take the oaths of allegiance and supremacy, failed to appear and was fined 500 pounds of tobacco unless he could excuse himself at the next court. In March he gave a satisfactory explanation for his absence, and nothing further was said of the oaths. On the surface, at least, no other criminal proceedings in Charles were or might have been related to political conflict.[70] In Somerset County, Francis Thorogood threw a brickbat through the courtroom window in November 1690, thereby wounding Justice John King. A jury found him guilty, and the court fined him for drunkenness and abusing the justices. Nothing more political than this probably unpolitical event appears in the Somerset County records after May 1690.[71]

Other surviving county records are equally barren, although Talbot County Courthouse was the scene of an alleged "tumultuous meeting & disturbance" in February 1691/92. More accurately, the gathering was a frolicsome drinking party which got somewhat out of hand and included several "men dissatisfied to the present Government." One of these gentlemen had wryly called their meeting "the Convention." There was no overt action against the government, and John Lillingston, the supposed leader, was acquitted and discharged when the case came before the new royal council some months later.[72]

On the whole the local leadership, regardless of its leanings, ruled without visible strain. After the convention of April 1690 most changes in local appointments were confined to those nor-

---

[70] Ch. Ct. and Land Rec., R no. 1, ff. 44–45, 46, 139, 163.
[71] Som. Jud. Rec., 1690–91, ff. 1–2.
[72] *Md. Archives*, VIII, 371–74, 378.

mally expected. Deceased justices were replaced and there were few additions. Sheriffs left office at death or after three years of service, a standard term. Furthermore, if one omits St. Mary's and Calvert counties, where the revolution had centered, the majority of justices serving at the arrival of the new royal governor in April 1692 had held Lord Baltimore's commission in July 1689.[73] Despite the uneasy position of the convention and its executive committee, in local government there was political as well as institutional continuity, and together these provided stability.

This stability was fundamental to the peaceful progress of the Associators' revolution. At the provincial level there had been a displacement of all the former leadership and disruption of most provincial services. The convention and its committee had minimal authority for legitimate exercise of more than caretaker powers. The willingness of county leaders to await a crown settlement, combined with their ability to keep the peace, prevented the development of factional strife that had kept alive the disorders of Bacon's Rebellion. Thus struggle for power at the top was kept under control by pressure for order at the broader based county level.

The provisional government received a further assist with the arrival of additional news from England in the spring of 1691. These new communications had some importance, for almost two years had now elapsed since the rebellion, and another year would pass before royal government officially began. Furthermore, the proprietary party had engaged in new efforts to foment opposition to the Associators during the previous winter. Gentlemen who had been abroad testifying for Lord Baltimore had returned to Maryland, bringing with them pamphlets and

[73] Appendix B, Table B-3. Only in Talbot and Baltimore did newcomers constitute a majority. For Anne Arundel and Kent, information is incomplete. Taking all the counties, furthermore, 46 per cent of the justices in April 1692 were holdovers from the proprietary period. "County Government," Appendix 1, Table 2, has a complete listing of replacements and additions with dates.

rumors about the development of affairs in England. They had strongly implied that Baltimore would retain his province.[74]

The Associators were therefore quite relieved to receive an additional endorsement from the crown and confirmation that Maryland would have a Protestant government. During the April session of the convention a packet of letters arrived from Coode and Cheseldyne. They conveyed the news that William and Mary approved of the proceedings in Maryland and were sending the colony a royal governor. Colonel Lionel Copley was the "Gentleman pitcht upon to come."[75]

The crown had not officially notified Maryland of its decisions until some of the attendant problems, especially resolution of the charter dispute, were resolved. On March 12, 1690/91, Their Majesties had finally written that "having heard what your deputies and Agents have offered to us Wee have thought fitt to take our Province of Maryland under our immediate Care and Protection, and by letters Patents under the Great Seale of England to appoint our trusty and well beloved Lionel Copley Esquire of whose prudence and loyalty we are well assured to be our Governor thereof, Untill whose Arrivall we do hereby Authorize and impower you to continue in our name the Administration of the Government and Preservation of the peace and property of our Subjects there."[76]

Between April 1691 and the governor's arrival a year later, the Associators maintained authority and, with one exception, marked time, leaving major issues for Copley's anticipated assumption of the government. The exception was the trial of four men for the murder of John Payne in the newly reconstituted Provincial Court. In addition to the formal record of the trial, never revealing of the details of procedure or evidence, there survives an account of the proceedings by a lawyer from whom

[74] *Md. Archives*, VIII, 249.

[75] *Ibid.*, 260.

[76] *Ibid.*, 235–36. See Chapter V below for full details on events in England.

the accused had sought assistance. It adds to the picture of the provisional government's uneasy basis during these years.[77]

According to the lawyer's narrative, he and several other leading attorneys, some of them Protestant, openly opposed the proceedings. They argued that the royal letter was insufficient authorization to establish a court with jurisdiction in so grave a matter and urged postponement until the new governor arrived. The convention, acting on firm ground, ignored the protests. It had received royal orders to provide a speedy trial and the crown had commanded the Virginia authorities to return the suspects to Maryland.[78] The judges selected, on the other hand, admittedly lacked "indifferency" to the issues; they were all "principall agents in these our unhappy Turmoyles."

Two days after the convention opened the prisoners were brought to St. Mary's, and the narrator of the account with some difficulty obtained leave to see them, but not in privacy. He advised them to petition for postponement until witnesses could be summoned. Meanwhile, they should ask the court to assign them counsel. Under English law of the time, representation by attorney was forbidden in felony charges, but at the discretion of the court the accused could seek advice from assigned counsel on points of law, although the prisoner had to stand alone before the bar and could not be prompted by his lawyer to request advice on any point.[79] The prisoners asked for Charles Carroll (Catholic), William Dent (Protestant), George Thompson, and the narrator.[80]

[77] The trial record is in *Md. Archives*, VIII, 245–48; the lawyer's narrative is on 251–62. Quotations in the paragraphs that follow are from 254, 259, 260, 257, 262.

[78] *Cal. S. P., Col., 1689–92*, no. 1349.

[79] William Hawkins, *A Treatise of the Pleas of the Crown . . .* , 2 vols. (London, 1719), II, 400–402.

[80] For Carroll's religion, see Wills 16, f. 179. On Dent, see n. 87, below. The narrator may have been Robert Carvile, long an active attorney in the Provincial Court and briefly attorney general in 1688 (*HLP*, 133; *Md. Archives*, LXV–LXX, *passim*; Prov. Ct. Judg., DSA, *passim*). Carvile was Roman Catholic (*Md. Archives*, VIII, 448). It appears that

The narrator had presented the petition to the clerk of the court, John Llewellin, within the next few hours, and had also chatted with the chief judge, Nehemiah Blakiston. Blakiston was still serving as speaker of the convention as well. Llewellin thought the narrator could be assigned as counsel, and Blakiston was full of promises that the "prisoners should have all the faire Dealeing Imaginable." The following day, however, the request for counsel was denied. The refusal was not illegal, but it probably was not consistent with frequent practice in the English courts.[81] The prisoners might have had the benefit of pretrial consultation, but all four lawyers were imprisoned temporarily on charges of treasonable agitation, and Carroll and the narrator were not bailed until the trial was over.[82] In addition, authorities seized papers which the narrator had prepared for the defense, despite the court's order that "they might have what yet they pleased." Those papers had included a defense that attacked the provisional government, apparently in preparation for a trial before a royal governor.

The account of the trial is hearsay, since the narrator was

Catholics were not barred from practice of the law (if they were willing to take the oath of allegiance and supremacy) until Copley's arrival (see *ibid.*, 448, 522–23). George Thompson, currently of St. Mary's, may be the gentleman of the same name who earlier served as clerk of Charles County (*ibid.*, LXX, 43, 252; *HLP*, 149).

[81] The tenor of Hawkins' discussion suggests that it was practice to allow such advice (*A Treatise of the Pleas*, II, 400–402). In 1695, 7 Will. 3, chap. 3, par. 1, finally permitted actual representation by attorney for defendants accused of treason. Danby Pickering, ed., *The Statutes at Large* (Cambridge, 1763), 389. See also Theodore P. T. Plucknett, *A Concise History of the Common Law*, 5th ed. (Boston, 1956), 434–35.

[82] The narrator complained also that no one could see the prisoners without a guard: "I never knew it denyed here for the friends to visitt Prisoners in prison" (*Md. Archives*, VIII, 254). Carroll and Dent were accused of "high misdemeanors," George Thompson "having d.d. a paper to some of the members by way of contrary advice how they proceeded . . . was Committed to Custody for a seditious and Treasonable Pamphlett." The charge against the narrator was "mutenous Rebellious Treasonable Practices and Endeavours . . . to Disturbe theire Majesties peace" (259).

then in custody. John Woodcocke twice denied the jurisdiction of the court but was overruled, and after a warning that a third refusal to plead to the charge would lead to his execution without mercy, he pleaded not guilty.[83] "Petty Iury Called the Prisoners made nott many Challenges. Mr. Geo Playton [Plater] the Kings atturney opened the Charge of murther and went to prove the mather of fact then the K[ing's] evidences were summoned which Consisted chiefly of those men Mr. Payne had pressed to goe along with him to seize the yacht." Chief among these were a John Keenaly or Keene and a Thomas Price, who testified that Payne, in pressing them into service, had explained that he was the king's collector and that the expedition was to seize the yacht as a trader between Maryland and Virginia in violation of the acts of trade. This was critical evidence, for the defense rested its case upon the argument that Payne was acting, not as king's collector, but as a captain of militia to seize Sewall and his boat on the basis of the warrant from Coode of early October. Payne was using his commission as collector to gain access to the yacht; once aboard he planned to seize it by virtue of the warrant. The narrator of this account argued "That if he were not in due Execution of his office & command as Collector (as without doubt he was not) he come at his perill," and the verdict could be at most second-degree murder or manslaughter. It was not usual, after all, for the collector to visit ships in the dark and to be accompanied by armed men.

The prisoners took exception to Keene and Price as witnesses on the grounds that they had previously been convicted of felonies, a fact that would render their testimony invalid. The records of those convictions could not be found, however, and the court accepted the evidence, despite the presence of men who could have testified to the truth of the charge.[84] The court clerk,

[83] This was proper procedure. See Sir Matthew Hale, *Historia Placitorum Coronae: The History of the Pleas of the Crown*, 2 vols. (London, 1736), II, 256.

[84] Including the narrator himself, who had drawn up the pardon for

John Llewellin, admitted later that he knew Coode had taken the record book with him to England, "butt att the tryall he was silent in that point."

The prisoners called for the papers seized from the narrator, which included evidence to support the contention that Payne intended to act by virtue of his militia commission, but these were refused. Blakiston in his charge to the jury not only insisted that Payne was killed in execution of his duty as collector, but denounced the accused as papists carrying arms (forbidden to Catholics by royal declaration) and harked back to the murder of Rousby six years before, a bias against the accused that could be found in many judges of the period in the courts of England.[85] The jury acquitted William Aylward but convicted John Woodcocke, George Mason, and William Burley. Woodcocke, whom Keene had identified as triggerman, was executed.[86]

The court apparently managed to avoid flagrant violations of the legal standards of the time. It allowed the prisoners to challenge members of the jury, for instance, and it ordered a search of the records to find the convictions of Keene and Price. On the other hand, the judges were not at all concerned to establish the truth or to give the prisoners the benefit of rights that were a matter of discretion. Furthermore, reputedly "all as well as prisoners were overawed by an armed force of horse and foot attending all that court of Tryall." The Associators were doubtless determined to obtain convictions and to execute the man

Price. He states that "I was sped, by the Sher to Testifye for the Prisoner yett nott permitted to goe to Court and were ready to depose the same in court and hundereds knew them both to be certainly true yett because the Record was nott produced and could nott be found they were admitted as good Evidence" (*Md. Archives*, VII, 261).

[85] See the accounts of English trials of the 1670's and 1680's in James F. Stephen, *A History of the Criminal Law of England*, 2 vols. (London, 1883), I, 369–416.

[86] The other two were pardoned after Governor Copley's arrival (*Md. Archives*, XX, 485). Aylward, the man acquitted, had been clerk of Somerset county (*HLP*, 153) and probably had better legal knowledge to argue his case than had the other defendants.

most responsible as a means of bolstering their authority. There were still men of prominence—and not all Roman Catholic—who were not afraid to challenge them.[87]

There is no account of the convention's specific transactions at its session in September 1691, except for the passing of a new ordinance appointing civil and military officers.[88] Presumably it also heard the report of William Blanckenstein, one of its members, on his trip to New York. The committee had made him its agent the previous July to consult with Governor Sloughter on possible Maryland assistance in the defense of Albany. There is no indication the convention took any definite action in September on aid to the sister colony.[89]

Six months later, just before the last meeting of the convention, the royal governor finally arrived, and the Associators' government came to an end. It had seized and retained power without bloodshed, beyond the deaths of Payne and Woodcocke; it had maintained order and public services under civilian rule; it had managed to avoid actions that could be used to discredit its leaders. These achievements reflected the stability of local institutions upon which law and order depended and the willingness of all men, including Lord Baltimore's supporters, to let the English crown be the final judge of who should rule in Maryland.

[87] For example, William Dent, imprisoned briefly for objecting to the trial, was the stepson of John Addison, who was a judge on that same Provincial Court conducting this trial. Dent later became attorney general of Maryland. Harry Wright Newman, *The Maryland Dents* (Richmond, 1963), 15–25.

[88] Ch. Ct. and Land Rec., R no. 1, f. 275.

[89] *Cal. S. P., Col., 1689–92*, nos. 1673 and 1702; Edmund B. O'Callaghan et al., eds., *Documents Relative to the Colonial History of the State of New York*, 15 vols. (Albany, 1853–1887), III, 788–89.

CHAPTER V

"A Case of Necessity": The Crown Settlement, 1689–1692

Contemporary events in England had an important bearing on Maryland's Glorious Revolution. The crown's attitude toward changing developments in Lord Baltimore's colony and its subsequent decision to make Maryland a royal province provide an informative case study of colonial policy-making in the late seventeenth century. The royal assumption of government and the appointment of new officials reflect a characteristic absence of consistent policy or recognized channels of authority, as well as the pre-eminence of domestic problems and personalities. Furthermore, these events forcefully reveal the increasingly significant role of the English trading community and colonial lobbyists in the determination of policy and patronage.

England's interests in Maryland were by no means new in 1689. There had been occasional royal involvement in, and intrusion into, the colony's affairs since Maryland's founding in 1634. After the restoration of Charles II, Stuart interest in the possible profits from a fertile tobacco-producing area prompted a desire for greater control over the Chesapeake colonies. Concurrently, problems of defense against the Indians and international rivals also began to dictate more centralized direction of colonial affairs, while the sporadic rebellions of Marylanders against their proprietors were heightening English suspicions of instability or despotic rule in the colony. The frequent posting of complaints to Whitehall by customs collectors and antipro-

prietary colonists did not endear Lord Baltimore to the embry-
onic gathering of young English bureaucrats anxious both to
extend royal authority and to create profitable careers for themselves in colonial administration.[1]

Conflicts between royal customs officials and Lord Baltimore's
government over enforcement of the Navigation Acts in 1683
provided Charles II with an excellent rationale for quo warranto
proceedings against the Maryland charter. This prosecution, still
under consideration at the time of the king's death, gained new
impetus upon reports that George Talbot, president of the Maryland council and Catholic cousin of the proprietor, had murdered
Christopher Rousby, the customs collector, on October 31,
1684. James II ordered the immediate initiation of legal proceedings.[2] For numerous reasons, the prosecution failed to de-
velop much further. James was neither consistent nor persistent
in his direction of this case. Charles Calvert, who had returned
to England in 1684 to defend both his boundaries and his charter, was successful in his personal lobbying for a delay, and the
presence of numerous Catholics among the membership of the
Lords of Trade after 1686 did not harm his cause. With this
"rudderless drift of events," the case against Maryland had not

[1] A fully satisfactory study of the emerging colonial bureaucracy has
yet to appear. Aspects of the subject are well treated in *Colonial Period,*
IV; Ralph Paul Bieber, *The Lords of Trade and Plantations, 1675–1696*
(Allentown, Pa., 1919); Gertrude Jacobsen, *William Blathwayt: A
Late Seventeenth-Century English Administrator* (New Haven, 1932);
Stephen Saunders Webb, "William Blathwayt, Imperial Fixer: From
Popish Plot to Glorious Revolution," and "William Blathwayt, Imperial
Fixer: Muddling Through to Empire, 1689–1717," *William and Mary
Quarterly,* 3rd ser., XXV (1968), 3–21, and XXVI (1969), 373–415; and
Michael G. Hall, *Edward Randolph and the American Colonies, 1676–
1703* (Chapel Hill, 1960).

[2] *Md. Archives,* V, 436–39; W. L. Grant and James Munro, eds., *Acts
of the Privy Council of England: Colonial Series,* 6 vols. (London, 1912–
23), II, 64; Philip S. Haffenden, "The Crown and the Colonial Charters,
1675–1688," *William and Mary Quarterly,* 3rd ser., XV (1958), 308–11,
453.

passed beyond the initial stages of prosecution when James himself was overthrown.[3]

Both the domestic settlement of the Glorious Revolution and developments on the international scene prompted the new government of William and Mary to move more forcefully in bringing the remaining charter colonies under royal control. The Catholic-dominated government of Maryland was now especially vulnerable in light of the growing English reaction against Catholics and the approaching war with France. Consequently, it was not surprising that the new Lords of Trade recommended in April of 1689 that the crown direct the necessary actions "as may better secure their Majestys Interests in those parts and putt them into a Condition of defense against the Enemy." The king approved their proposal that Parliament consider particular procedures.[4]

News began reaching England in the summer that Maryland officials had not yet proclaimed the new monarchs. Virginia's secretary, Nicholas Spencer, described the threatening prospects of civil unrest in two letters to William Blathwayt, secretary to the Lords of Trade. These gentlemen summoned Baltimore to account for his government's neglect. The proprietor at least temporarily assuaged concern by his explanation of the death of his original messenger and his immediate dispatch of a duplicate order to proclaim William and Mary.[5]

It was mid-December before English officials became aware of the bloodless overthrow of Lord Baltimore's government and

[3] Haffenden, 456–64 (quotation, 459); Journal of the Commissioners of Trade and Plantations, CO5/723/I, ff. 109–10. Baltimore placed much importance on the value of a personal appeal in England. See his letter to William Blathwayt, Dec. 7, 1683, printed in Edmund B. O'Callaghan, ed., *Documents Relative to the Colonial History of the State of New York*, 15 vols. (Albany, 1856–87), III, 339–40.

[4] Journal of the Commissioners of Trade and Plantations, Apr. 26, 1689, CO5/723/I, ff. 117–19.

[5] Spencer to Blathwayt, Apr. 27, 1689, Blathwayt Papers, XVI, Research Library, Colonial Williamsburg, Inc.; *Md. Archives*, VIII, 112; *Cal. S. P., Col., 1689–92*, nos. 389, 390, 417.

the assumption of authority by the Protestant Associators. The autumn tobacco fleet brought the rebels' "Declaration of the reason and motive for the present appearing in arms of His Majestys Protestant Subjects in the Province of Maryland" and the convention's petition for "such a deliverance to your suffering people, whereby for the future of our religion, rights and Lyberties may be secured, under a Protestant Government by your Majestyes gracious direction especially to be appointed." But that same fleet also brought members and supporters of the deposed government with their own accounts of the recent upheaval. It was immediately clear that confused and controversial sessions were ahead for Whitehall officials. The legal aspects surrounding the charter, now under renewed siege, were troublesome enough without the added difficulty of determining just what had transpired in Maryland and why. Nor could the Maryland problem be isolated for intensive and separate deliberation, for that uprising was only one of a number of colonial and international issues now vying for the attention of English officials.

In late December the commissioners reopened investigation of the Maryland charter. Lord Baltimore appeared before them with an array of witnesses, among whom were Henry Darnall, the ousted councillor, and Mrs. Barbara Smith, wife of an imprisoned proprietary supporter. The Marylanders were armed with personal accounts of the revolt, letters from fellow adherents to the old government, and copies of relevant colonial statutes, especially the important Act Concerning Religion. After hearing their testimony and reading the various documents, the Lords recommended on January 7, 1689/90, that the crown send a letter to the current authorities in Maryland approving the proclamation of William and Mary and empowering the Associators to continue their administration of the government for the present.[6]

[6] *Cal. S. P., Col., 1689–92*, nos. 656, 658; *Md. Archives*, VIII, 114–15, 118–21, 147–51, 153–57, 162. The other witnesses provided by Baltimore were traders Samuel Groom, Samuel Philips, and Bartholomew Watts,

Meanwhile, Lord Baltimore was launching a concerted effort to besmirch the rebels, protect his charter, and retain control of the colony. Darnall had brought the proprietor legal advice from Charles Carroll, a young Maryland lawyer who had wisely deduced that a quo warranto proceeding "is not much favoured by the King or Pariament much less I believe will they approve of such unheard of actions as were committed against your Lordship & Government by these evil speritts without Commission or order from any superior power."[7] Unknown to Carroll, the Parliament was at this very time in the process of invalidating most of the quo warranto proceedings completed under Charles II and James II.[8]

Aware of the official uneasiness about vacating his charter, Baltimore was prepared to make numerous concessions to forestall his enemies. He proposed to the Lords of Trade the full removal of the "Deputys, Councill & Justices" whom he had previously appointed. The new government would be comprised solely of "profest Protestants" to whose good reputation, credit, and estate the merchants who traded with Maryland could testify. Baltimore recommended Henry Coursey to head the new government, a nomination that reflected the proprietor's desperate desire to retain some control. Coursey, the protégé of Philip Calvert, twice had been a councillor (1660–1670, 1676–1684) but had incurred the proprietor's disfavor. When Baltimore left for England in 1684, he had omitted Coursey from the council, re-

and present or former Marylanders George Robins, Henry Coursey, Jr., Thomas Taylor, John Lillingston, and Charles Abington (163).

[7] Carroll to Lord Baltimore, Sept. 25, 1689, *Md. Archives*, VIII, 124–26. Carroll, a Catholic, had entered the Inner Temple in 1685. He served briefly as a clerk in the office of Lord Powis before emigrating to Maryland on the eve of the Glorious Revolution. His later career in the colony was particularly distinguished (Carroll T. Bond, ed., *Proceedings of the Maryland Court of Appeals, 1695–1729* [Washington, D.C., 1933], xxv).

[8] Historical Manuscripts Commission, *The Manuscripts of the House of Lords*, New Ser., 11 vols. to date (*London*, 1887–) II, 422–27.

placed him as chief justice of the Provincial Court, and later removed him from the court commission altogether. Even so, Coursey was now a preferable alternative to John Coode and his colleagues.[9]

Baltimore, recognizing that he was most vulnerable on the religious issue, hoped that the exclusion of Catholics would sufficiently appease English officials. He further promised "all the satisfaction the Inhabitants in general there can desire, and which his Lordship is also certain all the Merchants, Traders and Dealers for that Province will be very much satisfied with." Baltimore knew well the influence wielded by the merchant community in determining colonial policy. He was now willing to forego any punishment of the rebels, but he did request that the king direct a "full Examination of the truth of all such matters pretended by John Coode and those other persons joyned with him to be the cause of their taking up Arms."[10]

The spring fleet was due to leave England soon, and it was very important that it carry some indication of royal feeling to the anxious colony. The Lords of Trade hurried the preparation of a letter, which William signed on February 1. It commanded the Associators to proceed with their administration of the government, pending the crown's "full examination of all matters and hearing of what shall be represented to us on the behalf of the Proprietor and his Right." The current government was to enforce the acts of trade and, significantly, to allow Baltimore's agents to collect the traditional revenues due the proprietor. Those revenues were the two-shillings-per-hogshead duty on exported tobacco and the fourteen-pence-per-ton duty on ships trading in Maryland.[11]

---

[9] *Md. Archives*, VIII, 165–66. On Coursey's career and relations with the proprietor, see III, 326, 394; LVII, xiv; LIV, xxiv; *HLP*, 95, 96, 125, 179.

[10] *Md. Archives*, VIII, 165–66.

[11] *Ibid.*, 167–68. This letter, sent via Francis Nicholson, reached the Associators in late May (169, 193).

The Lords resumed their "full examination," only to discover the difficulty of piecing together the causes of the revolt or determining which parties were in error. New charges and countercharges arrived from the colony in early February in the form of petitions that had circulated at the previous November sessions of the county courts. Six petitions favored the revolt and the new regime, while three counterpetitions sharply denounced the overthrow and disparaged the motives and abilities of the Associators.[12] News arrived soon after of John Payne's death, the first bloodshed of the revolution. John Coode, skillfully seizing the incident as a "barbarous murder," effectively employed it as propaganda against the proprietary party; he had immediately written the Earl of Shrewsbury, then secretary of state, as part of the continuing effort to counter the adverse publicity being generated in England against the revolt.[13]

Coode's letters received additional support in England through a petition from Payne's brother, Dr. William Payne. At hearings in mid-April, the Lords studied these materials and concluded that "Some Papist confederates with Major Sewall" had committed the murder in the manner alleged, and they deplored the occurrence of "so heinous a Crime."[14] They prepared a letter, which the king signed on April 26, embodying these opinions and ordering the arrest and "Speedy Tryal" of the alleged culprits.[15]

The Lords had noted in their deliberations the disturbing parallel between the killing of Payne and the murder five years earlier of Rousby. Coode himself had carefully reminded them

[12] Endorsements noted that the petitions were received on February 7, 1689/90. See also pp. 91–93 above.

[13] Coode to Secretary of State, Feb. 18, 1689/90, and Mar. 24, 1690, *Md. Archives*, VIII, 169–70 and 170–73. See above, pp. 93–95, for further details on the incident.

[14] Journal of the Commissioners of Trade and Plantations, Apr. 24, 1690, CO5/723/II, ff. 170–72. See also *Cal. S. P., Col., 1689–92*, nos. 766, 785, 831, 832.

[15] *Md. Archives*, VIII, 174–76.

of Rousby's death in one of his letters. Whatever the motives for or the actual circumstances of the two deaths of Protestants acting in the king's service and killed by Catholics related to the proprietor, this second such occurrence greatly strengthened the natural predilections of the current English officials to favor the self-proclaimed Protestant rebels. Baltimore's situation appeared increasingly unfavorable as Coode hammered heavily on the religious issue in letters which reached England throughout the next few months. "Wee have been much disquieted and disturbed by the Papists and the discontents of that faction against their Majesties knowne Interest," he had written on March 24, when describing his problems in containing the opposition.[16]

Upon receipt of the letter, the Lords of Trade summoned Baltimore to attend a meeting of the Privy Council scheduled for June 25, 1690.[17] By this point, Baltimore had already suffered his first defeat. Despite the absence of a clear decision on the charter issue, officials had determined that the crown, and not the proprietor, would appoint the new governor; Baltimore was to have no voice in the selection. By mid-May, the crown had designated Lionel Copley as the intended governor of Maryland.[18]

Copley, the forty-two-year-old lieutenant governor of Hull, was a loyal Protestant with a history of anti-Catholic activity in the army. He had recently played an important role in securing Kingston-upon-Hull for William of Orange.[19] More par-

[16] *Ibid.*, 170. Other correspondence between the Associators and English officials during this period may be found on 123–24, 151–52, 169–70.

[17] *Ibid.*, 190.

[18] "I am told that the King has appointed Colonel Copley, who secured Hull for him, Governor of Maryland and Virginia," noted an entry in the Greenwich Hospital Newsletter of May 17, 1690. *Cal. S. P., Dom., 1690–1691*, 12. The precise date of the decision is unknown, but see also "A Paper Relating to Maryland, Rec'd from Coll Copley," marked June, CO5/713/I; *Col. S. P., Col., 1689–92*, no. 976.

[19] Annie Leakin Sioussat, "Lionel Copley, First Royal Governor of

ticularly, however, his present good fortune over other contenders for the Maryland post owed much to two very influential men, Thomas Osborne, the former Earl of Danby and now Marquis of Carmarthen, and William Blathwayt, the powerful secretary to the Lords of Trade. Osborne was governor of Hull, and therefore Copley's superior. He had earlier obtained the Hull position for Copley; now, as president of the Privy Council and "unquestionably the first minister of the Crown," he was in an even better position to aid his protégé.[20] Osborne's motivation to assist Copley further likely derived from two factors. Copley had recently fallen into serious trouble for tampering with the mail, an offense probably committed with Osborne's knowledge and approval. With the affair now public, it seemed judicious to remove Copley from the Hull area. In addition, Osborne wished to make room for his brother Charles, who now replaced Copley as the lieutenant governor.[21] Blathwayt had maintained a correspondence and a mutually profitable relationship with Copley for several years. As secretary of war and assistant to the Lords of Trade, he was an important man to know. Blathwayt had earlier helped to shield Copley from a suit for debt, and was now strategically placed to assist in easing Copley from his more recent indiscretion.[22]

Copley would not depart for Maryland for another year and a half. Indeed, it would be over a year before appointments to either the secretaryship of the colony or the council would be filled. Meanwhile, attention focused on the proceedings against the charter and the nature of Copley's commission. English legal officials were somewhat apprehensive over the crown's inten-

Maryland," *MHM*, XVII (1922), 163–77; Charles Dalton, ed., *English Army Lists and Commission Registers, 1661–1714,* 6 vols. (London, 1960), I, 188: II, 39; III, 99, 101; Webb, "William Blathwayt," 19–20.

[20] Andrew Browning, *Thomas Osborne, Earl of Danby and Duke of Leeds, 1632–1712,* 3 vols. (Glasgow, 1951) I, 446, 474–78 (quotation, 475).

[21] *Ibid.,* I, 486; *Cal. S. P., Dom., 1690–91,* 68.

[22] Webb, "William Blathwayt," 19–20, 377–78. Blathwayt and Copley parted ways soon after the latter's appointment, however.

tions. Chief Justice Sir John Holt expressed his misgivings to Osborne on June 3, 1690: "I thinke it had been better if an inquisition had been taken and the forfeitures committed by the Lord Baltimore had been therein founde before any grant be made to a new governor. Yet since there is none and it being in a case of necessity I thinke the King may by his Commission constitute a governor whose authority will be legall tho he must be responsible to the Lord Baltimore for the profits. If an agreement can be made with the Ld Baltimore it will be convenient and easy for the governor that the King shall appoint, an inquisition may at any time be taken if the forfeiture be not pardoned of which there is some doubt."[23]

The crown was clearly resting its position on "a case of necessity," for charter rights could not be forfeited without successful judicial proceedings, according to the very statute which placed William and Mary on the throne of England.[24] For a while, the advisors reflected their own uneasiness and concern about this procedure, for the initial drafts of Copley's commission still provided for its issuance in Lord Baltimore's name while the proprietor would retain most of his charter rights.[25] Copley, less concerned over the legal matters than over his own powers and perquisites, expressed dismay over this relationship and introduced demands that the commission be similar to those issued other royal governors. Such a commission would be revocable only by the crown, and would normally continue for the duration of Their Majesties' lives. With his eye on the pocketbook, a vision which would later prove to be very characteristic, Copley also demanded that Baltimore surrender half of the two-shillings-per-hogshead duty and the quitrents "with all the perquisitts that other Governors have in the neighboring Collonys."[26] The Lords of Trade forwarded a draft of the proposed

[23] *Md. Archives*, VIII, 185–86.
[24] Andrew Browning, ed., *English Historical Documents, 1660–1714* (New York, 1953), 122–28, especially 124.
[25] *Cal. S. P., Col., 1689–92*, no. 1029.
[26] *Md. Archives*, VIII, 200.

commission to Attorney General Sir George Treby for his opin-
ions on its fitness to pass the great seal. The crown also ordered
Treby on August 21 to proceed forthwith by *scire facias* against
Baltimore's charter "in order to vacate the same."[27]

Treby was no more enthusiastic than Holt about these proceedings. He prefaced his report with the observation that "I
understand the seizure of this Government to be for necessity,
as being the onely meanes of preserving the Province." He was
extremely cautious in his remarks and advice. Such a routine
commission might not be agreeable to the already established
"Lawes and manner" of the colony, or might "be prejudicall
to the Interest of the Inhabitants," matters about which he was
insufficiently informed to rule conclusively. Consequently, in
what may have been a delaying action and was certainly an unwillingness to approve the current policy, Treby recommended
returning to a shorter and more general commission which would
avoid legal pitfalls: "I did draw a commission generall reciteing
the confusion that was there and the danger of loosing the Province to the Enemyes and the necessity of takeing it into their
Majesties' hands and thereupon constituting a Governor there
to Govern according to the Laws of the Place (and as the administration ought to have been by the former Governor) and
to defend the Province and take and apply the Public Revenue
to that purpose. And I see noe cause to depart therefrom or to
recommend this present Draught."[28]

A satisfactorily worded commission continued to elude the
royal officials. In October, the king requested that Baltimore
submit copies of previous commissions by which he acted as
governor during his father's lifetime. These were referred to
Treby and the solicitor general for review and assistance in preparing the commission and instructions they would judge "most
Conduceing to the good Government of the said Colony, taking

[27] *Ibid.*, 200–204.

[28] Report of Treby, Sept. 1, 1690, *ibid.*, 204. The preamble to the final
commission stresses the problem of defense (263).

Care that there be inserted therein a Salvo for his Majesty's **Right and Prerogative.**"[29]

Baltimore had thus far retained a tenuous hold on his charter, although the right of appointing a governor had escaped his grasp. As the months passed, new information from America regarding the state of affairs in Maryland attested to the importance of a prompt decision on the part of the crown and the immediate dispatch of the governor. In November, Baltimore led a new parade of eleven proprietary witnesses, all Protestants, before the Lords of Trade with new statements of grievances against the Associators. Baltimore used this same occasion to renew his protests and efforts to discredit the rebel government, including charges that the Associators had refused to heed royal orders sanctioning the collection of proprietary revenues.[30]

The testimony before Whitehall officials was not all weighted against the Associators, however. Coode and Cheseldyne had arrived in England and made their first official appearance before the Lords of Trade on November 20, presenting new explanations and justifications of the overthrow and its aftermath. They successfully placed Baltimore on the defensive once again with their paper leveling fifty-two "Articles Against the Lord Baltimore, his Deputies, Judges, & Ministers employed by him in the Government of this Province." These articles rehearsed and elaborated upon the earlier list of grievances.[31]

In response to the Lords' request, Coode and Cheseldyne also prepared a rebuttal to the charges submitted by the eleven proprietary witnesses. They here elaborated more extensively than

[29] *Ibid.*, 207; CO5/723/II, f. 178.

[30] "Petition of Severall of the Ancient Protestant Inhabitants" and "The Humble Petition of Charles Lord Baltimore," CO5/713/I, nos. 30 and 32; *Md. Archives*, VIII, 210–13. The assistance of the Bishop of London had been solicited by one ardent Anglican who supported Lord Baltimore (192–93).

[31] *Md. Archives*, VIII, 215–20. The charges are discussed more fully on pp. 116–20 above. For unexplained reasons, Rebert King, the third agent, had accompanied them no further than Plymouth (Edward Randolph to Blathwayt, June 28, 1692, *Randolph Letters*, VII, 379).

anywhere else their account of the actions of the deputy governors in the winter and spring of 1688–89 and their own moves to obtain control of the government. They noted that three of the proprietary witnesses, Abraham Wilde, Thomas Taylor and John Lillingtson, were not even in Maryland at the time of the uprising.[32]

The Lords of Trade conducted a brief interrogation of both parties to the dispute, studied the numerous petitions and read all the available correspondence and papers. They could still come to no resolution, and their report to the king suggested that the problem be referred to the new governor for a full investigation upon his arrival in the colony. Again, the crucial decision was avoided, and the responsibility shifted to another individual. The king acquiesced, approved the report, and on January 1, 1690/91, he ordered the secretary of state to prepare instructions for the governor accordingly.[33] Meanwhile, the Lords of Trade forwarded a draft of the originally proposed commission to Lord Baltimore on January 3 that he might register any objections.[34] When over a week had elapsed with no response, they sent Baltimore a second note requesting his opinion. They were displaying a new sense of urgency prompted in part by the recent hearings but also by a letter from Governor Francis Nicholson in Virginia. Commenting on developments in Maryland, Nicholson had voiced a hope that the situation would soon be settled "or the King will lose by it."[35]

Baltimore had many objections to register and undoubtedly had spent the intervening days in reassessing his position and preparing his defense. He employed the wrong strategy, how-

[32] Journal of the Commissioners of Trade and Plantations, Dec. 5, 1690, CO5/723/11, f. 199; *Md. Archives*, VIII, 225–28.

[33] *Cal. S. P., Col., 1689–92*, nos. 1195, 1201, 1228, 1263, 1278; *Md. Archives*, VIII, 229.

[34] *Cal. S. P., Col., 1689–92*, no. 1281; *Md. Archives*, VIII, 200–203, contains the commission draft sent to Baltimore.

[35] *Cal. S. P., Col., 1689–92*, nos. 1287, 1023.

ever, for his response proved too adamant and unrealistic in light of the events which had already transpired. He informed the Lords that he found many clauses "very prejudiciall" and "utterly destructive of the Rights Powers and Priviledges granted to his Lordship by his Charter." That charter was still Baltimore's refuge, and until the crown successfully proceeded against it, he was staunchly determined to oppose any such commission. His most foolhardy contention, however, was the assertion that he alone should hold the right of nomination and appointment of the governor; he promised once more to nominate a "Protestant of unquestionable Credit for Governour, as likewise Protestants of very good Repute to be of the Councill and to repose the command of the Militia together with the Magazine of Armes and Ammunition in the hands of the Protestants." Baltimore was stubbornly refusing to accede to any commission by which he was to share with the crown the right to appoint or remove the governor and the right of veto over legislation.[36] Baltimore had perhaps forgotten that the crown had declined to accept his "Protestant" nominees almost a year earlier. Now, in reasserting powers already "trimmed" by the royal advisers, Baltimore sufficiently provoked these men to go even further in usurping his proprietary rights, which they proceeded rapidly to do.

The Privy Council heard a reading of Baltimore's objections on January 15, after which the king directed Holt and Treby to settle the commission dispute.[37] Most likely these gentlemen also received ample indications of displeasure over Baltimore's uncooperative stance. Their new commission was much changed in form. It differed in no essential way from those issued for other colonies immediately under royal control. The new governor would derive his powers from the crown with no responsibility to the proprietor. Baltimore would continue to own the land and to receive certain revenues from Maryland, but his powers and authority in governmental affairs stood negated.

[36] *Md. Archives*, VIII, 230–31.
[37] *Ibid.*, 231; *Cal. S. P., Col., 1689–92*, no. 1288.

Treby had also incorporated into the opening paragraph the brief justification for the seizure which he had earlier recommended: "Whereas by reason of great neglects and miscarriages in the Government of Our Province and Territory of Maryland in America, the same is fallen into disorder and confusion, by means whereof not only the publick Peace and Administration of Justice (whereby the properties of Our Subjects should be preserved there) is broken and violated, but also there is an utter want of Provision for the Guard and Defence of the said Country against our Enemies, and thereby the same is exposed and like to be lost from the Crown of England. And whereas Our said Province and our good subjects the Inhabitants thereof cannot be defended and secured by any other means than by our taking the Government thereof into our hands and into our immediate Care. . . ." On January 21, the two men sent the document to the Privy Council with their signatures scrawled beneath the statement "I do approve of this draught."[38]

Baltimore was understandably outraged. He petitioned the king with a request that final action be withheld until he could once more state his rights and objections. The Privy Council granted him a hearing on February 5, but his protests went unheeded. He could not reverse the decision, and to his dismay, most of his charter rights now slipped from his grasp.[39] A week later the commission draft was transmitted to Secretary of State Viscount Sydney in preparation for the royal signature. Queen Mary signed the warrant on February 14.[40]

Apprehension still prevailed in some quarters, however, about this course of action, and it was four and a half months before

[38] Draught of Commission to Lionel Copley, CO5/713/I, no. 42. For a critical assessment of the roles played by Holt and Treby, see George Chalmers, "Political Annals of the Present United Colonies From Their Settlement to the Peace in 1763," in *Collections of the New-York Historical Society for the Year 1868* (New York, 1868), I, 76–78.

[39] *Md. Archives*, VIII, 232–33; CO5/719/I, no. 7.

[40] CO5/719/I, no. 8; *Cal. S. P. Col., 1689–92*, no. 1297; the full commission is in CO5/724/I, ff. 1–17, and *Md. Archives*, VIII, 263–70.

the great seal was affixed to Copley's commission. It finally required a summary order from the Privy Council to the Commissioners of the Privy Seal to dispatch the document immediately "unless they have any reason for stopping or further delay of it. In which Case, they are to acquaint the Lords . . . on Thursday next in the morning, with their reason for stopping the Said Commission."[41] This apparently sufficed; the great seal was affixed on June 27, 1691, and within two more months the governor's instructions had also been completed. These instructions, like the commission, followed the standard pattern for other royal colonies.[42]

Without normal judicial action, Baltimore's charter had in effect been suspended, "by reason of great neglects and miscarriages" as the commission explained. The crown later initiated prosecution against the charter, but again it encountered difficulties with legal advisers. The proceedings were never completed.[43] As long as the Calverts remained Catholics and England was at war with France, the proprietary family would be without full control of the colony. The crown would rule until 1715, when a Protestant proprietor was then able to assert his charter rights and regain most of his governing powers.[44]

[41] *Md. Archives*, VIII, 240–41.

[42] *Cal. S. P., Col., 1689–92*, no. 1297. For the text of Copley's instructions, see *Md. Archives*, VIII, 271–80. Six months later, a commission was drafted for Francis Nicholson as lieutenant governor of Maryland (CO5/724/I, ff. 41–42).

[43] Chalmers, "Political Annals," 79, 93. Also *Cal. S. P., Dom., 1690–91*, 376; *ibid.*, 1697, 255–58; Historical Manuscripts Commission, *Manuscripts of the House of Lords*, IV, 30, 141, 314, 342. Lord Baltimore had been outlawed in Ireland in 1689, but later legislation reversed the outlawry. See Clayton Colman Hall, *The Lords Baltimore and the Maryland Palatinate* (Baltimore, 1904), 100–101, 136–37. Lady Baltimore and her daughters had been briefly held in custody in late 1688 but were released upon orders from members of the Privy Council (Johnson Papers 1638–1699, f. 139, Add. Mss. 22,183, British Museum).

[44] "Royal Period," 316–47. The question of proprietary rights and powers surfaced with the appointment of each new governor to the colony (Hall, *The Lords Baltimore*, 125–40).

During the final months of the struggle over the commission, other business proceeded. On March 12, the queen signed a letter notifying the colony that "having since heard what your deputies and Agents have offered to us, Wee have thought fitt to take our Province of Maryland under our immediate care and Protection." She announced the appointment of Copley and the decision that half of the two-shilling duty on exported tobacco would henceforth go for support of the government, while Baltimore would retain the remaining half and all of the fourteen-pence tonnage duty.[45] This proclamation in effect legitimized the revolution in Maryland and ended the uncertainty that had plagued its affairs for more than two years.

There was still the task of staffing the new royal government with provincial officeholders to assist the governor, and Whitehall personnel now focused their attention on this priority. The deliberations over Maryland's future were entering their third year, and the Lords of Trade realized that a rapid determination of these remaining appointments was a necessity. Hoping that Copley might sail with the convoy departing in mid-September, the Lords posted his sailing instructions while hastily sifting recommendations and making appointments.[46]

Recommendations came from a variety of sources. The Lords were no more knowledgeable of specific residents of the colony than of Maryland affairs in general. They turned for advice quite naturally to others who were more informed, particularly the colonial trading community, a traditional source of such information, and Lord Baltimore. Each had some firsthand acquaintance with the colony's leadership and social structure, even if they did not possess the most up-to-date intelligence on the alliances and rivalries emanating from the revolution. Lionel

---

[45] *Md. Archives*, VIII, 235–36. Baltimore had renewed protests about his inability to collect the revenues due him, which prompted a strong restatement of his rights in the queen's letter. For the discussions of his protests and the taxes, see CO5/723/II, ff. 219–20; *Md. Archives*, VIII, 233–35.

[46] *Cal. S. P., Col., 1689–92*, no. 1709.

Copley was also consulted, although his information was clearly secondhand.

The first position to be filed was the lucrative and powerful post of secretary. The Lords of Trade agreed on July 29 that the position should go to Sir Thomas Lawrence, English baronet, and the Privy Council concurred on the following day.[47] Little is known about Lawrence's earlier career or the source of his patronage. Born about 1645, he was the son of Sir John Lawrence of Chelsea, Middlesex. He matriculated at Oxford in 1661, received his A.B. degree in 1664/65 and an A.M. from University College in 1668. Lawrence was also a student at the Middle Temple during the same time that William Blathwayt studied there; Blathwayt may have used his influence in obtaining this appointment, for the two men maintained a cordial relationship during Lawrence's tenure as secretary. Between 1668 and 1691, Lawrence's activities remain a mystery, except for his marriage to Anne English of St. Clement Dane's in 1674 and the births and deaths of members of his family.[48]

Lawrence had had no previous contact with Maryland, but this was not to be the case with the men selected for the council. Copley had submitted a list of his own nominees on September 1.[49] In all likelihood, he had determined upon these names after consultation with Coode, for seven of his eight nominees were prominent Associators who were among the major figures in the government at the time of Coode's departure from Maryland one year earlier. In addition to Coode himself, the list in-

[47] Board of Trade Journal, 1691–1695, f. 40, transcribed copy in Pennsylvania Historical Society, Philadelphia; Privy Council 2/74/218, PRO.

[48] G. E. Cockayne, *Complete Baronetage, 1611–1800,* 5 vols. (Exeter, 1900–1906), II, 61; Sir Henry F. MacGeagh and H. A. C. Sturgess, comps., *Register of Admissions to the Honourable Society of the Middle Temple,* 3 vols. (London, 1944–1949), I, 170–71; Joseph Foster, ed., *Alumni Oxoniensis: The Members of the University of Oxford, 1500–1714,* 4 vols. (Oxford, 1891–1892) III, 889; Chelsea Parish Register, 1653–1704, P74/LUK/162, Greater London Record Office.

[49] List Received From Coll Copley's Agent Sept. 1, 1691," CO5/713/II, no. 49.

cluded John Addison, George Robotham, David Browne, Henry Jowles, Nicholas Greenberry, and Nehemiah Blakiston, all of whom were influential members of the Grand Committee of Twenty.[50] The eighth nominee, James Whitwood, remains unidentified; he may have been a friend of Copley.[51] Strangely, the list did not include Kenelm Cheseldyne, who may have quarreled with Coode in England or was not to Copley's liking.

The new governor was undoubtedly in close contact with the Lords of Trade during this crucial period. He apparently supplied additional names later in the month, while withdrawing some of his earlier recommendations. A final master sheet listing individuals under consideration contained five more names with Copley's endorsement and six of the original eight names he had submitted. Significantly, the two omissions were Coode and Whitwood.[52] Most likely, these changes of mind followed a meeting with Captain John Hammond of Maryland, who had arrived from America in mid-September and immediately asked for Copley. Most of the new nominees were men whose ascendancy in the colony had come after the departure of Coode and Cheseldyne.[53]

Hammond, a merchant who resided in Anne Arundel County, was to play a most decisive role in the selection of the council. Although he had lived most of his life in Maryland, Hammond was well known in Engish circles through his own and his family's trade connections. He was probably the nephew of John Hammond, author of the celebrated pamphlet "Leah and Rachel, or the Two Fruitfull Sisters Virginia and Mary-land" pub-

[50] See pp. 97–98 above.

[51] Copley did bring a coterie of friends to the colony in 1692 and established them in profitable posts ("Royal Period," 78–79).

[52] "List of Persons Recommended to be of Their Majestys Councill in Maryland," undated, CO5/713/II, no. 53. The list is also available in *Md. Archives*, VIII, 282–83, but the printed version does not include the added pencil markings nor does it reflect the different handwritings shown on the original, both of which are very important in this analysis.

[53] *Ibid.*, 282. The new names were Thomas Tench, Charles Hutchins, John Courts, Henry Hamand, and John Dent.

lished in London in 1656. Captain Hammond had been originally a Quaker but had deviated from Quaker beliefs in the 1680's and later embraced the Anglican communion.[54] First appointed a justice in 1685, he had led the opposition against Richard Hill when the latter opposed the rebels' call for elections in August 1689. The Associators had gratefully promoted Hammond to justice of the quorum at their first convention and later made him a militia officer. When his business necessitated a voyage to England in 1691, Hammond became the logical person to entrust with information for London officials.[55] Hammond's knowledge was also to have a wide-ranging influence on other participants in the selection of the council.

Lord Baltimore, now without the final authority he had always possessed on council appointments, proposed eighteen "most Substantial Protestant Inhabitants of Maryland," none of whom had actively supported the revolutionary cause in 1689. His suggestions primarily encompassed members of old proprietary families like George Wells, James Frisby, and Thomas Brooke.[56]

Thomas Povey, a clerk in the Trade and Plantations Office, forwarded this list to Micajah Perry, probably the most prominent London merchant trading in the Chesapeake area and currently the chief spokesman for the merchant community in

[54] Harry Wright Newman, *Anne Arundel Gentry*, rev. ed. (Annapolis, 1970), 187–96; Quarterly Meeting for the Western Shore, Minutes, 1682–1709, 3; Yearly and Half Yearly Meeting of Friends in Maryland, Minutes, 1677–1758, 248, both microfilm in Hall of Records, Annapolis; *Md. Archives*, VIII, 196; XVII, 379. Clayton Colman Hall, ed., *Narratives of Early Maryland, 1633–1684* (New York, 1910), 279–308, contains "Leah and Rachel."

[55] Hill, who had been forced to flee Maryland for his personal safety in early June of 1690, was also then in England. Both Hill and Henry Darnall had been released from bail and exonerated for alleged words against the crown by Privy Council action of January 1690/91 (*Md. Archives*, VIII, 181–82, 191–92, 196–98, 229). Hammond was later appointed to the council under Governor Nicholson (XXV, 51).

[56] "List of Names of Substantial Protestants Submitted by Lord Baltimore . . . ," undated, CO5/713/II, no. 50.

advising Whitehall on colonial affairs. Perry returned Baltimore's list on September 17 after marking it with the opinions of his fellow merchants. He checked the names of eight "which we believe are honest and good men; some of them we corrispond with: and we know not but they are well affected to the present Gouvemt: not haveing heard anything to the contrary at any time." Perry also indicated approval of two other men whom the merchants understood to be under consideration although not included on Baltimore's list. The traders thought very highly of other Marylanders, but these men had "espoused my Lords Interest" and would thus "be unwilling to engage in the Government." These were Perry's "best thoughts at present."[57]

One of Perry's two additions was the name of John Hammond. Later that same afternoon Hammond paid an unexpected visit to Perry's office, which resulted in a change of the earlier "best thoughts." Perry quickly dispatched to Povey a new list of fourteen nominees with eleven new names. The "gentleman lately arrived from Maryland" had obviously impressed Perry.[58]

Hammond's suggestions to Perry represented a combination of Associators and nominal proprietary men, although he had assured the London merchant that all were "good honest Substantiall Protestants and such he can and will be ready to give satisfaction are well affected to the present Government."[59] They embodied, nonetheless, definite degrees of affection. James Frisby, for example, a duplication from Baltimore's list, had certainly been responsible for much opposition to the rebels in Cecil County. In contrast, eight men were currently members of the Grand Committee.[60] Eight names appearing on Perry's recon-

[57] Perry to Povey, Sept. 17, 1691, CO5/713/II, no. 51 and enclosure 51i; also *Md. Archives*, VIII, 281.

[58] CO5/713/II, no. 51 and 51ii.

[59] *Ibid.;* letter is also available in *Md. Archives*, VIII, 282.

[60] Regarding Frisby's opposition, see *Md. Archives*, VIII, 332–33; XIII, 318–19. Members of the Grand Committee on the list were George Robotham, John Brooke, David Browne, William Harris, Nicholas Gassaway, Nicholas Greenberry, Henry Jowles, and Nehemiah Blakiston.

sidered list duplicate Copley's final recommendation, presumably influenced as well by Hammond.[61] It is significant that the final council contained nine of Hammond's fourteen nominees.

The Lords of Trade relied basically upon these three sources in the determination of names to submit to the crown. First, someone in the office, perhaps Povey, constructed a list of the proposed councillors in three columns, headed by the titles "Supposed to be my Lord's party," "these by Captain Hammond," and "these by I know not whom"; the latter were undoubtedly Copley's nominees, for the list corresponds exactly with the names he submitted.[62] This information was subsequently transferred to a neatly compiled master sheet designated "List of Persons Recommended to be of their Majestys Council in Maryland." The names were arranged in five categories in the following order: those nominated (1) by both Copley and the merchants; (2) by Copley alone; (3) by both Baltimore and the merchants; (4) by Baltimore alone; and (5) by the merchants alone.[63]

Following this working form and the extensive checks and notations made in several different handwritings, one can draw some conclusions about the principal factors operative in the final selection. Whitehall obviously wanted a Protestant council of substantial estate and integrity which would please as many parties as possible. For example, it is noteworthy that neither Coode nor Cheseldyne ever received serious, if any, consideration. They were the two men most indelibly associated with leadership of the revolution and its promotion in England, and the two individuals perhaps most offensive to the proprietary party. Cheseldyne was apparently never nominated, and Coode,

[61] Duplications were Jowles, Blakiston, Greenberry, Hutchins, Robotham, Browne, Tench, and Thomas Greenfield, although there is some question about Greenfield's having Copley's endorsement; significantly, he was the only member of this group not appointed to the council.

[62] CO5/713/II, no. 52; *Md. Archives*, VIII, 284.

[63] CO5/713/II, no. 53.

proposed originally by Copley, had been eliminated by mid-September.[64]

The Lords reached agreement on the six individuals shown by the sheet as endorsed by both Copley and the merchants: Colonel Henry Jowles, Captain Nehemiah Blakiston, Captain Nicholas Greenberry, Mr. Charles Hutchins, Colonel George Robotham, and Colonel David Browne. One other name unmistakably nominated by both groups had been momentarily overlooked; it was obviously an oversight and was soon corrected. Someone other than the sheet's original compiler detected "Thomas Tench Esquire" entered in both blocks two and five, scratched them out there and inserted his name in the first column. Tench became the seventh councillor to be selected.[65]

The eighth and ninth selections, Captains John Addison and John Courts, were the top two nominees in the second category, men proposed by Copley alone. All nine men decided upon at this point had been delegates to the Associators' Convention, seven were members of the Grand Committee, and six had been appointed to the reconstituted Provincial Court in April of 1691.[66] Only Charles Hutchins was serving on neither the committee nor the court. He still bore impressive credentials. Promoted to justice of the quorum for Dorchester County in 1689, he had risen from no militia office to the ranks of colonel and county commander by 1691.[67]

[64] It is conceivable, based upon contemporary accounts, that English officials and merchants found Coode and Cheseldyne personally objectionable. Remarks suggesting this explanation can be found in Edward Randolph to Blathwayt, June 28, 1692, *Randolph Letters*, VII, 376. The two were currently under charges of embezzlement; see CO5/713/I, nos. 32, 43, and 44; and Blathwayt to Copley, Feb. 28, 1692/93, Blathwayt Papers, XVIII.

[65] CO5/713/II, no. 53.

[66] Justices of the Provincial Court included Blakiston, Jowles, Robotham, Greenberry, Tench, and Addison, plus five other colonists (*Md. Archives*, VIII, 242).

[67] *Ibid.*, XIII, 244; Dor. Land Rec., O no. 4½, ff. 9, 195. Tench was the other nonmember of the committee. An Anne Arundel delegate, he did not sit in the convention until 1690, but rose rapidly thereafter.

With the selection of these nine men, some officials apparently considered the task completed; proprietary councils had usually numbered eight men. A suppposedly final list containing the nine names was prepared for submission to the Privy Council. Before royal approval was obtained, however, three additional names were attached, again in a different handwriting. Sir Thomas Lawrence, the new secretary, now headed the list, while James Frisby and Thomas Brooke became the eleventh and twelfth ranking councillors. The amended heading now read "List of Councill of Maryland," rather than "List of Persons Recommended. . . ."[68]

Frisby and Brooke had headed the group nominated by both Baltimore and the merchants, and they were the only men proposed by the proprietor who were selected. Apparently, some Lords felt that the two men selected from the second category, Copley's list, should be balanced by two from the third block. It is not unlikely that Blathwayt himself, a close friend of Lord Baltimore, instigated and succeeded in carrying out this attempt to compensate in some way for the proprietor's otherwise complete loss of influence.[69]

The foremost criterion, then, in selecting the councillors was the source of each's recommendation. A second important consideration was to ensure geographical distribution. Proprietary councillors from 1666 to 1689 had been predominantly residents of only four counties on the southern half of the Western Shore. During that time only four men from other areas sat on the council, and at the outbreak of the revolution the Eastern

[68] CO5/713/II, no. 54. The final list was approved October 27, 1691, (Privy Council 2/74/268).

[69] Jacobsen, *Blathwayt*, 116–17, speaks of the close friendship between the two men. For information on the two appointees, see Francis B. Culver, "Frisby Family," *MHM*, XXXI (1936), 337–44, and Christopher Johnston, "Brooke Family," *MHM*, I (1906), 66–73, 184–88, 284–89. Copley never allowed Frisby to take his seat, and the latter left with his family for temporary residence in England (*Md. Archives*, VIII, 331–33; XX, 16; *Cal. S. P., Col., 1689–92*, no. 2472).

Shore and the northern counties of the Western Shore were without a voice.[70] In contrast, the new royal council drew its membership from eight of the colony's ten counties, including four from the Eastern Shore, an area long neglected. Both Copley's original list and Hammond's recommendations to Perry had explicitly stated the county where each man resided and had revealed a conscientious attempt to avoid duplication.

Religious affiliations were of fundamental importance. No Catholic received consideration, and the absence of Quakers, an able segment of the Maryland population, is also notable. There is no evidence of a Quaker nomination, despite the active role of some Friends in the revolution. John Edmundson, for example, was an ardent Associator and a member of the convention, the Grand Committee, and the Provincial Court.[71] Current English attitudes probably accounted for this discrimination, for Copley strictly applied oath requirements and rapidly moved against Quaker burgesses upon his arrival in Maryland.[72] The twelve men were all at least nominal Anglicans with the exception of David Browne, a Presbyterian. It is unlikely that English officials were aware either of his religion or that he was a native Scotsman.[73] Only Brooke, Baltimore's nominee, had any "papist" tinges. A member of a prominent Catholic family, he had con-

[70] See Table 1.

[71] Frank B. Edmundson and Emerson B. Roberts, "John Edmundson— Large Merchant of Tred Haven Creek," *MHM*, L (1955), 219–33. Tench and Robotham had shadowy Quaker ties, having formerly been Friends or having married Quakers; there is no evidence of continued Quaker affiliation in 1691, however. See their biographies, pp. 275 and 284.

[72] *Md. Archives*, XIII, 254, 256–57. Four Quakers, including John Edmundson, were dismissed from the first royal assembly as ineligible for service.

[73] *Old Somerset*, 212–13, 292, 363, provides a well-documented biography of Browne. Under an English statute of 1696, only "natives" of England, Ireland, or the plantations became eligible to be justices or occupy similar places of trust. Some native Scotsmen resigned or were removed from these offices (*Colonial Period*, IV, 167–68, 175).

verted to Anglicanism, while three brothers remained devout Catholics and one entered the Jesuit order. Brooke's stepfather was Henry Darnall, the former councillor who was now the colony's foremost Catholic and the principal resident agent for Lord Baltimore. Enemies of Brooke periodically stressed these family ties in recurrent efforts to discredit him.[74]

These new councillors shared other striking similarities when one compares their career profiles. Many of these same characteristics have already been noted in the description of the initial Associators. There is an interesting pattern of mercantile activity among the councillors. At least half of them pursued their livelihood through trade as well as planting, illustrative of the growing importance of mercantile wealth and connections. With the exception of Lawrence and the two last-minute proprietary appointees, the council was almost unanimously composed of first-generation Marylanders who had settled in the colony between 1668 and 1675, John Courts being the only native. Only Nicholas Greenberry among the eight immigrants had brought a wife and family to the colony. The other men had married the daughters or widows of more established families in Maryland and had prospered greatly. By 1688, however, most of the future councillors had reached points in their careers from which their prospects for upward mobility appeared to them to be blocked.

The significance of this perception is not easy to assess. One might argue that some of these new councillors had already risen by 1689 to the political position and status they had any right to expect at that time. This certainly would seem to be true of Courts, Hutchins, and Greenberry. One might also contend that others were in line for promotion. Perhaps Baltimore would soon

[74] Johnston, "Brooke Family," *MHM*, I (1906), 66–73, 184–88, 284–89. Brooke was absent from the council during much of Copley's tenure. In 1708 he was dismissed from the council (*Md. Archives*, VIII, *passim*; XXV, 245; XIX, 99). Baltimore reappointed him to the council in 1715 (XXV, 327).

have appointed either Browne or Francis Jenkins, the two leading Somerset County figures, to replace the recently deceased
William Stevens as a representative of the lower Eastern Shore
on the council. But to a number of these men who actively participated in the revolution and gained seats on the new royal
council, such expectations of future mobility probably did not
look bright in 1689. Robotham, a leading figure in Talbot
County, could always see the Catholic Lowe family or Catholic
Peter Sayer above him. Henry Jowles's progress was stymied in
Calvert. Blakiston, the ambitious son-in-law of a former councillor, had too angered Lord Baltimore to ever expect proprietary favor. Thomas Tench was obviously a newly settled merchant on the rise who would take advantage of all opportunities
to advance his position. John Addison's progress had probably
been curtailed by his conviction for violating the Navigation
Acts in the late 1670's, and he had to move his residence from
St. Mary's to a remote frontier in Charles County in order to
become even a justice of the peace. For all these men the revolution had offered an opportunity to attain power, and all possessed the political skill to exploit the situation.[75]

Many older families who had previously dominated the colony
would continue for another generation to regard these men as
their inferiors, although this hostility diminished in the next two
decades, as strategic marriages united many of the older and
"newer" families. Peter Sayer spoke, nonetheless, for the older
power structure in 1692 when he "presented his Service" to the
new governor by sending word "he would waite upon him when
he kept better company."[76] The aspiring customs collector Edward Randolph found the council basically "a contemptable
crew" and "silly Animalls," who "strutt it like New Beadles of

[75] See Biographies of the Members of the Associators' Convention, pp.
232–88.

[76] Quoted in Randolph to Blathwayt, June 28, 1692, *Randolph Letters*,
VII, 376. "Royal Period," chapter V, discusses these marriages and the
emergence of a new "country party." Sayer himself had only arrived in
the early 1670's.

St. Martin's parish."[77] Nonetheless, even the diehards would soon have to admit that the revolution had promoted a new social and political group in Maryland.

Although the crown now had a governor, a secretary, and a council for the new royal colony, it would be another six months before that government began to function in America. In the interim, London was the scene of avaricious contests for power and financial preferment. The battles were both comic and tragic, indicative of the rivalries for power and deepseated hostilities which would almost undermine the government in its initial year. Copley, an ambitious and covetous individual, postponed his sailing in the fall of 1691 and remained in London in an effort to extend the emoluments and authority of his office to the detriment of both Charles Calvert and Thomas Lawrence. He only succeeded in antagonizing the two men, who retained impressive support in influential circles. Each man, sensitive to his own rights, showed great combativeness in responding to the governor's action.

Copley's first request upon his nomination, it will be recalled, was to demand the powers and revenue enjoyed by other royal governors. To Copley's dismay, Baltimore had retained the quit-rents, half of the two-shilling tobacco duty, and all of the four-teen-pence tonnage tax. Furthermore, Copley's instructions re-quired that he set aside one-fourth of the one shilling allowed him from the tobacco duty to provide arms and ammunition for the province; he was also to lend his full assistance to Baltimore in the collection of proprietary revenues. The instructions were explicit: "You are not in any wise yourself or any other by your Order to intermedle with the said Moiety of the said impost of two shillings per Hogshead or the said duty of fourteen pence per Tun. But to permit the same to be collected . . . without any hindrance or molestation whatsoever." Lest Copley forget, Baltimore renewed his petition in November and December of

[77] *Randolph Letters*, VII, 376, 377. Randolph's numerous other letters of this period contain similarly uncomplimentary comments.

1691 that back revenues be collected and paid the proprietor. The king ordered still another letter written to ensure Baltimore's proper reimbursement. Protests over Copley's failure to comply continued for the next two years.[78]

Baltimore made Copley's final months in England uncomfortable in other ways as well. Copley's personal finances were in a humiliating state, as he stood substantially indebted to several Englishmen. Lord Baltimore staged a determined effort to purchase the debts in the hope of imposing some bar to prohibit Copley's sailing. The latter petitioned the Privy Council for aid, and it advanced £600, later reduced to £500, from his expenses and salary. Even with this assistance, Copley later reported he had narrowly escaped the proprietor's "arbitrary, unchrystian and ungentlemanly practices."[79]

Secretary Lawrence's successful defense against the governor placed other restrictions on Copley's financial ambitions in Maryland. The secretary's post was potentially the most lucrative in the colony after that of the governor. The only operating expense was provision of paper, ink, and other supplies, and the shrewd Lawrence had carefully arranged a special grant from the king to cover that encumbrance. The secretary could anticipate innumerable sources of income from his plural duties as chief public notary and keeper of both the Provincial Court and Land Office records. His position entitled him to receive license fees required to operate an ordinary, and he could expect additional income from his power to appoint all county clerks and deputy notaries.[80]

---

[78] *Md. Archives*, VIII, 274–75; *Cal. S. P., Col., 1689–92*, nos. 1825, 1873, 1924, 1932, 2050, 2089; William Blathwayt's Journal, 1680–1717, I, 425–30, transcript in PRO-Treasury Papers, Library of Congress.

[79] Copley to Blathwayt, June 20, 1692, Blathwayt Papers, XVIII; *Cal. S. P., Col., 1689–92*, nos. 1820, 1839, 1945.

[80] *HLP*, 30–34. Lawrence received £80 to purchase stationer's supplies because Maryland was a new royal colony. William A. Shaw, ed., *Calendar of Treasury Books*, 32 vols. to date (London, 1904–), IX, part IV, 1375, 1380–81, 1390.

These last two prerogatives in particular attracted the envious eye of Copley in his search for more personal revenue. Lawrence asked the Lords of Trade for a ruling on "the ancient laws and constitutions of Maryland so far as relates to the said office," and for information regarding any intention Copley had of altering the conditions or profits of the office.[81] Copley angrily denied any designs, promised never to infringe upon "any law of Maryland to hurt Sir Thomas," and castigated the secretary's "early shewing me his temper by raising disputes with me on such imaginary suggestions."[82] Lawrence had accurately assessed his superior and in this instance had official support. After hearing the testimony of a notable array of witnesses on December 15, 1691, the Lords of Trade ruled that Lawrence had the right to appoint clerks of the county courts, but he was admonished not to sell these positions. In return for posting sufficient security for the good behavior of his appointees, he was "to receive yearly a Fee or Gratuity of the Tenth part of one year's value and no more, of each place from such clerks as shall be nominated by him, the said value to be estimated [by] the Governor and Council upon a vacancy." The secretary's victory was won at the cost of the governor's enduring enmity, as Lawrence soon learned when he tried to enjoy the rewards of that victory in the New World.[83]

Not until February 1, 1691/92, did Copley manage to set sail on his "very ill passage." Lawrence was supposed to sail with

[81] Memorandum of Sir Thomas Lawrence to Lords of Trade and Plantations, CO5/713/II, no. 58. The memorial was read November 15, 1691 (*Cal. S. P., Col., 1689–92*, no. 1903; Blathwayt to Copley, Nov. 19, 1691, no. 1912).

[82] Copley to Blathwayt, Dec. 10, 1691, CO5/713/II, no. 63.

[83] Board of Trade Journal, Dec. 15, 1691, ff. 75–76; CO5/713/II, no. 67. Lawrence had the support of former Virginia governor Lord Howard of Effingham; Nicholas Sewall, whom Lawrence succeeded as secretary; former councillor Thomas Taylor; and Cheseldyne. (*Cal. S. P., Col., 1689–92*, nos. 1944, 1946; CO5/713/II, no. 65). Lawrence's struggles with Copley and successive royal governors and eventually with the assembly itself continued for well over a decade.

him, but reneged at the last minute; he claimed, according to Copley, that the ship was unseaworthy. One suspects that the growing schism between the two men led Lawrence to employ any excuse to avoid a long voyage with his superior. Copley reached Maryland in April and Lawrence arrived six months later.[84]

One of the governor's first tasks was to conduct the "full examination" which English officials had entrusted to his care. There should have been little doubt of the outcome. With a council composed almost entirely of Associators and with the new assembly also prejudiced in favor of the revolution, Copley was not likely to search widely for evidence either defending Lord Baltimore's claims or incriminating the rebel government. Indeed, he quickly allied with the Associators, whom he favored with the patronage at his disposal, while omitting opponents of the revolution from his judicial commissions. He even removed James Frisby from the council and allowed, if he did not encourage, the expulsion from the lower house of some delegates who had been forthright in their opposition to the Associators.[85]

The first royal assembly considered the "Severall Articles of Impeachment or Charge Exhibited by our Agents against the Lord Baltimore and his Deputies." This not impartial jury conducted what it termed a "strict search" of the charges and evidence. Not surprisingly, the investigation concluded that the accusations against the proprietary government were "Punctually & Exactly true," although it introduced no additional documentation. The councillors and thirty-six burgesses signed the petition summarizing the results of this "full examination" and

[84] Copley described the circumstances of his sailing in his letter to Blathwayt, June 30, 1692, Blathwayt Papers, XVIII; and in a letter to his patron Thomas Osborne, June 20, 1692, *Md. Archives*, VIII, 328.

[85] "Royal Period," 73–130, provides a full discussion of Copley's tempestuous seventeen-month tenure as governor. He died in September 1693. In his letter of Dec. 26, 1691, to Blathwayt, Copley discussed the inquiry he was to make into the charges against Lord Baltimore (*Cal. S. P., Col., 1689–92*, no. 1961).

indicated they remained "ready and willing to prove defend and maintain by such further Testimony proofs and evidences as may be reasonably required of us."[86]

Throughout the 1690's, many English officials remained uncertain over the basis of the crown's seizure of the colony, which some regarded as illegal. In 1701, while Parliament was considering legislation for vacating the charters of Maryland and other colonies, the Board of Trade requested the Maryland council to detail the "ill conduct" of the proprietary government prior to 1689. The council could now muster only five basic grievances. Three of these complaints, such as dissatisfaction with the requirement of an oath of allegiance to the proprietor rather than to the crown, were in fact directed against rights conveyed to Lord Baltimore by his charter. A fourth indictment, concerning use of the tonnage duty, had been overruled by a decision of the Privy Council in 1691. The final charge was the "murder" of the two royal customs collectors, Rousby and Payne. The councillors failed to mention that one of these deaths had occurred nearly five years prior to the revolution, and that the other came six months after the Associators had assumed control. Undoubtedly they felt no pressure to justify in any detail a revolution now twelve years past nor to provide carefully documented evidence to support a legal vacating of Baltimore's charter. Significantly, they did remember that English officials had been most concerned in 1690 with charges of the proprietor's failure to accord sufficient allegiance to the crown, his possible dereliction in furnishing an adequate defense of the colony, and the seeming pattern of violent opposition to royal agents.[87]

[86] *Md. Archives*, XIII, 344–45; CO5/713/II, no. 86. Among those who did not sign were William Whittington, Thomas Robins, and John Bigger, who had either supported Lord Baltimore during the revolution or at least refrained from endorsing the Associators.

[87] *Md. Archives*, XXV, 115–17; Hall, *The Lords Baltimore*, 136–37. Of the original councillors, Tench, Addison, Brooke, and Courts were still alive; apparently only Tench and Brooke were present the day this business was conducted.

Maryland's political leaders were to demonstrate in the early years of the new royal government that they had learned and remembered other lessons as well from the transatlantic settlement of their revolution. They were far more aware of the pressures that operated most persuasively on the English crown and bureaucracy in the determination of colonial policies and patronage. They particularly sensed the problems of communication and the pressures of time which would often necessitate essentially pragmatic and often uninformed decisions. They learned the important concerns of defense and economics which motivated most colonial decision-making. They further detected which individuals, among the myriad of committees, councils, and Whitehall offices, had the greatest potential influence. It had been quite clear in 1690–91 that policy had not been and was not likely to be determined by any one group of highly trained personnel with sufficient time and information to investigate matters properly or with sufficient power to implement its recommendations.

Marylanders, like other English colonists during this period, drew several important conclusions. They were not long in observing that second-level bureaucrats and secretaries like William Blathwayt and Thomas Povey were quite influential and potentially of more value to aspiring colonists or anxious assemblies than the various lordships who were their superiors. When these second-level men were assiduously courted and cultivated, they performed significant favors for the Maryland government; when they were not so patronized, the consequences were quite evident to the dismayed colonists.[88]

Ranking only slightly beneath these secretaries in importance was the powerful merchant community. The Chesapeake trad-

[88] See, for example, Council & Assembly to Blathwayt, Oct. 18, 1694, and Nicholson to Blathwayt, Oct. 18, 1694, and June 15, 1695, Blathwayt Papers, XV; Council and Assembly to Blathwayt, July 10, 1696, Blathwayt Papers, XVIII; *Md. Archives*, XXII, 128–29, 357; XXIV, 384–87; XXVI, 80–85.

ers constituted the single most influential source of information and advice on matters affecting the colony. Mindful of the strategic role played by individual lobbyists during this interim period, the first royal assembly provided for the appointment of a standing agent in London who would attend to the best interests of the colony; not surprisingly, the appointment went to Peter Pagan of London, a Chesapeake merchant who had been handling several financial matters for the Associators since the revolution.[89] His successors later in the decade, Thomas Povey and the merchant Micajah Perry, reflect the importance which the colony continued to attach to obtaining strategically placed individuals to watch over its affairs.[90]

Maryland warmly greeted Governor Copley in April of 1692, but some questions still remained unanswered and some issues disturbingly unresolved. There was the peculiar status of the proprietor's charter, usurped by the crown but perhaps not legally invalidated. There was also the uncertain role of Lord Baltimore himself, who continued to clamor over revenues and powers. Furthermore, with Maryland now under control of the crown, what would be its new transatlantic ties, to what extent would the mother country intrude into the daily affairs of a colony which had had litle supervision from England except for the Navigation Acts in its earlier history? These questions would be answered in the chapter of Maryland's history known as the royal period.

[89] *Md. Archives*, XIII, 467. On Pagan's earlier services to the Associators, see VIII, 240, 292–93, 296–97.

[90] *HLP*, 49. Ella Lonn, *The Colonial Agents of the Southern Colonies* (Chapel Hill, 1945), covers the history and development of this office.

CHAPTER VI

The "Revolution of Government" Assessed

What was this "revolution of government"? Was it an attempt to accomplish extensive social or political change, and, if so, had it a popular base? Or was it merely a successful *coup d'état* by a small group primarily interested in increasing its own power? Could Charles Calvert have avoided losing his governmental powers, or were there pressures that made this outcome inevitable? Did the change in rulers precipitate basic alterations in the institutions of Maryland or lead the way to major social or economic upheaval? Or did the overturn of the proprietary in itself have little effect on the development of the colony?

Resolution of these questions requires understanding of the structure of Maryland society in the 1680's and 1690's. While a complete picture of that structure is not yet available, the preliminary results of current research suggest a general outline.

Until the 1690's, the majority of planters, rich and poor alike, were immigrants. Unbalanced sex ratios and high immigrant mortality had postponed the moment when births exceeded deaths and population could grow by natural increase. White immigration had been heavy, particularly during the 1660's and 1670's, but it declined precipitately about 1680 until the late 1690's. By that time, the native population had begun to dominate Maryland society.[1] But in the years that preceded and im-

[1] Russell R. Menard, "The Growth of Population in Early Colonial

mediately followed the revolution, the tipping point had not been reached.

Maryland in the 1680's and 1690's was a land of small planters. A study of Maryland inventories has established that at least 75 per cent of the planters who died between 1690 and 1699 and left a record of their assets owned personal property valued at less than £100 sterling. Such estates reveal a standard of living aptly described as a "rude sufficiency."[2] Analysis of Maryland rent rolls compiled between 1700 and 1707 confirms this conclusion. Seventy per cent of the landowners of Prince George's County, a frontier tidewater county, owned less than 500 acres, and 50 per cent owned less than 350 acres. Among resident landowners, the median was about 240 acres. The rent roll for the oldest area, St. Mary's County—excluding the manors, for which information about subdivision is lacking—shows medians that are somewhat lower; for Somerset on the Eastern Shore they are slightly higher, but still well under 500 acres.[3] About

Maryland, 1631–1712," ms. prepared for the St. Mary's City Commission, on file at the Hall of Records, Annapolis. Wesley Frank Craven, *White, Red, and Black, The Seventeenth Century Virginian* (Charlottesville, Va., 1971), 25, suggests that immigrants were also a majority in Virginia until sometime in the last quarter of the century.

[2] Aubrey C. Land, "Economic Base and Social Structure: The Northern Chesapeake in the Eighteenth Century," *Journal of Economic History*, XXXV (1965), 639–54.

[3] For Prince George's County, see "County Government," text, 597. Information on St. Mary's comes from the files of the St. Mary's City Commission, St. Mary's City, Md., for which Mrs. Carr is the historian. Information on Somerset has been supplied by Russell Menard from his manuscript "Politics and Social Structure in Seventeenth-Century Maryland." Menard also prepared the analysis of the St. Mary's County rent rolls.

Fifty years ago Thomas Wertenbaker showed that planters of seventeenth-century Virginia usually owned less than 500 acres. The Virginia rent rolls of 1705, which he printed, show aggregate landholdings of planters by county. Median holdings on these rent rolls run about 230–250 acres if one discounts planters who owned land in more than one county (Thomas J. Wertenbaker, *The Planters of Colonial Virginia* [Princeton, N.J., 1922], 41–59, 183–247).

one-third of the planters resident in Prince George's rented land without lease or on short-term, uninheritable leases, a fact that greatly increases the proportion of small planters.[4]

Planters were heads of households and the household was the basic social unit. Besides wives and children or other relatives, many households contained servants, both bound and "hireling." In several counties about 1704, such servants may have constituted more than 40 per cent of the males over fifteen years of age. Since those who were bound would soon be free, they must have moved into an ever increasing pool of unpropertied freemen—called "laborers" in the records—unless there was opportunity to become a householder or to migrate. Such opportunities were available and turnover in the pool may have been high, but as yet little information exists about this element of Maryland society.[5]

[4] "County Government," text, 605. Carvile Earle, "The Evolution of a Tidewater Settlement System: All Hallows Parish, Maryland, 1650–1783" (Ph.D. diss., University of Chicago, 1973), chapter VI, and unpublished work of Menard on Somerset and St. Mary's counties also show substantial leasing.

[5] The figure is for Prince George's, Talbot, Baltimore, and Charles counties. It is derived from the census sent to England in 1704, allowing 9 per cent for sons and the same for other male relatives and wards. Anne Arundel County shows only 33 per cent servants and laborers (*Md. Archives*, XXV, 225). There are difficulties in interpreting population figures for the other counties. See Menard, "The Growth of Population in Early Colonial Maryland." The allowance of sons is based on the number of nonheads of households with the same surname as the household head found on lists of taxables for Baltimore County, 1692, 1699, and 1706. Figures upon which the calculation is based are taken from Barbara Lathroum, "Changing Labor Patterns, The Case of Baltimore County, 1692–1706" (ms. seminar paper, Johns Hopkins University, 1972), Table II; from Balt. Ct. Pro., F no. 1, ff. 225–29; and from Baltimore County Tax Lists, 1699–1706, microfilm, Hall of Records. The allowance for other male relatives and for wards is an arbitrary doubling of that for sons. The number of servants and laborers in Maryland in 1704 was high because there had been a heavy importation of servants from 1698 to 1700. From 1704 to 1710 considerable outmigration can be demonstrated. See Menard, "The Growth of Population in Early Colonial Maryland." The Baltimore County tax list for 1692 yields a figure for

The polities of Somerset County about 1690 and Prince George's about 1700 have been studied in some detail.[6] Men without households, some sons of landholders excepted, did not participate in local government. The same was generally true of leaseholders, although they occasionally sat on juries. Probably the majority did not have the £40 visible estate required to vote. There was, however, almost 100 per cent participation in local government by landowners. These men served as justices, sheriffs, coroners, constables, road overseers, pressmasters, and jurors. Rich and poor alike shared the burdensome local offices and jury duty. Appointments to the bench went when possible to men who had wealth and some education to enhance their positions as figures of authority, and the limited number of men who had achieved such status ensured that most of them would be asked to serve. At the same time, the need to distribute justices among all areas of the counties made it necessary on occasion to appoint men with lesser qualifications. Sheriffs and coroners were also usually men who had achieved wealth and its consequent status. Study of seventeenth-century leadership in other counties shows a similar policy in appointments to the bench and the shrievalty, although opportunities for men of medium fortune were greater before 1690 than they were by 1700. Appointments to the council, of course, always went to substantial men.

---

servants and laborers of 46.5 per cent, since at least 6.3 per cent of the nonheads of households had the same surname as the household head and again doubling the number to include other relatives and wards. Even if these are grossly underestimated, servants and laborers will still be a sizable group.

[6] The following discussion draws upon "County Government," text, 585–86, 601–56, and information supplied by Menard. See his "Major Officeholders in Charles, Somerset and Talbot Counties, 1676–1689," on file at the Hall of Records. Under the sponsorship of the St. Mary's City Commission and Temple University, P. M. G. Harris, Carr, and Menard are conducting a study of inventories of four Maryland counties, 1658–1705, which demonstrates that few tenants who died in this period had as much as £40 in personal estate.

By 1690 membership in the lower house of assembly also tended to go to the most prominent of the county leaders, although this was as yet far from an invariable rule. Since the lower house of the 1680's was still struggling for status that the proprietor was reluctant to grant, its seats were probably valued somewhat less before 1690 than they came to be under the royal governors. Unfortunately, the records do not tell who voted and are mostly silent as to candidates and the issues, if any, on which they ran. What information there is begins in the royal period. The potential electorate was sizable, even though it did not include the majority of the leaseholders or any unpropertied freemen, but complaints appear in the 1690's that men often did not bother to vote, and in 1715 a law finally passed to penalize voters who failed to appear at the election courts. In Prince George's County for the first fifteen years after its establishment in 1696, issues such as church establishment, with its high attendant taxation, do not appear to have influenced elections. Factions organized around issues evidently were as yet undeveloped there. Although elsewhere in the colony by the 1690's the church tax or a governor's unpopular act may occasionally have been a factor in elections, the chief signs of political consciousness lay, not in contested issues, but in contested seats in an increasingly powerful lower house.[7]

Given this general social and institutional structure of the late seventeenth century, the men who exercised political influence in 1689 must have had unquestioned social and economic qualifications for holding local or provincial offices of power or profit, whether or not they held office at that time. In Prince George's county in the early eighteenth century, 1,000 acres or more of land provided a rough criterion for such eligibility, and

---

[7] "County Government," text, 388, 602, 685–91; "Royal Period," 82–86, 147–48, 186–88, 212–20, 253–54. Warren M. Billings, "The Causes of Bacon's Rebellion, Some Suggestions, "*Virginia Magazine of History and Biography*, LXXVIII (1970), 408–35, emphasizes that politics in Virginia during this period revolved around local personalities, not political issues, and the same was undoubtedly also true of Maryland.

about 1706 the group so qualified constituted about 8 per cent of the householders. Their counterparts twenty years earlier may have been less wealthy, but they were probably not a larger percentage of the population. Given an estimated 25,000 people in 1689, distributed among, say, 3,600 households, there were probably no more than 290 heads of households who were clearly eligible for major office. The vast majority of men were subject to masters, were struggling leaseholders, or were small freeholders who served their communities in local offices but who did not expect to exercise power.[8]

On the other hand, there was a certain amount of social and economic mobility in this society, a mobility which undoubtedly had political effects. A Randall Hanson who came to Maryland as an indentured servant and was illiterate all his life could become a merchant of sufficient influence to be a justice of the peace. A Henry Hawkins who came as a tanner could die a gentleman on the bench of Charles County after years of service in the assembly.[9] The presence of illiterate men on several county benches from the 1660's is further testimony to a rise in status and power that would have been impossible within a lifetime in England and would soon be more difficult in Maryland. The careers of the members of the Associators' Convention clearly

[8] Menard, "The Growth of Population in Early Colonial Maryland," 20, suggests the figure 27,000. Arthur E. Karinen, "Maryland Population, 1631–1730; Numerical and Distributional Aspects," *MHM*, LIV (1959), 373, accepts the figure 25,000 published in Evarts B. Green and Virginia Harrington, *American Population before the Federal Census of 1790* (New York, 1931), 124. He also accepts their ratio of households to people of 1:7.1, which may be high for the seventeenth century (*ibid.*, xxiii). Using this ratio, 25,000 people would be distributed in about 3,520 households. Menard's essay revises Karinen's pioneering work in a number of respects. In Prince Georges' County in 1706, there were about 460 heads of households, and 37 men over twenty-one who owned 1,000 acres or more, hence the figure 8 per cent.

[9] For Hanson, see Patents 4, f. 18; Ch. Ct. and Land Rec., G no. 1, f. 128; *Md Archives*, III, 490; XVII, 380; VIII, 243; PG Land Rec., A, f. 21. References supplied by Russell Menard. For Hawkins, see his biography, pp. 258–59.

show these opportunities.[10] Thus, although the number of politically active men may have been small, and was necessarily
smaller earlier in the seventeenth century, such men represented
a broader spectrum of society than might be supposed.

A very large percentage of planters in Maryland seem to have
shared the varied responsibilities of local government, according
to abilities and stations. If the participation found in Somerset
and Prince George's counties was typical, it may account for the
quick acceptance of law and authority in areas where settlement
was new. It may also help account for the stability of local government when rebellion put it to the test.

This stability had foundations as well in the sense of responsibility which clearly had developed by 1689 in men with recognized economic and social standing that made them eligible for
positions of power. Only in Cecil County, the newest and most
remote area of settlement, were there men so determined to oppose the revolution that they countenanced disruption of routine
governmental functions. There the influence of the wealthy
merchant James Frisby evidently kept alive active resistance,
and warring factions in the county prevented normal operation
of government and required intervention by the Grand Committee. But Frisby's counterparts elsewhere clearly put law and
order and public service before their personal preferences.
Whether in or out of office, the county leadership wished to
avoid bloodshed and its members found their self-interest
grounded in community stability.[11]

This self-interest was not yet the self-interest of an established
ruling group. The justices sitting in July 1689 were predominantly immigrants—90 out of 104—and their origins were diverse. A large proportion were also newcomers to the exercise
of power. Of these 104 men, 81, or 77.2 per cent, had served

[10] See Biographies of the Members of the Associators' Convention.
Fourteen justices of the 1680's were illiterate (information supplied by
Russell Menard).

[11] Billings, "The Causes of Bacon's Rebellion," suggests that the de-
centralization of local government was a source of instability in Virginia
in the years before 1676. This was not the case in Maryland in the 1680's.

less than eleven years; 50, or 47.6 per cent, had served less than six years. The mean number of years of service was 7.18. These figures reflect the fact that a large majority of seventeenth-century immigrants died before their children were of age and ready to succeed them in office. Early death among immigrants slowed down the formation of hereditary local power groups in Maryland and even curtailed the development of a well-entrenched and experienced magistracy.[12] The stable behavior of the county leaders during the crisis of 1689–1692 must have been due more to the traditions of behavior established for exercising power than to the development of a secure and self-aware class of rulers.

At the top of the social and political structure in 1689 were the proprietor and his deputy governors or council, a small number of men who through plural officeholding controlled all the powerful and lucrative posts of the central government. This narrow, proprietary party was the group overthrown by the revolution—or coup—of 1689 in Maryland. How that overthrow was accomplished has been discussed in some detail. It remains to assess the result.

The earlier "rebellions," combined with the constitutional struggles of the 1670's and 1680's, suggest that dissatisfaction with the proprietary ran deep enough that its overthrow could be considered a revolution based on real grievances that had broad appeal. Two trends of strong feeling can be detected in the various lists of complaints, beginning with the "hue and Crye" of 1677 and continuing through the various justifications made by the leaders of 1689: fear of popery and fear of the regal powers of the proprietor.[13] Parallel fears were to be found in

[12] Information on immigrant status and length-of service is from unpublished research of Russell R. Menard. Of the 1,735 decedents analysed in the inventory study cited in n. 6 above, at least 1,249, or 72 per cent, had never married or had died before any children came of age. Only 273, or 16 per cent, are known to have left offspring who could have been old enough to take charge of property.

[13] *Md. Archives*, V, 134–44; VIII, 108–10, 215–20; "Mariland's Grevances," 396–409.

the England of the period, where the Titus Oates plot of 1678 created months of hysterical persecution of Catholics and where memory of earlier Stuart efforts to rule without Parliament kept propertied Englishmen alert to circumvent expansion of prerogative power. In Maryland the regular arrival of new settlers must have kept information flowing about the events in England and brought men ready to be aroused to fears of similar dangers. In Maryland, however, the danger lay in the proprietor, not in the crown. Not only English law but the strength of the crown itself seemed the safest bulwark against the powers of a Catholic palatine prince.

Among the propertied groups in the colony, perhaps proprietary exercise of kingly powers had produced the greatest unease during the decades that preceded the Associators' seizure of power. By virtue of his charter, the proprietor could dictate election procedures and thus might control membership of the assembly. Election of four rather than two delegates and election procedures controlled by act of assembly rather than prerogative might provide some protection and were major objectives that prerevolutionary assemblies failed to attain. The proprietor could veto legislation that the assembly passed, hence the unsatisfied need to contain this power by a reasonable time limit. He could raise an army, hence the necessity not to make it too easy for him to fund it. He appointed all judges, hence the unsuccessful struggle to check this power by a strict transfer of English law where the laws of Maryland were silent. He appointed all sheriffs; they were his arm in the counties and their combination of police and financial powers gave them considerable independence of county court control, hence the recurring effort to limit their terms. All these were powers exercised by the crown in England, but should a proprietor have the powers of the crown? And in England three years of Catholic rule and the threat of a Catholic succession had produced its own bloodless revolution.

However, the argument for a revolution in response to fundamental grievances has a weakness. The assemblies of 1676–1684, which actively fought Lord Baltimore on the issues of defense and proprietary prerogative, contained many of the most adamant opponents of the revolution. Thirty of these delegates were still alive in 1689, and seventeen, a majority, declined to support the Associators (see Table 3). Furthermore, this num-

Table 3. Attitudes toward the revolution of survivors* of proprietary assemblies, 1676–1688, by religion

Assembly and religion	Cooperate	Oppose	Unknown	Total
Assemblies of 1676–1684				
Catholics	0	3	0	3
Quakers	1	4†	0	5
Other Protestants	10	10	1	21
Religion unknown	0	0	1	1
Total, 1676–1684	11	17	2	30
Assembly of 1686–1688				
Catholics	0	2	0	2
Quakers	2	0	0	2
Other Protestants	13	4	0	17
Religion unknown	0	0	2	2
Total, 1686–1688	15	6	2	23
Combined assemblies, 1676–1688				
Catholics	0	4	0	4
Quakers	2	4†	0	6
Other Protestants	18	12	1	31
Religion unknown	0	0	3	3
Total, 1676–1688	20	20	4	44

Note: The combined membership of the 1676–1688 assemblies totaled 78: 8 Catholics, 12 Quakers, 35 other Protestants, and 23 whose religion is unknown.

* "Survivors" are those who were alive in 1689. Omitted is James Mills, whose whereabouts in 1689 are unknown.

† These four men remained aloof; they signed no petitions and held no offices. For Quaker opposition or neutrality, see pp. 195–99.

ber included fourteen non-Catholics, a majority of the twenty-six known surviving Protestant delegates. Among these Protestants, representing all areas of the colony, were such stalwart defenders of the proprietor as Richard Hill, William Hatton,

James Frisby, George Wells, and Miles Gibson.[14] Only the last proprietary assembly (1686–1688), elected after Lord Baltimore's departure, contained a sizable number of future Associators or their followers. Twelve of the twenty-three survivors of this assembly were to sit in the Associators' Convention.[15]

The unwillingness of many former burgesses to condone the overthrow reflected the conservatism of men accustomed to exercising power in an age that regarded "well ordering" and "quiet rule" as the foundation of society. Some men thought upheaval not only illegal and dangerous but immoral. Thomas Smithson wrote the Bishop of London that "only the sence of our duty and the doctrine of our Church obliges us nott to stand in [the Associators'] Councill." Many members of these assemblies might have accepted or even welcomed the vacating of Lord Baltimore's charter and the establishment of crown government, but these survivors saw no "necessity to justify risinge in armes" against a lawfully constituted authority.[16] They were also men who had achieved public recognition during the proprietor's personal rule, an element missing in the careers of the majority of the revolutionary leaders. Over the years the Calverts had built up a following among these and other leading

---

[14] See Table 3 and Appendix A. Hill, Frisby, and Gibson actually went to England to support Lord Baltimore's case before the crown (*Md. Archives*, VIII, 213). Religion is not proved for Thomas Smith, who cannot be identified, but he may be the Thomas Smith who signed the anti-Associator petition from Kent in June 1690. Joseph Wickes, a Protestant, had retired from public life by 1689; he may be the Josh Wukes who signed the same petition. Supposing that Wickes and Smith were both Protestant supporters of Lord Baltimore, the assembly of 1676–82 would favor the proprietor 15 to 8; that of 1682–84, 8 to 4. For the assemblies together, the figure would be 16 to 11 in favor of the proprietor.

[15] Two of the twelve, John Stone and Henry Hawkins of Charles County, were lukewarm in their support of the revolution until May 1690. This last proprietary assembly contained only six active opponents of the revolution, four of whom were Protestants: Richard Hill, George Lingan, George Wells, and William Dare.

[16] *Md. Archives*, VIII, 192–93.

Protestant merchants and planters in every county who were willing to stand by the proprietor after the revolution.[17]

The composition of the last proprietary assembly might suggest that, in the years 1685–1688,[18] the electorate of small planters was speaking its mind after the failures of the two preceding assemblies to obtain constitutional changes from Lord Baltimore. Unfortunately, nothing is known of these elections. It seems probable that there was increasing competition for seats in the assembly, but unlikely that voters of little or no education gave much heed to legal or constitutional arguments. The willingness of so many members of this assemby to stand for election for the Associators' Convention probably reflects shrewd opportunism and their anger against misgovernment of the deputy governors rather than the informed conviction of a small-planter electorate. Such willingness may also have reflected the absence of a proprietor who had evidently been able to build support among his Protestant burgesses even while they opposed him on issues of importance.

If the majority of those who had fought the constitutional battles of 1676–1684 did not lead the "revolution of government," was there instead a powerful uprising of the small landowners, leaseholders, and other freemen? Clearly many such men from the southern Western Shore counties joined the march

[17] See Table 4 below and Carr and Jordan, "Service of Civil and Military Officers, July 1689–April 1692," table on file at the Hall of Records, Annapolis. With six exceptions, all Protestant delegates opposing the revolution had been justices or sheriffs before the proprietor's departure (see Carr and Jordan, "Assembly, 1676–1688, Members Alive in July 1689, Attitudes to Revolution," on file at the Hall of Records; *Md. Archives*, XV, 38, 42, 65–73, 77, 131, 136, 253–55, 328, 346, 395). Four of the six who had not been justices or sheriffs—William Richardson, John Goddin, John Stevens, and Francis Billingsley—were Quakers.

[18] The last assembly was elected in 1685, but several by-elections were held to fill vacancies created by death or appointments to the council or a shrievalty. For example, John Coode replaced Richard Gardiner of St. Mary's, who died late in 1687 (Wills 4, f. 276). Coode was thus not elected until 1688. See Appendix A.

on St. Mary's. The proprietary adherents asserted that these men were merely dupes of their leaders, who were playing on fears that the council had betrayed the province to the papist French and Northern Indians.[19] Such assertions receive support from the fact that these followers had no organized long-run objectives, for unlike the protest of 1677, the various lists of grievances contain no complaints that pertain specifically to this group. Maryland's small planters and unpropertied freemen had little to gain one way or another from the change in government. Their anti-Catholic prejudices seem to have provided the main incentive for mobilizing behind the leaders of the rebellion.[20]

It has been suggested recently that the unpropertied freemen or laborers of Chesapeake society constituted a restless and dangerous element that contributed to all the various uprisings against authority in seventeenth-century Virginia and Maryland without necessarily having organized objectives.[21] Hitherto little attention has been given to the size of this group in the society and the extent to which opportunities for household formation were available. The absence of women for men to marry and the difficulties of acquiring the capital to establish a plantation must have influenced the way these men viewed their opportunities. The meager evidence so far on hand suggests that laborers were a sizable group in Maryland. For most of the 1680's the price of tobacco was so low that credit must have been hard to come by, a fact that probably restricted more than ever the opportunity for laborers to become planters.

Were the Maryland laborers or even servants a substantial source of support in bringing the revolution about? None of the firsthand comments on the events of 1689 indicate that laborers or servants played a major role. Henry Darnall, Peter Sayer,

[19] *Md. Archives*, VIII, 156.

[20] *Ibid.*, 161. See also references cited in n. 13 above.

[21] Edmund S. Morgan, "Slavery and Freedom: The American Paradox," *Journal of American History*, LIX (1972), 24–28.

Charles Carroll, and others, all supporters of Lord Baltimore, left accounts that emphasize the temporary fears of "the people," but do no call them rabble or describe them as without estate. Coode's followers were clearly identified as "the less cautious sort of people" and not of the "better sort"; but when Peter Sayer called the men in arms in Talbot "silly mobiles," he then described efforts to quiet them through reminders of the estates they risked losing by rising in arms against lawful authority.[22]

On the other hand, it is likely that laborers and possibly even indentured servants did constitute part of Coode's army. His abortive order to raise the St. Mary's County militia against Anne Arundel County in late September 1689 explicitly summons "servants and freemen" and makes it clear that some had already been armed. The existence of many unpropertied laborers—theoretically, at least, subject to muster—may have provided a pool of potential soldiers for leaders capable of organizing a military coup.[23]

Still, the evidence as a whole does not suggest that unpropertied men constituted the military base of the revolution. Maryland county courts kept the peace under conditions of tension and uncertainty from September 1689 until Governor Copley's arrival in April 1692. Surely, if the Associators had had to depend mainly on laborers and servants to establish their position, such men would not have quieted down completely once the council had been deposed. There should be signs of their restlessness in the records of the county courts and complaints of their activities in the accounts of the revolution sent to England.

Indeed, the revolution does not seem to have divided the province along any recognizable economic lines, although economic stress surely added to unrest. The only economic complaint was Lord Baltimore's abortive attempt to collect his quitrents

[22] *Md. Archives*, VIII, 115–22, 124–28, 147–51, 153–54, 158–62. Richard Johns, in a letter written September 27, 1689, does allude to "the long soard in the Rables hands" *ibid.*, (127).

[23] *Md. Archives*, VIII, 121.

and fines in coin. This impractical policy can have been in fact imposed only on men of large estate, since most planters simply had no coin with which to pay. Yet substantial planting and mercantile interests were to be found both among the Associators and their opponents. Neither group seems to have supposed that their economic ills would be much affected by retaining or overthrowing the proprietary government.[24]

Nor did the revolution divide the inhabitants of Maryland strictly according to religion. A substantial number of Protestant leaders opposed Coode and his party. The strongest resistance came from Anne Arundel, Baltimore, and Cecil counties, each almost exclusively Protestant in population, but there were non-Catholics defending Lord Baltimore in every county. Evidence on the attitudes of 187 former burgesses or current officeholders as of July–September 1689 unmistakably documents this point (see Table 4). Of these 187 men, at least 79, or 42 per cent, seem not to have cooperated with the revolution. More than half of the 79 were certainly Protestant, while only 25 per cent have definitely been identified as Catholic. Depending upon whether or not the unknowns were Catholic, 28 to 35 per cent of these Protestant leaders either supported the proprietor or were unwilling openly to support the Associators.[25]

This Protestant support, or at least neutrality, was to be found among all identified sects. Thomas Smithson spoke for other "True sonnnes of the Church of England" in his letter to the Bishop of London written from prison in June 1690. Michael Taney, who in 1685 had joined his wife in pleading for help in settling an Anglican minister in Calvert County, also languished in prison for many weeks. Henry Hanslop of Anne Arundel, Simon Wilmer of Kent, Nicholas Lowe and James Murphy of

---

[24] *Ibid.*, 216–17; Russell Menard, "Farm Prices of Maryland Tobacco, 1659–1710," *MHM*, LXVIII (1973), 80–85; inventory study cited in n. 6, above.

[25] For a discussion of the characteristics of the Protestant opposition, see p. 72 above.

Talbot, and Matthew Scarborough of Somerset, all of whom explicitly refused cooperation with the Associators, sat on Anglican vestries in the 1690's.[26] The Quakers also generally remained aloof or supported Lord Baltimore, except in Talbot County. Richard Johns, an active Calvert County Quaker, refused the convention's plea to persuade Anne Arundel to send delegates. Two identified Quakers signed the Calvert petition favoring Lord Baltimore. Otherwise known Quakers outside of Talbot failed to sign any petitions.[27] A letter sent from the London meeting some months later, which enjoined abstaining from political battles, suggests that this aloofness was deliberate. Several men known to be closely associated with the Friends, however, signed the anti-Associator petitions from Calvert and Cecil.[28]

[26] Carr and Jordan, "Service of Civil and Military Officers," July 1689–April 1692," Hall of Records; *Md. Archives*, XXIII, 17–22.

[27] *Md. Archives*, VIII, 126–27; XIII, 235–36. Henry Orton and Daniel Rawlings are Quakers who signed from Calvert (VIII, 131–32; Monthly Meeting at the Clifts, Minutes, 1677–1771, ff. 5, 6, 18, 20 [entries covering years 1681–93], microfilm in the Maryland Hall of Records). See also Third Haven Monthly Meeting, Minutes, 1676–1746; Yearly and Half Yearly Meeting of Friends in Maryland, Minutes, 1677–1758 (microfilm in the Maryland Hall of Records). These are the extant minutes of seventeenth-century Quaker meetings in Maryland. Quaker registers of births of this period are difficult to interpret, since they are transcripts which collected entries by families. It is impossible to tell whether a man entered all his children at the time of his conversion or whether the original entries were scattered across the years as children were born. Burial and marriage records have been used (Third Haven Monthly Meeting, Burials, 1672–1952, Marriages, 1678–1935; Monthly Meeting at the Clifts, Register, 1649–1784, 1655–1809, Marriages, 1682–1824, microfilm, Hall of Records). None of the names on the petitions from any county except Talbot appear in these minutes or registers. There are no records for the Somerset meetings, but no one Torrence has identified as a Quaker appears on the Somerset petition (*Old Somerset*, 167; *Md. Archives*, VIII, 139–41).

[28] George Fox to Friends in Maryland, Nov. 12, 1690, Epistles Sent, 1683–1701, I, ff. 62–63, Friends House Library, London. Signer Francis Hutchins's daughter was married to a prominent Quaker (J. Reaney Kelly, *Quakers in the Founding of Anne Arundel County* [Baltimore, 1963], 127). Elisha and Benjamin Hall, sons of Quaker Richard Hall,

Table 4. Attitudes toward the revolution of former burgesses and of men holding office in July or September 1689, by religion

Attitude and group	Religion			Total
	Catholic	Religion unknown	Protestant	
Opposition				
Officers, July 1689, not appointed by Convention	20	16	7	43
Former Protestant burgesses in opposition (not included above)			2	2
Refused service under Convention				
Reappointed, Sept. 1689			19 ⎫	21
Newly appointed, Sept. 1689			2 ⎬	
Served under Convention but in opposition				
Reappointed, Sept. 1689			6 ⎫	6
Newly appointed, Sept. 1689			0 ⎬	
Probably refused service under Convention				
Reappointed, Sept. 1689			3 ⎫	4
Newly appointed, Sept. 1689			1 ⎬	
Former Quaker burgesses, probably opposed*			4	4
Total opposition	20	16	44	80

Cooperation

Served under the Convention		
Reappointed, Sept. 1689		
Civil	64	
Military	3	
Newly appointed, Sept. 1689		
Civil	23	
Military	13	103
Probably served under the Convention		
Reappointed, Sept. 1689	3	
Newly appointed, Sept. 1689	1	4
Total cooperation	107	107
Unknown		
Unknown if served under the Convention	8	8
Former burgesses, attitude unknown (not included above)	1	4
Total unknown	9	12
Grand totals	160	199

Additional column values: Former burgesses — 3; Total unknown — 3; Grand totals — 19, 20.

* There is no evidence to prove the position of these four men. For a discussion of Quaker opposition, or neutrality, see pp. 195, 198–99.

Source: Lois Green Carr and David William Jordan, "Service of Civil and Military Officers, July 1689–April 1692"; "Members of the Assemblies, 1676–1688, Religion"; "Assembly in July, 1689, Attitudes to Revolution"; "Members of the Assembly, 1676–1688, Dead by July 1689," tables on deposit at the Hall of Records, Annapolis. Copies may be obtained at cost. Note that this table cannot be constructed from the tables in Appendix B, which organize the data differently.

This Quaker inclination toward Baltimore's cause is not surprising. After some initial persecution, the Friends had found a haven in proprietary Maryland. Their refusal to swear oaths or serve in the militia had led to friction with the secular authorities, as did their objections to using secular courts for settlement of disputes among their members. Nonetheless, Lord Baltimore and his governors had made some efforts to accommodate these views and to keep this able segment of the population active in community affairs. Quakers elected to the assembly had been seated without objection to their refusal to be sworn. Quakers had been occasionally appointed to the county benches, although after 1678 they had begun to refuse service "for conscience's sake." In 1688, faced with a determined effort of Quaker meetings to establish their own control over administration of Quaker estates and supervision of Quaker orphans, the Maryland authorities had agreed to waive the oath-taking requirements in these matters. The Friends still paid fines for refusing militia service, but they doubtless felt that these penalties were preferable to the prospects open to them under a government pledged to deprive Catholics of political rights.[29]

---

also signed. Elisha became a Quaker in 1704; Benjamin married a Catholic and converted (*Md. Archives*, VIII, 131–32; XX, 465; XXIV, 360; All Saints Vestry Minutes [Calvert Co.], 1703–1717, entries for Jan. 25, 1703/4, Feb. 15, 1704/5; Christopher Johnston, "Hall Family of Calvert County," *MHM*, VIII [1913], 292–94). George Warner, a justice of Cecil, signed the Cecil petition. By 1692 he was surely a Quaker, but his name is absent from the minutes of the meetings before that date (*Md. Archives*, VIII, 135; XIII, 351, 354; Third Haven Monthly Meeting, Minutes, 1676–1746; Yearly and Half Yearly Meeting of Friends in Maryland, Minutes, 1677–1758).

[29] There is discussion of Quaker sufferings for refusing to swear oaths or serve in the militia and of the decisions to let Quakers make affirmations in testamentary matters in Kenneth Carroll, *Quakerism on the Western Shore* (Baltimore, 1970), 62–65. For a discussion of Quaker efforts to control administration of Quaker estates, see "County Government," text, 355–57. For the number of Quakers who served in the assembly of 1678, see Table 3.

Quakers who were appointed to the county benches but failed to

The only enthusiastic Quaker response to the rebellion centered in Talbot, where John Edmundson, a wealthy Quaker merchant, endorsed Coode immediately and rallied others of his religion. Edmundson had been one of the handful of Quakers who had sat in the assemblies of the 1670's and 1680's, and with another Quaker merchant, William Sharpe, he represented Talbot in the Associators' Convention.[30] Thomas Thurston of Baltimore County was a third Quaker Associator, but he was obviously no longer entirely bound by Quaker discipline; during the interregnum he accepted a military commission.[31] Edmundson played an important role in the interim government. He not only sat on the Grand Committee but he became a justice of the Provincial Court, possibly with permission to make an affirmation rather than take the usual qualifying oaths. He must have been dismayed when the first royal assembly refused to seat him, thus confirming the good judgment of those Quakers who had been reticent in extending their support to Baltimore's enemies. Edmundson was re-elected in 1694 and was again refused a seat in the assembly.[32]

---

qualify were: William Dorrington of Dorchester, 1681 "for Conscience sake" (*Md. Archives*, VII, 44); William Sharpe, William Stevens, and Ralph Fishbourne of Talbot, 1685 (*ibid.*, 380; Third Haven Monthly Meeting, Minutes, 1676–1746, ff. 30, 32, 38, 69, Marriages, 1688–1935, f. 2; Talb. Judg., 1682–85, ff. 200, 221, 229, 240, 264; Talb. Land Rec., NN no. 6, ff. 1, 35, 66, 97, 118, 125, 146); and Edward Day of Somerset (Som. Jud. Rec., 1687–89, ff. 4, 27). Others appointed but for whom insufficient records makes their service or refusal impossible to prove were: John Goddin of Somerset, 1680/81 (*Md. Archives*, XV, 332; *Old Somerset*, 467); Samuel Chew II of Anne Arundel, 1685 (*Md. Archives*, VII, 379; Monthly Meeting at the Clifts, Register, 1655–1809, f. 15); and Thomas Evernden of Somerset, 1685 (*Md. Archives*, XVII, 380; Yearly and Half Yearly Meeting of Friends in Maryland, Minutes, 1677–1758, ff. 28–29). Before about 1678, Quaker practice with respect to such appointments varied.

[30] See his biography, pp. 285–87.

[31] Kenneth Carroll, "Thomas Thurston, Renegade Maryland Quaker," *MHM*, LXII (1967), 170–92; Kelly, *Quakers in Anne Arundel County*, 56–57; *Md. Archives*, VIII, 378.

[32] The 1692 expulsion was not well received in Talbot County, where

Presbyterians, the only other sizable dissenter group which can be to some degree isolated and identified, were much warmer in their response to the revolution, but by no means unanimously so. They were concentrated on the lower Eastern Shore, where their leaders were powerful in Somerset, the county most whole-hearted in its endorsement of the revolution outside the three southern Western Shore counties. Three of the Somerset delegation were active Presbyterians; two, David Browne and Robert King, became leading provincial figures. Ninian Beale, one of the original rebel leaders, was a "father" of Presbyterianism on the Western Shore. On the other hand, another prominent Western Shore Presbyterian, William Hatton, refused cooperation. Protestant support for the rebellion was not universal.[33]

Still, religion was, no doubt, a major factor in determining revolutionary alignments. All Catholics apparently opposed the revolution, while in the population at large probably most Protestants accepted the overthrow of Lord Baltimore. Fears of popish plots were easily aroused among the majority of small planters, particularly in the southern Western Shore counties and in Talbot, where there were active Catholic congregations and where the revolution originated. Without this undercurrent of popular feeling, the Associators could not have captured the militia of these areas and prevented the deputy governors from mustering an opposing force. The success of anti-Catholic appeals was a measure of the small planter's outlook. Insofar as the overturn of the proprietary government had a popular base, it was provided in antipopery.

Edmundson's supporters in "a Riotous & Tumultuous Manner" affirmed "they would Choose John Edmundson to be a Burgess and none other urging divers approbrious & Manacing Speeches to the Justices and Sheriff in Contempt to the King and the Law" (Talb. Land Rec., NN no. 6, f. 33b [rear]). In 1694 the assembly also refused to qualify Richard Johns, a Quaker elected from Calvert County (*Md. Archives*, XIX, 20).

[33] *Old Somerset*, 211–71; J. William McIlvain, *Early Presbyterianism in Maryland*, Notes Supplementary to the Johns Hopkins Studies in Historical and Political Science, series VIII, nos. 5–6 (Baltimore, 1890), 10–13; "County Government," Appendix VI, Table 4B, 234–35.

Yet, it seems doubtful that these fears were irrepressible or that leaders of the revolution were simply responding to uncontrollable pressures from below. During the months before the revolt, they seem to have encouraged popular fears and alarms which they could instead have helped to assuage. Their later behavior suggests fear that they might not succeed, that the crown might restore the province to Lord Baltimore and that the colonists would accept such a decision. They exercised extreme care and great political skill in courting the support, or at least ensuring the neutrality, of the small group of men in each county substantial enough to exercise authority, and enough of these men opposed the revolution to cause its leaders anxiety.

The presentation of grievances justifying the overthrow of the deputy governors reflected the same careful planning. Even the declaration of July 25, 1689, although it referred to popish plots, emphasized the constitutional and legal issues that had occupied the attention of Lord Baltimore's last assemblies: the calling of two delegates instead of four; the proprietary veto; the proprietor's suspension of a law previously approved; the severe sedition laws; the lack of a clause reserving allegiance to the crown in the oath of fidelity.[34] By the time the Associators were presenting their case to neighboring colonies and to the English authorities, they had refined their complaints with a lawyer's skill. The contrast to the tone of the "hue and Crye" of 1677 is striking. Item by item the accusations constitute a legal, not an emotional, argument tailored both to the responses of English lawyers and administrators and to the men in Maryland who exercised local power. The main accusations were based on events well known to everyone, and at least one example probably could have been brought forth from the history of the preceding thirty years to bolster any of the more petty allegations of judicial or administrative injustice or incompetence. The more absurd accusations—that the deputy governors had connived at murder (of Rousby and Payne), that they had

[34] *Md. Archives*, VIII, 101–7.

conspired with Indians, and that they had concealed these sub-versions—were treated in the same legalistic tone. The strategy was to emphasize the rational necessity of overthrowing Lord Baltimore's rulers, thereby persuading local leaders to keep the peace until the crown could establish a properly authorized gov-ernment. Had the Associators been riding an irresistible wave of antipopery and fear of Calvert tyranny, their chances of keeping order and avoiding ultimate personal disaster would have dimin-ished greatly.

Nonetheless, there was much discontent in Maryland during the last two decades of the proprietary regime, and the impact of the Glorious Revolution made Maryland ripe for a change. Before making final judgment as to the meaning of "this revolu-tion of government," its consequences—economic, institutional, political, and social—should be examined.

The Revolution of 1689 in Maryland did not bring economic change. The substitution of crown for proprietary authority did not affect the operation of the tobacco economy. The pro-prietor retained his title to the land and its quitrents and no one tried to reverse his decision, in effect since 1683, to abandon the headright system. His right to the revenues from the shilling per hogshead and the fourteen pence per ton of shipping was upheld by the crown. The structure of fees paid to public offi-cials, furthermore, did not change, although it is true that they were paid to royal rather than proprietary appointees and the most lucrative offices enriched a different group.[35] The Navi-gation Acts were as much in effect as ever; they were more vig-orously enforced, but there is no reason to suppose that the re-sults would have been different under a proprietary regime, given royal determination to make the laws effective. Some of

[35] "Royal Period," 78–79, 104–6, discusses Copley's appointments. Jor-dan points out that Francis Nicholson, appointed governor in 1694, re-turned many proprietary supporters to office (145), but these were not the people who had held lucrative positions before 1689. Members of the council continued to hold many of the major fee-paying offices, and they were an entirely new group. See *HLP*, 122–34.

the merchants to suffer prosecutions under the acts during the 1690's were members of the Associators' Convention.[36] The royal governors were more eager than the seventeenth-century Calverts had been to see Maryland fit the developing imperial system; but otherwise pressures on the economy—tobacco prices, British trade policy, population growth, problems of capital formation, labor shortages, market organization—do not appear to have hinged in any way on the overturn of the proprietor.

Institutional consequences were greater, but mostly in religion. The assembly of 1692, under Governor Copley's instructions, passed the first act for the establishment of the Anglican church. Although an act agreeable both to the colonists and to the English authorities did not pass until 1702, establishment proceeded meantime. Every taxable, regardless of religion, paid forty pounds of tobacco annually for the support of the Church of England. The province was divided into parishes, and in each the freeholders elected a vestry to collect and administer these funds, build churches, and pay ministers. During the 1690's, vestries became active in all the parishes. Churches were built and ministers began to arrive.

These changes did not encounter very forceful protest, except on the part of the Quakers, who actively lobbied in Maryland and Virginia for approximately ten years to forestall the official establishment of the Anglican church. Catholics were in no position to make very vocal complaints, and the Presbyterians seem to have cooperated. The objections that did materialize were directed against the new and heavy taxation. Governor Francis Nicholson observed in 1696 that the tax "is much balked at by papists, Quakers, and dissenters who are pretty numerous." De-

---

[36] Copley's administration did its best to sabotage enforcement, but under Nicholson prosecution was vigorous ("Royal Period," 98–104, 112–13, 122, 129, 143). The names of the merchants prosecuted in 1696 were circulated to the counties, and included William Sharpe and Michael Miller (Joseph H. Smith and Philip A. Crowl, eds., *Court Records of Prince George's County, Maryland, 1696–1699* [Washington, D.C., 1964], 215).

spite his fears that an "influence from heaven" might be necessary, the assembly twice again passed legislation establishing the
church with the mandatory tax support after the original act
had been disallowed.[37]

In explaining support for establishment, it is important to remember that in 1689 there were few churches and fewer ministers for the more than 70 per cent of the population who were
not Catholics or Quakers. Had the non-Catholic and non-Quaker
families been organized into active congregations, more resistance might have arisen against the establishment of one church
at the expense of others. There might have been pressure to
adopt the suggestion made by the Lords of Trade in 1678 that
public taxes support churches of any Protestant denomination.
As it was, however, the need for religious institutions and the
routines and habits of thought and feeling they perpetuated was
apparently overriding. Added to this need was the pressure from
the English authorities to establish the Anglican church. In these
circumstances, there was little incentive to conceive and fight
for an alternate plan.[38]

[37] Nicholson to Thomas Tenison, June 12, 1696, Fulham Palace Papers,
II, ff. 53–54, Lambeth Palace, London; *Md. Archives,* XIII, 435–40; Nelson
Waite Rightmyer, *Maryland's Established Church* (Lebanon, Pa., 1956),
20–52; "Royal Period," 95–96, 169–76, 267–84; Kenneth Carroll, "Quaker
Opposition to the Establishment of a State Church in Maryland," *MHM,*
LXV (1970), 149–70. Significantly, Presbyterians sat on early Anglican
vestries through the beginning of the early eighteenth century ("County
Government," text, 538, 669–70). Richard A. Gleissner, "Religious Causes
of the Glorious Revolution in Maryland," *MHM,* LXIV (1969), 327–41,
oversimplified the politics of creating the religious establishment in Maryland by assuming that the Associators continued to dominate the assembly
through the 1690's. Until 1702, the Maryland vestries voted in new members to replace those who had died or removed or resigned. Thereafter
the freeholders put out two members and elected two each year.

[38] Commissary Thomas Bray, an active force in the growth of the
Anglican Church in Maryland, observed to the Archbishop of Canterbury in 1700 that Quakers were the main opponents and that "four years
ago before ministers were sent, people on the Eastern Shore (I am told)
were well disposed to turn Quaker. . . . This drift has changed now"
(Fulham Papers, II, ff. 139–40). On the educational function of seven-

It was important also that other denominations were not forbidden to support their own churches. English acts passed in 1688 protecting the rights of dissenters to establish congregations were assumed to apply in Maryland, and the Act for Religion of 1702 made this assumption explicit. Even the Catholics finally received permission to conduct private services.[39] Nevertheless, public taxation in favor of one group was strong discouragement to the others. Church establishment must have had a real impact on the lives of all the inhabitants.

Otherwise, there was very little refashioning of the legal and governmental institutions developed under the proprietor. Evidently, both the planters of Maryland and the English authorities considered them to be satisfactory in most respects. In Massachusetts and New York, where governments had also fallen, the whole legal system was revamped,[40] but in Maryland little was necessary.

The most important changes in the legal system were in arrangements for appeals and in the decrease of plural judicial appointments. The king in council became the final court of appeal in causes or suits in which the judgment or decree ex-

---

teenth-century churches, see Lawrence A. Cremin, *American Education: The Colonial Experience, 1607–1783* (New York, 1970), 138–66. His comment on Maryland (164–65), however, does not address itself to the problems considered here.

[39] County courts exercised powers that in England were assigned to two justices of the peace for authorizing the establishment of dissenting congregations. Talb. Judg., 1692, 1696, 1698, f. 248 (1698); Acts 1702, c. 1, Thomas Bacon, *Laws of Maryland with Proper Indexes* (Annapolis, 1765); PG Ct. Rec., C, ff. 59, 209a. For restrictions on Catholics, see Acts 1704, c. 59, *Md. Archives*, XXVI, 340–41; Acts 1704 c. 95, XXVI, 431–432; Acts 1707, c. 6, XXVII, 146.

[40] See Joseph H. Smith, ed., *Colonial Justice in Western Massachusetts (1639–1702): The Pyncheon Record, An Original Judges' Diary of the Administration of Justice in the Springfield Courts in the Massachusetts Bay Colony*, Legal Studies of the William Nelson Cromwell Foundation (Cambridge, Mass., 1961), 82–88; Julius Goebel, Jr., and T. Raymond Naughton, *Law Enforcement in Colonial New York: A Study in Criminal Procedure (1664–1776)* (New York, 1944), 24–32.

ceeded £300 sterling, and the governor and council replaced
the upper house of assembly as the final tribunal of appeal in the
province, in effect adding the governor to this court.[41] The
thoroughly justified complaint of the revolutionaries that the
Provincial Court judges had reviewed their own decisions as
members of the upper house resulted in the selection of Provincial Court justices largely from the ranks of men who were not
councillors. This reform, however, did not occur until the arrival
of Governor Nicholson in 1694. Once in power, the Associators
had been in no hurry to alter the former policy. The Associators'
Convention had appointed the Provincial Court established in
1691 in large part from the ranks of the Grand Committee, and
Governor Lionel Copley's Provincial Court consisted mostly of
his councillors; the majority of these judges had been leaders
during the interregnum.[42]

The battle over the extension of English law was settled temporarily in favor of the assembly. Passage in 1692 of an Act for
Proceedings at Law without a clause giving judges discretion
and repeal of the Act for Judicature returned the status of English law to that of 1678. This debate was to take on a different
character with the passage of time. Within a decade the act
would be dropped and there would be judges on the Provincial
Court who believed that no English statute should extend that
did not explicitly mention the plantations.[43]

More striking was the immediate growth both in power and
procedural sophistication of the lower house of assembly. The
change was a natural development already begun but hastened
by the new political arrangements. The chief executive was now
a royal governor rather than a proprietor or his deputy; and the
upper house was no longer tied to the executive by close per-

[41] Carroll T. Bond and Richard B. Morris, eds., *Proceedings of the
Maryland Court of Appeals* (Washington, D.C., 1933), xxxiii.

[42] C. Ashley Ellefson, "The County Courts and Provincial Court of
Maryland, 1733–1763" (Ph.D. diss., University of Maryland, 1963), 113–
15, 150, 320; "Royal Period," 76–77, 144.

[43] "County Government," text, 92–96.

sonal connections. A royal governor and council were not concerned to protect a family fortune and assumed that the assembly was a lawmaking body comparable in many ways to Parliament. Copley, for example, allowed the speaker of the lower house to issue writs for by-elections. Nicholson called a general election in 1697 simply because three years has passed since the last, thereby setting an explicit precedent for holding elections at least every three years. In this climate the lower house rapidly developed standing committees, improved its skills in drafting legislation, and forced more open recognition of its claims to parliamentary privileges. In addition, the governor's loss of control over land grants, a power now vested in a proprietary agent, undoubtedly encouraged the development of political independence. Also helpful to this growth was the makeup of the first royal council, which consisted largely of men not previously superior in position to many members of the lower house.[44]

No important shifts in the governmental structure had been necessary to increase the importance of the lower house. The executive still had powers to call, prorogue, or dismiss an assembly and to veto its legislation; the upper house was still the council; and the lower house was still elected by the same procedures on the same franchise—although four, not two, delegates were now required. Laws, even though signed by the executive and in effect, could still be disallowed.[45] Royal Maryland inherited from proprietary Maryland a constitution that already fitted its needs.

This fact was evident also in local government. The grievances of the Associators had disclosed little discomfort with its structure or functions, except as related to the patronage dis-

[44] "Royal Period," 88–92; Newton D. Mereness, *Maryland as a Proprietary Province* (New York, 1901), 206.

[45] Royal disallowance was perhaps a greater threat to the "True Force and Validity of the Laws" than proprietary disallowance had been, since when the proprietor was his own chief executive and signed an act, he was not able to disallow it later.

pensed by central authority,[46] and the first royal administrations made few changes. Only one might be classified as a reform: Councillors no longer were empowered to sit on county courts— another attack on plural judicial powers. In addition, single justices acquired sole jurisdiction over actions in very small causes; this extension of power surely had not required a rebellion to attain.[47]

The creation of the vestries might have brought about major change in local government, for in England and in Virginia they performed vital governmental functions, but in Maryland such functions had long resided in the county courts. Local government as already constituted had justly proved itself in Maryland and the local leaders showed no eagerness to give up power. The only function released to the vestries was that of keeping vital records. The only power granted that might instead have been located in the county court was to admonish couples suspected of illegal cohabitation from "keeping company"; a second offense required the vestry to inform the county court, which could then proceed to punishment for fornication, even though this crime remained otherwise unproven. This effort to endow the vestries with a judicial function similar to that enjoyed by English courts of the ordinary is a fascinating topic in itself, but its effect on local government was minimal. The powers of the

---

[46] The main complaint that affected county government concerned poor record-keeping by clerks, who were appointed by the provincial secretary. John C. Rainbolt, "The Alteration in the Relationship between Leadership and Constituents in Virginia, 1660–1720," *William and Mary Quarterly*, 3rd ser., XXVII (1970), 411–34, suggests that one cause of Bacon's Rebellion was the small planters' resentment of taxation laid by secret sessions of the levy court. In Maryland the levy was laid in open court, where any taxpayer could object and if necessary a levy court determination could be appealed to the Provincial Court ("County Government," text, 411–12, 555). In 1697 a petition from Somerset County to the assembly requested that some freeholders join the justices in laying the county levy, but the upper house rejected it on the grounds that in Maryland the levy was laid in open court (*Md. Archives*, XIX, 516). The issue never arose again.

[47] "County Government," text, 115–17, 128–29.

vestry remained primarily parochial until the middle of the eighteenth century. Its failure until then to play a significant part in county government reflected a well-established county constitution in 1689.[48]

The first royal assembly, which was dominated by supporters of the rebellion,[49] revised all the laws and had an opportunity to promote changes in institutions and policies; but except for establishment of the Church of England, it sought little that was fundamental. Its members addressed themselves, of course, to the grievances of the preceding fifteen years. The Act for Elections of 1692 put election procedure on a statutory basis and provided for four instead of two delegates per county. Sheriffs' terms, previously set by the executive, were limited by act. The Act for Proceedings at Law was passed. The Act for Deserted Plantations was repealed; Lord Baltimore now would have to sue for his back quitrents. Most of the laws passed were familiar, however, and most of those repealed were simply obsolete.[50]

There were a number of reasons for this conservative approach. Many of the burning issues of the 1680's were settled when the proprietor lost his governing rights. His power of veto was no longer a grievance, and the royal power of disallowance went unquestioned. His sedition laws could be repealed as obsolete; sedition against the crown could be prosecuted under English law. He could no longer require an oath of fidelity; such oaths were now taken for Their Majesties. And under a crown governor, Protestant settlers no longer feared that arms and ammunition might be used to betray them to the Catholic French.

Other issues took on a different aspect when the proprietor was no longer in control. The Associators had complained that Lord Baltimore created offices and set their fees without an act

---

[48] *Ibid.*, 221–23, 313, 530–31, 535–36.

[49] "Royal Period," 80–82. It should be noted, however, that only in Dorchester did all the delegates represent active support of the Associators (84–86).

[50] "County Government," nn. 34, 39 to chapter V.

of assembly; but the assembly of 1692 took no action to authorize or eliminate the offices in question or to establish fees for them. The leaders of the new government were no longer anxious to dispense with the patronage and profits that these offices and their uncontrolled fees represented. An act of assembly created deputy commissaries for the counties, answering another complaint, but the double fees that had accompanied commissions for local probate were not eliminated.[51] The new commissary general was not about to lose a major portion of his income.

The Associators had made accusations of maladministration—selling of offices, taking of illegal fees, poor recordkeeping, failure to pay at least for repair of arms out of the shilling-per-hogshead duty—and these charges undoubtedly had some basis in fact; but these were problems that plagued the royal government as well. Sir Thomas Lawrence must have been at least as venal a provincial secretary as any of his predecessors, and Governor Copley far more venal a governor. Governor Nicholson enraged his judges and other officeholders by his efforts to improve administration, yet many of those who refused to cooperate were men who had supported complaints against the proprietor.[52] And it proved as necessary as ever to use public taxes to keep the county arms in repair.[53]

Whether under the proprietor there had been gross abuses of judicial process that the royal administration could or did remove is not easy to determine. The Associators had complained that the council or Chancery Court had heard causes adjudicable only at common law, but evidence of real abuse of this kind is

[51] Acts 1692, c. 3, *Md. Archives*, XIII, 436–37; Acts 1694, c 27, XXXVIII, 22. For double fees, examine any administration account recorded in I&A.

[52] "Royal Period," 69–73, 97–130, 231–42, discusses the role of Copley and Lawrence and later reaction to royal appointees and the disputes over their fees. "County Government," text, 541–53, covers Nicholson's efforts to improve local administration. For membership of the benches during Nicholson's time, see *Md. Archives*, XX, 138; XXIII, 127–30.

[53] "County Government," text, 407.

hard to find. The editor of the first chancery record of Maryland, which covers the years from 1669 through 1679, describes the court as "punctilious" in its adherence to English procedure and finds only a few minor instances of questionable jurisdiction.[54] The council record does not reveal evidence of usurped common law jurisdiction. Nevertheless, there may have been instances. The same may be said of accusations that judges sometimes sat in their own causes,[55] and that writs of error—coming to be considered a matter of right in England—were denied. The practice of "fineinge of men absent without giveing day in Court to Answer by sci[re] fac[ias] or otherwise oftentimes without Juryes where matter of Fact ought to be enquired of and found" probably referred to efforts to force various officers to carry out their duties. Ordinarily once a man appeared in court with a reasonable excuse or the work completed, his fine would be remitted. The same procedure was common and went uncriticized under the royal governors. Empaneling jurymen who were not freeholders also occurred from time to time after as well as before 1689.[56] Why the Associators objected to the appointment of a court of delegates to review determinations of the Prerogative Court is unclear, and such courts continued to be appointed when the need arose.[57]

More serious, perhaps, were the charges of illegal procedures in law enforcement. The worst accused the judges of the Provincial Court of determining criminal matters of fact, whereby men had been convicted and even executed. Unfortunately many criminal proceedings of the Provincial Court are missing before 1689, but those remaining show no man executed without conviction by a jury. It was also charged that papists had apprehended Protestants without warrant or cause of commitment ex-

[54] *Md. Archives*, LI, xxii.
[55] This accusation appears only in Abington's account sent to New York ("Mariland's Grevances," 400).
[56] "County Government," text, 264–67, 487, and n. 136 to chapter VI.
[57] *Md. Archives*, XX, 47–48, 58.

hibited and had confined them to long imprisonment before trial; or they had been forced to find high bail; or they had been sentenced to cruel punishments under "unjust unreasonable illegal tyrannical Acts of Assembly craftilly obtayned from the unwary Representatives of the Province." These accusations seem to refer primarily to the arrest of Fendall, Coode, and Godfrey in 1681; to the arrest and long imprisonment of the Indian trader Jacob Young accused of treasonable negotiations with the Northern Indians; and to the punishments that could be inflicted under the sedition act of 1649. Examination of the remaining provincial and county court records for the 1670's and 1680's does not indicate that such practices were standard. Nevertheless, Lord Baltimore probably had not troubled himself much with the rights of men he supposed had plotted rebellion or treason. On the other hand, the transcript of Fendall's trial, and the trial record for Coode and Godfrey, show great care to follow English procedures, and Young was eventually sentenced only to a good-behavior bond.[58]

Whatever the validity of the accusations that there had been administrative and judicial misgovernment, even the Associators did not assert that it had been sufficient to justify a revolt. They emphasized instead the patience with which they had endured such evils until the danger of the supposed papist conspiracy had driven them to action.[59] These complaints were part of the legal brief drawn up against Lord Baltimore, but the fact that major change in policy or procedure did not follow the institution of crown government suggests that they were not a fundamental cause of discontent.

The political and social consequences of the "revolution of government" were more serious and must have reflected more of its basic causes. One of the most immediate results was the exclusion of Roman Catholics and Quakers from public office,

[58] *Ibid.*, V, 311–34; VII, 370–72, 386–92, 472–73, 475–76, 477, 479, 480, 485, 500.
[59] "Mariland's Grevances," 402; *Md. Archives*, VIII, 105.

including jury service, through oath-taking requirements. The oath of fidelity to the king was no problem to Roman Catholics, but the oath of abhorrency required the admission that no "foreign Prince, person, prelate State or Potentate hath or ought to have any Jurisdiction, power Superiority or Authority Ecclesiasticall or Spirituall within the Kingdom of England or the Dominions therunto belonging"—in other words, that the Pope had no authority over Roman Catholics in Maryland. Even more drastic was the so-called test, which the governors' instruction required them to demand of all officers appointed under the provincial seal. This was a declaration, signed under oath, that denied transubstantiation. No mental reservation or papal dispensation could enable any Roman Catholic believer to sign it. And for a believing Quaker—at least for those under the discipline of the Maryland meetings—any oaths whatever were forbidden.[60]

Exclusion of Quakers was partly self-inflicted, but it also was the result of a shift in provincial policy. During the last fifteen years of the proprietary regime, Quakers had been refusing judicial office, and Quaker efforts to avoid use of the courts suggests that most Friends would have refused appointment even if oaths had not been demanded.[61] But Quakers had served in the assembly and three were elected to the assembly of 1692. Their refusal to swear allegiance to the crown led to refusal to seat them.[62] From that time Quakers no longer participated in government at any level, although they probably exercised the vote. The effect of this exclusion in the community is not easy to assess, given the small numbers of Quakers in any one county and their unwillingness to serve in the courts.

The effects of Roman Catholic exclusion must have been felt

---

[60] "County Government," text, 447, 449, 478. See Smith and Crowl, eds., *Court Records of Prince George's County*, xxiv, xxv, for the text of the oaths as found in Maryland.

[61] See n. 29 above.

[62] *Md. Archives*, XIII, 354, 366.

more widely, if only because the council, and thus also the upper house of assembly, had previously been dominated by Roman Catholics. In St. Mary's County, where one-third to one-
half the white population was Catholic,[63] the effect must have
been particularly pronounced; many offices of power changed
hands there, and if oath-taking requirements were enforced, it
must have been difficult to fill the necessary jury panels and local
posts of constable and pressmaster. Calvert and Charles were
probably similarly affected, although less so, and even counties
with a small Catholic population faced the problem. Although
ony perhaps 5.6 per cent of the popuation of Prince George's
County in 1706 was Catholic, this segment included nearly a
quarter of the heads of households substantial enough to qualify
for office of power or major profit.[64] Such drain of potential leadership cannot have gone unfelt. Governor Nicholson commented
on the difficulty of procuring men for responsible positions, some
of the best qualified being Catholic or Quaker.[65]

Another consequence of this exclusion was to help reduce the
terms of banishment from office of Protestants who had opposed
the Associators. Copley and his council had excluded opponents
of the revolt from all offices within their power to grant, but by
1696 nearly all of the non-Quaker Protestants still alive who had
refused service under the Associators' government were at least
county justices once more. This shift was paralleled in assembly membership after the election of 1694. Twenty-four of the
forty-two delegates elected in 1692 were replaced, and half of the
newly elected members had openly opposed the Associators. Governor Nicholson, Copley's successor, was determined to make

[63] In 1710 there were about 3,130 white inhabitants in St. Mary's
County, and in 1708, 1,238 Catholics (*ibid.*, XXV, 258). There were also
668 Negroes in 1710. Whether any Negro converts would have been
included in the Catholic count is unclear.

[64] "County Government," text, 693. In 1708 there were 248 Catholics
in Prince George's County and about 1,684 taxables or 4,041 people (*Md.
Archives*, XXV, 258; PG Ct. Rec., D, f. 101).

[65] "Royal Period," 142.

use of the best talent available, and quite apart from other political considerations, there was a shortage of men in the province of a caliber he considered suitable for posts of authority. The factions organized around the conflicts of 1689–1692 were coming to an early end.[66] In this respect the political effects of the revolution were minimal.

One of the most important and longest-lasting political results was reflected in the new appointments to the council and the rise of new men to positions of political importance. The Calverts had favored Catholic relatives and had demanded personal loyalty of other appointees, usually sealed by marriage alliances. Under the crown the council ceased to be a family conclave. Most of the new councillors were Associators, men who probably would not have acquired these posts under the former regime. Some of these men established families that remained powerful through the eighteenth century. John Addison, as just one example, was particularly successful in this regard; Thomas Addison received an appointment to the council soon after his father's death. However, several others of the first royal council died within a few years without sons to follow in their immediate steps, and there was consequently room for other families to obtain a council seat. A new constellation of power was forming, and entrance to it would be for the moment more open. Offices on the provincial level would no longer be dominated so completely by one or two families especially close to the proprietor, and when the Calverts regained their governing rights after 1714, they would confront a much enlarged circle of political leaders.

Ironically, the families of the immediate ringleaders of the revolution would not be among that enlarged circle of officeholders in 1715. No second-generation Blakiston, Coode, Cheseldyne, or Jowles was to attain high provincial office. Blakiston started the royal period in a position of great power. He quickly

[66] *Ibid.*, 140–48; Carr and Jordan, "Service of Civil and Military Officers, July 1689–April 1692," Hall of Records.

became the confidant of Governor Copley. Before the governor's death in 1693, that brief alliance had brought increased power and wealth, the latter through a number of illegal escapades. The alliance also spawned bitter factional struggles in the colony and investigations by English customs officials. Blakiston died a few months after the governor's death and left his young son with a tarnished family name and a personal estate in great disarray. John Blakiston apparently never overcame these handicaps, for there is no record that he ever held office.

John Coode never exercised real power under the royal governors. He had returned from England in 1692 without an appointive office and was soon opposing Copley and Blakiston. A perennial malcontent with antiauthoritarian tendencies, Coode seemed quite unable to work effectively for very long within a government. He achieved limited prominence in 1694 when Governor Francis Nicholson appointed him militia officer and sheriff of St. Mary's County. Within two years, Coode was at odds with Nicholson and stirring up an unsuccessful rebellion against his former benefactor. Despite complaints about his drunkenness and a conviction for blasphemy, Coode was elected a burgess again in 1708, but the assembly refused to seat him. He died within a few months. None of his sons ever attained offices above the county level, and their local appointments came during their father's lifetime.

Cheseldyne was likewise plagued by personality problems and drunkenness, although his career was more stable and successful than Coode's. Cheseldyne served again as speaker of the lower house and held the lucrative post of commissary general before his eventual promotion to the council in 1703, where he sat until his death. His son, however, served just one term in the assembly before personal scandal apparently terminated his political career.

Among the initial four leaders, only Henry Jowles clearly left at his death a positive reputation upon which a son might easily build. Indeed, Henry Peregrine Jowles at the end of the royal period seemed to have begun a distinguished political career, which was interrupted by his untimely death in 1719 during his third term in the assembly. Consequently, only two of the four original organizers of the revolt enjoyed high office for any considerable length of time and in no case did their sons achieve the coveted seats of power on the provincial council.

In the two decades following the overthrow of Lord Baltimore, then, it was not the men who plotted and openly led the coup itself who reaped its major benefits so much as the men elected to the Associators' Convention who proved themselves capable of political skill and leadership. The benefits extended also to other supporters, some of whom for the first time became justices or sheriffs. Such men bequeathed to their sons improved prospects of political influence. Indeed, in counties where Catholics formed part of the group eligible for office, all Protestants now found the opportunities for political advancement somewhat greater than might have been possible had the proprietary regime continued.[67]

Another way to assess the consequences of the overturn of the proprietor is to look at its effects upon the lives of individuals. The ordinary Protestant planter, since he was not a member of the group eligible for office of power, may have been little affected, except in his religious life. Most important to him during the interregnum must have been the success with which bloodshed was avoided, property protected, and the usual public services maintained. Under the royal governors, he may have welcomed the exclusion of Roman Catholics from decision-making, and the establishment of crown authority may have lessened his anxiety. But he raised and sold his tobacco, paid his rents or quitrents, trained in the militia, mended roads, and, if he were a freeholder, voted in elections and served his turn on juries or in

[67] See Biographies of the Members of the Associators' Convention and Appendix B. For a detailed discussion of the conflicts that developed among the former Associators under Copley and subsequent repercussions, see "Royal Period," 76, 81, 100, 102–3, 107–30, 178–97, 206–7, 220–25, 252, 353, 361–62; *Md. Archives*, XX, 453; XXIII, 197–98.

local office as he always had during both decades. The most noticeable change, from his point of view, must have been his higher taxes—sometimes one-third more than they would have been without the church establishment[68]—and the increased possibility of going to church, receiving the sacraments, and participating in the personal drama and community organization that these made possible. In 1676, heavy taxation for defense had inspired a rebellion supported by the small planters; the lack of significant protest in the 1690's of the forty pounds of tobacco per poll suggests that the expenditure for churches to which the tax was directed satisfied a deep need, whether or not settlers often actually attended services.

The ordinary Catholic planter felt greater change. He escaped the burdens but also the privileges of participation in the county polity, such as the opportunity to air grievances that grand jury service provided.[69] He could no longer receive the sacraments in a public church, and for a while he may not have dared to receive them at all. Under the English penal statutes, furthermore, which were now considered to extend, he could suffer severe legal disabilities. On the other hand, there is little evidence that these were in fact imposed. Officeholding aside, Catholics retained their legal rights, including for the moment the right to vote.[70] In addition they continued to be accepted as sureties on

[68] In Charles County in 1697, for example, the provincial levy was 41 pounds of tobacco per poll, the county levy was 48¼, and the parish levy was 40 (Ch. Ct. and Land. Rec., V no. 1, f. 292). In 1701 the figures were 17¾, 37¼, and 40 (Y no. 1, ff. 329–30). In Prince George's County in 1696, the figures were 81 (provincial), 56 (county), 40 (parish); total, 177 (Smith and Crowl, eds., *Court Records of Prince George's County*, 53).

[69] For the powers of the grand jury, see "County Government," text, 485–88.

[70] The laws and the extent to which Catholics actually were persecuted under them are discussed in *ibid.*, 163–64, and n. 295 to chapter III. There were occasional observations that Catholics and Quakers would combine their efforts and votes to elect candidates favorable to their cause ("Royal Period," 186–88, 253–55, 287). David Jordan, "A Plea for

bonds, to be appointed appraisers of estates, and in general to perform all the various functions the society required that did not involve exercise of authority or decision-making.[71] In consequence, most details of the day-to-day existence of most Catholic planters probably suffered little change, although they must have felt uncertainty, especially at first. Letters sent to England about 1710 indicate that the Jesuits in St. Mary's and Charles counties were still ministering to the Catholic families there and had not lost any to heresy. Indeed, some years before, the Anglican commissary Thomas Bray had complained of numerous "perversions made to Popery." Still, the Jesuit fathers had to exercise care.[72] Where Catholics were numerous, conducting religious education and observance in secret may have had long-run effects on patterns of community behavior as yet unstudied.

Those Catholics who had or might have had offices of power or major profit felt the greatest deprivation. They no longer participated in decision-making at any level of government and no longer could aspire to expand fortunes on the profits from fees. Yet, they may not have lost all their influences. The lawyers Charles Carroll and Robert Carvile, for example, were allowed to practice in the Prerogative and Chancery courts, and Governor Nicholson consulted both on legal points of importance.[73] Catholics still controlled large investments, and there

---

Maryland's Catholics," *MHM*, LXVII (1972), 429–35, discusses treatment of Catholics and one particular effort to aid them.

[71] "County Government," text, 691–94.

[72] Thomas Hughes, *History of the Society of Jesus in North America, Colonial and Federal*, 4 vols. (London, 1907–17), *text*, II, 437–39, 443 (quotation). The Jesuits wrote under the guise of commercial correspondence.

[73] *Md. Archives*, XX, 314, 316–19, 439–42. The dockets in the Chancery Court proceedings mark the initials of the attorneys for each party. CC and RC appear frequently. Examination of the Provincial Court and county court records for the period show no other attorneys who could be meant. Carvile and Carroll appear as procurators in the Testamentary Proceedings. See, for example, Test. Pro. 16, ff. 90, 97, 99; 18, f. 84; 22, ff. 133, 487; Chancery Proceedings, PC, f. 336, 609; PL, ff. 113, 387.

had been much intermarriage with powerful Protestant families. In Prince George's County the Catholic Henry Darnall was the stepfather of Protestant councillor Thomas Brooke and brother-in-law of Provincial Court justice William Hatton; Brooke, in turn, was married to the stepdaughter of Protestant councillor and former Associator John Addison, and Addison and Hatton were business partners. Through these connections, as well as through his position as proprietary agent and major landowner, Darnall must have been able to make his influence felt.[74] Nor did the revolution put an end to such intermarriages or by itself threaten the economic position or social status of well-established Catholic families.[75] During the eighteenth century the Hills and Gardiners of Prince George's, the Neales and Brents of Charles, the Carrolls of Anne Arundel, the Fenwicks and Brookes and Sewalls of St. Mary's, and many more continued in varying degrees to maintain or build their fortunes.[76]

The greatest opportunities under the new government fell to the Protestant members of the group eligible for exercise of

[74] "County Government," text, 679–81, Appendix, VI, Table 8A, 272–78, 304–7, 325–27.

[75] For example, during the 1690's William Bladen, connected to an important English family and a man who achieved prominence in Maryland, married Anne Vanswearingen, daughter of the Catholic Garret Vanswearingen; and Benjamin Hall, son of the Quaker Richard Hall, married Mary Brooke Bowling, sister of Councillor Thomas Brooke and also of his three Jesuit brothers. Hall eventually became a Catholic (Johnston, "Hall Family," 294; *Md. Archives*, XX, 402; *HLP*, 43, 95, 127, 130, 133, 136, 138, 143, 145, 162, 163, 167, 178, 182, 183).

[76] For Hills, see Effie Gwynn Bowie, *Across the Years in Prince George's County: A Genealogical and Biographical History of Some Prince George's County, Maryland, and Allied Families* (Richmond, Va., 1947), 426–30. See also Christopher Johnston's genealogies in *MHM:* "The Neale Family of Charles County," VII (1912), 201–18; "The Brooke Family," I (1906), 184–89, 284–89, 376–78; "Sewall Family," IV (1909), 290–95; Charles E. Fenwick, "The Fenwick Family of Southern Maryland," ms. in possession of the author. Inspection of any of the wills cited in these genealogies will reveal substantial landholdings and many show Catholic affiliations. For the Carrolls, see, for example, Ellen Hart Smith, *Charles Carroll of Carrollton* (Cambridge, Mass., 1942).

power. For this group the eclipse of the proprietor and their Catholic competitors opened up new possibilities for provincial office. All ambitious Protestants could set their sights higher than before, even though few would be chosen. And for those who achieved such office, with its accompanying fees and province-wide prestige, there were opportunities to improve their life style as well as to gain wealth and exercise power. It is possible to misinterpret the significance of these expanded opportunities, however. As the population grew, competition for office within a growing class of eligible men would also become greater.[77] Forces were at work in Maryland that the revolution did not bring about.

The basic consequences, then, of the "revolution of government" in Maryland were primarily political and religious. There were three key changes: The Protestant crown replaced the Catholic proprietor as the source of ultimate authority, a substitution that ended when the proprietor later became a Protestant. The Anglican church received state support in order to ensure rapid creation of Protestant congregations. And Catholics were excluded from office, in line with English law and practice. These changes relieved major anxieties—fear of Lord Baltimore's regal powers, fear of popery, and dismay at the absence of Protestant churches. Equally important was the consequent broadening of opportunity for political advancement of Protestants. If consequences reflect causes, then it was the failure to relieve these anxieties and pressures that led to the overthrow of the proprietor.

The most immediate of these underlying causes was the pressure to broaden opportunity for Protestants to attain provincial office. A growing and predominantly Protestant population had been providing an expanding pool of qualified men at the same time that the proprietor had increasingly reserved appointments

---

[77] In Prince George's County this competition was becoming evident after 1710 ("County Government," text, 696).

to his council for Catholics or for Catholic and Protestant relatives. From 1666 to 1676, seven of fifteen councillors were Protestants unrelated to the Calverts, but from 1677 to 1684 only
one of ten new appointments went to an unrelated Protestant.
Complaints to the crown during these years that Catholics were
preferred to Protestants reflected awareness of narrowing opportunity. During Charles Calvert's absence in England, the predominance of Catholics increased even more. Two Catholics, and
no Protestants, were added to the council. By 1688 death had
reduced to one the Protestants not related to the proprietor. This
situation not only frustrated the ambitions of men who aspired
to provincial power, but it also aroused the suspicions and uneasiness of numerous other Protestants who possessed no realistic expectations or desires for office above the county level,
where opportunity was still broad. Both groups could support
an effort to place non-Catholics in the higher offices, thereby
satisfying the ambitions of some men while strengthening the
confidence of others in the government that so affected their
lives.

The overthrow of the proprietor, then, was the work of a
small group primarily intent on increasing its own power but
able to play on real anxieties and grievances perhaps heightened
by long-continued hard times. The opportunity for a coup arose
from a combination of circumstances. The revolution in England
set a precedent for removing a Catholic ruler, while James's
flight to France encouraged rumors that the French and their
Indian allies would make war on English Protestants in the colonies. At the same time the five-year absence of Lord Baltimore
had left Maryland without necessary leadership. Charles Calvert's father, the first proprietor, had had his brothers Leonard
and Philip and then his son to act for him in Maryland while
he maintained his position in England. But Charles had no son
of age and his uncle Philip and cousin William, the son of Leonard, both died shortly before his departure. Strong leadership
was needed on both sides of the Atlantic if the proprietor were

to keep his charter on the one hand and political control of the colony on the other. The multiple executive that ruled the colony after 1684 proved too weak to function effectively. The failure of the deputy governors to proclaim William and Mary in the absence of orders from Lord Baltimore provoked a crisis they were incompetent to handle. The Associators exploited that crisis to obtain crown government for Maryland and to acquire power for themselves in the new regime.

The reasons for this double success are to be found both in England and in Maryland. Two considerations influenced the English authorities in their decision to suspend Lord Baltimore's power to govern: They preferred to put the colony in Protestant hands; and they wanted to eliminate the proprietor's virtual independence of royal control and ensure both revenues for the crown and profits for English merchants. The second objective had led to moves to rescind the charter even under the Catholic James, who had experimented in more centralized imperial organization with the Dominion of New England. Crown government in Maryland need not have resulted in appointments of Associators to the council, however. Contacts in the merchant community of London were of major importance in obtaining this preferment, but success depended also on the progress of events in Maryland. There the Associators maintained civilian rule without major disruption or visible misgovernment that could be held against them in the negotiations with crown officials. This achievement was a tribute both to their political skills and to the effective system of local government, developed under the Calverts, upon which they had to depend.

From one point of view, the fall of Lord Baltimore's government brought to an end an experiment that had achieved a remarkable success. Before 1689, while men in Europe had been fighting wars to establish state religions and to suppress political participation of dissenters, men in Maryland of drastically differing religious persuasions had sat as equals at the same table and had made decisions together. At the provincial level, Catholics had dominated, but cooperation with Protestants had been an essential element in a colony that was part of a Protestant empire and peopled mainly by Protestants. The Calverts had been careful to woo Protestant leaders with patronage and marriage alliances. At the local level, Protestants and Catholics had served together on the county benches and had shared community responsibilities. Local as well as provincial cooperation had been a success, for by 1689, local government was so well founded that it could provide both the political and institutional stability necessary to maintain order and services under stress.

Thus the question arises whether a more prudent course and better luck might have enabled Charles Calvert to weather the accession of William and Mary and retain political rights for Catholics. The answer is: Possibly. His return to Maryland probably would have been necessary to keep him more in touch with political realities. His personal control would have been especially critical during the months after the Glorious Revolution in England. A strong governor might have prevented maladministration in his absence and might have been able to check indiscreet expression of hopes that James II would prevail against William of Orange, but even such a governor might not have announced the accession of Their Majesties without orders from the proprietor. A proprietor resident in Maryland could have proclaimed Their Majesties immediately and would have had a much better chance of mustering forces to subdue an attempted coup. His presence in the colony, however, would have required finding an able and powerful representative to protect his position in England.

Equally important, Charles Calvert would have needed flexibility he may not have possessed to make many accommodations. Legitimate complaints both from Maryland settlers and the English authorities needed attention. He would have had to give greater recognition to his assembly and make high provincial office less of a preserve for Catholics and close family connections. He would have had to take more responsibility for encouraging Protestant churches. Given the developing English imperial system, he probably would have had to accept the charter modifications that his Protestant successors after 1715 inherited from the royal government: appeal from his courts to the king in council and royal review of Maryland legislation. In short, he would have had to learn to see Maryland less as a family property with himself as its benevolent ruler and more as an English colony with himself as its royal steward.

Imperial plans at Whitehall that threatened the Maryland charter and kept the proprietor in England foretold of other changes he might have had to accept. Recent studies of Massachusetts and Virginia show that as the English crown began to set its colonies to serving the ends of the mother country, traders in New England and the Chesapeake were beginning to rely on their direct connections with influential Englishmen to build and maintain positions in the colonies.[78] Charles Calvert had endeavored to make himself the power center through which a career could be promoted in Maryland, and he had had considerable success. But his experiences after the revolt in negotiating for at least partial control of the Maryland government proved that his personal influence was insufficient. The Associators had connections with English merchants and crown bureaucrats that helped them gain complete dominance of the council. Had there been no rebellion, or had his governing powers been returned, Charles Calvert would have needed all the influence his Protestant supporters in Maryland could muster in the developing English imperial system to help him maintain his position. He might have had to share control of influence in England as well as power in Maryland.[79]

[78] Bernard Bailyn, *The New England Merchants in the Seventeenth Century* (New York, 1964), 170–97; Bernard Bailyn, "Politics and Social Structure in Virginia," in James Morton Smith, ed., *Seventeenth-Century America: Essays in Colonial History* (Chapel Hill, 1959), 90–115.

[79] For an indication of how one proprietor skillfully retained his colony and maintained successful relations with English officials, see Alison G. Olson, "William Penn, Parliament and Proprietary Government," *William and Mary Quarterly*, 3rd ser., XVIII (1961), 176–95.

Even if Calvert had had the necessary foresight and flexibility to adapt to changing circumstances, there is still some question whether he could have forestalled indefinitely the demise of Catholic-led rule in Maryland. Two flaws in his position, not clearly apparent to a seventeenth-century mind, evidently fed the colonists' anxiety. First, an inherent conflict existed between Lord Baltimore as landowner in control of the most accessible form of wealth and Lord Baltimore as the dispenser of justice and protector of the common weal. Any European monarch occupied this position, but the Maryland settlers questioned whether the proprietor should be a monarch. The charter modifications of 1691, which later Lords Baltimore found perfectly workable, might have sufficiently relieved fears of Calvert prince-ship. However, the continued presence of Lord Baltimore in his colony—also an essential ingredient of proprietary success—might have aggravated rather than minimized this tension. There are hints of real resentment against the visible signs of Calvert prince-ship before 1689.[80]

Second, and more critical, the proprietors and their governors had not undertaken the social education that might have helped to make their experiment a success. Neither in the public record nor in the Calvert Papers is there any indication that those in positions of public leadership saw toleration and full political participation as more than a device to keep peace between Cath-olics and Protestants. Little is known about the original ideas and motivations of George and Cecil Calvert in establishing Maryland toleration, but any ideas of future societies they may have thought they were promoting were not transferred to Maryland. There, practical men fairly enforced the toleration law against Catholic and Protestant alike and found it possible

---

[80] Catholics as well as Protestants exhibited this resentment. In 1683, the Catholic attorney Robert Carvile, for example, had to be disciplined for calling Lord Baltimore, a "ffart" and saying "he was as good a Mann as my Lord, What are the Calverts? My ffamily is as antient as the Calverts" (*Md. Archives*, XVII, 184).

to share power regardless of religious persuasion, but they took no positive action to promote belief in these policies as ideal goods. This may have been unconscious wisdom. To ignore explosive differences allowed men to discover in action that cooperation was possible, and if the population had not been continuously augmented from outside, practice might have provided education enough. However, newcomers were constantly arriving. Between 1670 and 1690, the taxable population doubled, and the major part of this increase must have been via white immigration. Most of the immigrants were Protestants from the British Isles.[81] They may have needed indoctrination to accept practices that in England were illegal, such as Catholic services held in public and attended by public leaders.

Even if anyone had glimpsed the nature of this problem, furthermore, mechanisms for indoctrination were lacking. In the seventeenth century, when illiteracy was common and books were few, exhortations of preachers were the most usual means of reaching the mind. In Maryland, where public support of churches and ministers was forbidden, there were few preachers, but it is not clear that if there had been, they could have been enlisted in a general effort to promote toleration. The Maryland experiment was the policy of secular, not religious, leaders. Few seventeenth-century religious leaders were ready to support such ideas. The Elizabethan and Stuart rulers could use the church to reinforce their idea of the union of church and monarchy, but the Calvert proprietors had no phalanx of churchmen ready for active espousal of separation of church and state.

The revolution in Maryland followed closely upon the revolution in England, and there are interesting parallels. In both, an uprising attracted sufficient support to accompish the overthrow

[81] Menard, "The Growth of Population in Early Colonial Maryland," 9, 17–18, 20. Men not from the British Isles applied for naturalization, usually granted by act of assembly. There were only 113 granted before 1689 (*Md. Archives*, II, 94, 144, 205, 271, 282, 331, 400, 403; VII, 78, 79, 169, 216, 330, 387, 444, 461, 487, 489; XIII, 126, 144).

of a Catholic ruler and his ministers without bloodshed; an elected convention, not the military, was recognized as the ultimate authority until the question of who should rule was answered; and the outcome was a stable settlement at the expense of Catholic liberties. The loss to Catholics was greater in Maryland than in England, however, and the gain in constitutional guarantees against tyranny was less significant.

The Maryland revolution deposed a Catholic ruler, but he was not a ruler who had seized or was attempting to seize illegal powers; his powers had been granted by a charter that the English authorities never found legal ground to repeal. The leaders of the overthrow sought to prove that Lord Baltimore had exercised tyrannical rule and had violated the terms of his charter, but their arguments were not convincing. In the end, part of the proprietor's charter rights were suspended as an emergency measure without other clear statement of justification. In this respect, the establishment of temporary crown rule for the colony was an anti-Catholic act.

In Maryland a major political experiment foundered partly for lack of leadership. Whether Charles Calvert could have supplied that leadership is uncertain, given the changes that were inevitable. What is certain is that ambitious and discontented men were able to exploit the tensions unavoidable in a collaboration of Catholics and Protestants and make the most of grievances that creative leadership would perhaps have been able to settle.

In some respects the events of 1689–1692 are more interesting for what they show about stability in Maryland than for what they show about conflict or impending change. Stable local governments kept order without resort to military rule or even much repressive exercise of magistratical powers. A stable local leadership, whether pro- or antiproprietor, refrained from engaging in local power struggles that could have led to disorder and bloodshed. What might have happened is clear from events on the edge of settlement in Cecil County. Had other leaders behaved like those of Cecil, the Grand Committee, with its ambiguous powers, would surely have found the situation too difficult to handle, as did the leadership in Virginia during Bacon's Rebellion fifteen years earlier. Instead, local leaders, despite sometimes bitter disagreements, maintained the safe routines that would minimize tension.

This is not to say that there yet existed in Maryland a ruling class with a sense of identity and awareness of the role it performed; the social origins of immigrant justices were still much too diverse and their governing experience too limited. Nor were factions and conflicts absent. It is rather to suggest the stabilizing influence of established and workable local institutions. Maryland inhabitants of all social levels knew what to expect of their local government and what their government would expect of them. They accepted these obligations. When more distant centers of authority were in suspension, the local framework of powers and duties proved adequate to keep communities functioning. The habits of behavior that this framework fostered enabled men who exercised influence, whether in or out of power, to see in orderly process an identification of their own and the public interest.

This identification underlay the clear concern with legitimate derivation of power. Both sides eagerly claimed to represent lawful authority. The rebels emphasized their loyalty to the crown and the Protestant church and the supposed disloyalty of Lord Baltimore's deputy governors. The discussions of grievances painstakingly set out to demonstrate that Lord Baltimore had committed illegal acts and had violated his charter. The opponents of the revolution referred constantly to Lord Baltimore's charter rights conferred by the crown and to the inability of any man to terminate a legitimate government without lawful authority. Two common assumptions underlay the debate: that the crown was the ultimate source of legitimate power and that the purpose of legitimate power was to maintain social order. Each party saw the ability to keep orderly rule as a buttress to its position. Neither wished to be forced into action that could undermine such proof.

The Associators had the weaker theoretical position, since they could never claim crown authorization for their seizure of the government. Circumstances obliged them to rely instead on an imaginary emergency and then later, and more importantly, on a supposedly popular mandate made orderly through the procedures of electing representatives. The precedent set by the English convention in 1688 strengthened this second justification. Nevertheless, if the Maryland convention had failed to maintain order, the precedent might have lost much of its value. The Associators depended heavily on the legitimacy supplied by their proven capacity to enlist the cooperation of men who could keep orderly civilian rule.

The revolution in Maryland began with a military coup and the displacement of all provincial officeholders. The provincial administration remained in complete abeyance for two years and was only very partially restored with the re-establishment of the Provincial Court a year before Copley's arrival. Yet a supposition that these events were visible evidence for a period of great social disruption is false. The struggle for power at the provincial level did not destroy underlying stability. Such stability depended upon the existence of a sound institutional structure and a conscientious magistracy. Clearly it is necessary, in studying political change, to look beyond provincial politics and conflicts to the local communities. The recent interest in local history may lead to study of the role of local government in other colonial disorders and the development of further speculations about the nature of stability and change.[82]

In 1715 the Fifth Lord Baltimore, another Charles Calvert and

[82] Richard Maxwell Brown, *The South Carolina Regulators: The Story of the First Vigilante Movement* (Cambridge, Mass., 1963) is a revealing discussion of the problems that flow from the absence of local government.

a Protestant, regained governing rights to Maryland. By then, the province was quite different from what it had been during his grandfather's reign. It was no longer a family-owned and -dominated outpost of settlement; it was an English colony contributing to an imperial system organized around the interests of the mother country. Over twenty-five years many changes had occurred in the social and political structure, some paralleling developments in other colonies—the growing dominance of native-born figures, for example, and the clearer definition of local as opposed to imperial interest.[83] The transformation could have taken place, however, without the hiatus in Calvert rule. The basic forces at work did not necessarily hinge on the overthrow of proprietary authority. On the other hand, supposing the Proprietor had not lost his government, his relationship to his people in Maryland and to the crown in England would have had to change. A period of isolated development was ending for all the mainland English plantations, and Maryland had to take her place with the others as subordinate parts of a system that was developing slowly, clumsily, but for the most part irreversibly. The revolution of 1689, by precipitating royal government in Maryland, unquestionably hastened this adjustment. Thus the revolution marked, even if it did not cause, a new era in Maryland history.

[83] "Royal Period," chapters V, VI.

Biographies of the Members
of the Associators' Convention

Short biographies are provided below for each of the forty-one identified members of the Associators' Convention, 1689–1692. These profiles place primary emphasis on the public careers of the delegates.

Where information is available, there are estimates of land-holdings and economic status on the eve of the revolution and at the death of each member. The Associators died over the period 1690 to 1718. An unpublished consumer price series, 1660–1720, constructed by Russell R. Menard for the St. Mary's City Commission, indicates that over the period 1690–1718 values given for personal estates at death are roughly comparable.

On the basis of signatures appended to wills and deeds, all of the Associators but John Cambell were literate.[1]

Russell Menard has generously provided a number of references used in the preparation of these biographies.

JOHN ADDISON
?–1705 or 1706

John Addison had come to Maryland from western England by the summer of 1674. He belonged to a prominent family of

---

[1] There are admitted limitations to judging literacy in this manner, but it is at least one crude test. See Lawrence A. Cremin, *American Education: The Colonial Experience* (New York, 1970), 546–49.

merchants and clergymen. Two definite brothers, Thomas and
Henry, were merchants of Whitehaven; all three were probably
younger sons of the Reverend Launcelot Addison, and therefore brothers of Launcelot Addison, the dean of Litchfield and
chaplain to Charles II, and of Anthony Addison, the rector of
Abingdon and chaplain to the Duke of Marlborough.[1]

Addison appears to have settled initially in Charles County.
By early 1677, he had married Rebecca Dent, the daughter of
the Reverend William Wilkinson and widow of Thomas Dent,
a prominent planter. The Addisons lived in St. Mary's County
until 1687 when they moved to a plantation in Charles County
purchased from Addison's stepson Peter Dent. By 1689, Addison
owned at least 1,500 acres of land.[2]

A merchant and Indian trader as well as a planter, Addison
was a partner with several English merchants. Their vessel, *The
Liverpool Merchant*, was condemned and its cargo seized for
violation of the Navigation Acts in the early 1680's. During this
period, Addison was transporting many servants into the colony.[3]

Other than performing jury duty, Addison played no significant public role and held no office before his appointment as a
justice of Charles County in September 1687. Whether this delay was attributable to his problems with the Navigation Acts
or the difficulty of upward mobility in the Catholic-dominated
St. Mary's County is uncertain. Perhaps the latter was a factor
in his change of residence.[4]

Addison was active in spreading and later discounting the
rumors of a Catholic-Indian conspiracy in March of 1689.[5] It

[1] *Md. Archives,* LXVII, 420; "County Government," appendix, 272–74.

[2] "County Government," appendix, 274–75; I&A 4, f. 74; Harry Wright
Newman, *The Maryland Dents* (Richmond, 1963), 13–14.

[3] *Md. Archives,* V, 334–42; LXIX, 172–79; LXVII, 420; XX, 36. In
1680, Addison claimed headrights for transporting seventy-five persons
to Maryland (Patents WC#2, ff. 308–9).

[4] *Md. Archives,* LXIX, 265, 355; V, 565.

[5] *Ibid.,* VIII, 86–87; Fairfax Harrison, *Landmarks of Old Prince William,* 2 vols. (Richmond, 1924), I, 130.

appears that he was an early supporter of the rebels that summer. The Associators' Convention continued him as a justice
and made him a militia captain and coroner as well. He sat on
the special committee appointed to assess the levy and soon became a member of the Grand Committee of Twenty and of the
reconstituted Provincial Court.[6]

Under the royal government Addison's career continued to
prosper. He sat on the council from 1692 until his death. He
served for brief periods on the Provincial and Chancery courts
and was a militia colonel. A prominent Anglican, he was consistently a vestryman for his parish.[7]

Addison died sometime between November 1705 and April
1706. He left a landed estate of 6,478½ acres and a personal estate of £1,840.0.1½. His son and heir, Thomas Addison, had a
distinguished career; he received appointment to the council in
1708/09 and served until his death in 1727.[8]

NINIAN BEALE
c. 1625–1717

Ninian Beale was born in Scotland in approximately 1625 and
spent his early life there. As a coronet, he was captured at the
Battle of Dunbar in 1650, then transported first to Barbados and
later to Maryland as a political prisoner.[1]

In 1667, Beale, termed a "planter," claimed fifty acres of land
for his service to Richard Hall. Soon thereafter he began an active career in land speculation. By 1689 he had patented over

[6] *Md. Archives,* XIII, 243, 247; VIII, 199; Ch. Ct. and Land Rec.,
R No. 1, f. 275.

[7] "County Government," appendix, 276; King George's Parish Vestry
Minutes 1693–1779, *passim.*

[8] I&A 29, ff. 193–98, 229–30; "County Government," appendix, 275–77,
278–81.

[1] J. Ninian Beale, "Ninian Beale, 1625–1717: Immigrant to Maryland,"
Maryland and Delaware Genealogist, II (1960–61), 46; "County Government," appendix, 291.

12,000 acres, at least 4,263 of which he retained in his own possession.[2]

Beale's home plantation was "Bacon Hill" in Calvert County, where he was active in the militia. Appointed a lieutenant in 1668, he became a captain by 1678 and a major by April of 1689. He held no civil office other than the deputy surveyorship of Charles County in 1684 and an appointment as commissioner of towns for his own county that same year.[3]

Beale was active in the initial stages of the revolution under Henry Jowles and was one of the latter's "soldiers" elected to the assembly in the disputed Calvert election. He later sat on the Grand Committee.[4]

Despite his advanced age, Beale remained on the public scene through much of the royal period. He served as sheriff of Calvert from 1692 to 1694 and chief militia officer during Jowles's suspension from the council during the same period. After Jowles's reinstatement in 1694, Beale served under him as a lieutenant colonel. After Prince George's County was erected in 1696, Beale sat as one of its delegates for four years. At no point in his career did he hold a judicial office.[5]

A Presbyterian, Beale was generous in his gifts to that church and active in founding that denomination in Maryland.[6]

None of Beale's children attained the father's prominence. Beale himself died in 1717 after several years of inactivity. He left an estate before the payments of debts of £87.13.5. The inventory included no servants or slaves. His will listed more than 2,117 acres of land.[7]

[2] "County Government," appendix, 290–92.
[3] *Md. Archives*, XV, 181; VIII, 89; XVII, 319; V, 502.
[4] *Ibid.*, VIII, 108, 117, 199.
[5] *Ibid.*, 445, 410; XX, 75–76, 130; XIX, 318; XXII, 77.
[6] Beale, "Ninian Beale," 46; PG Land Rec., C, ff. 116b–116c.
[7] Wills, 14, ff. 504–7; Inv. 1, f. 455.

NEHEMIAH BLAKISTON
?–1693

Nehemiah Blakiston was a younger son of John Blakiston, once mayor of Newcastle and one of the judges who pronounced the death sentence for Charles I in 1649.[1]

Blakiston migrated to Maryland in 1668, probably with his uncle George Blakiston. Within a year he had married Elizabeth Gerard, daughter of Thomas Gerard, a prominent Maryland Catholic and former councillor whose battles with the proprietor were legendary. Two years earlier Gerard himself had moved to Virginia.[2]

Blakiston embarked on an active law practice in the county and provincial courts. He served in several minor royal posts before the crown appointed him collector of customs for North Potomac River in 1685. Blakiston's complaints of obstructions to the performance of his duties brought him into considerable conflict with the proprietary government.[3]

With his brothers-in-law John Coode and Kenelm Cheseldyne, Blakiston was an early leader of the revolution, although his public role was not as prominent initially. The convention appointed him a justice of the quorum for St. Mary's, a militia captain, and a coroner. His growing importance is signaled by his total assumption of leadership upon the departure of Coode in the summer of 1690. Blakiston then headed the Grand Committee; he became speaker of the convention after its third session and became chief justice of the Provincial Court upon its re-establishment.[4]

[1] Christopher Johnston, "Blakistone Family," *MHM*, II (1907), 55; *Md. Archives*, XXII, viii.

[2] Johnston, "Blakistone Family," 56; Edwin W. Beitzell, "Thomas Gerard and His Sons-in-Law," *MHM*, XLVI (1951), 189–206.

[3] *Md. Archives*, LXIX, *passim*; XVII, 449ff.; Donnell M. Owings, Supplement to *His Lordship's Patronage*, ms, 101–3, MHS.

[4] *Md. Archives*, XIII, 241; VIII, 199, 206–7, 244, 250.

Governor Lionel Copley made Blakiston his principal confidant on the new council and rewarded him with such preferments as chancellor and commissary general. The actions of the governor and Blakiston with regard to royal revenues were not completely legal, and they tangled extensively and heatedly with Edward Randolph, the surveyor general of customs. After Copley's death in early 1693, Blakiston unsuccessfully fought for control of the government. He himself died in October with his finances in great disarray.[5] It was almost impossible then or now to separate Blakiston's personal assets and debts from the official accounts of the offices he held.

Blakiston was survived by his wife and a young son, John, who apparently never held public office and died in 1724.[6]

WILLIAM BLANCKENSTEIN
1660–?

William Blanckenstein, possibly the youngest member of the Associators' Convention, was born in 1660. He was transported to Maryland eighteen years later by William Dare of Cecil County. The Maryland assembly passed a bill for his naturalization in 1682.[1]

A resident of St. Mary's City, Blanckenstein was a factor for a St. Mary's merchant. Edward Randolph called him "a Hofsteiner born: & a Tayler." He was also active in Indian affairs, which probably influenced his being assigned as an agent to New York to consult on defense matters in 1690 and 1691.[2]

[5] "Royal Period," 76–122. Blakiston served briefly as a vestryman (*Md. Archives*, XXIII, 18). One can follow efforts to settle Blakiston's estate in Inv. 32A, ff. 66–67, and in I&A 10, f. 403; 12, f. 27; 13B, ff. 58, 62; 15, ff. 35, 122; 17, ff. 81, 152, 153, 164, 254; 19, f. 159.

[6] Wills 14, ff. 224–25; Inv. 10, ff. 292–96.

[1] *Md. Archives*, XIII, 80; VII, 420; Patents 15, f. 530.

[2] Ch. Ct. and Land Rec., R no. 1, ff. 200–201, 230–31; *DHNY*, II, 140; Edmund B. O'Callaghan *et al.*, eds., *Documents Relative to the Colonial*

By 1689, Blanckenstein had patented 1,682 acres in Cecil County, of which he retained 1,200. A 500-acre plantation had also been surveyed for him in Baltimore County.[3]

The convention made Blanckenstein an alderman of St. Mary's City at its first meeting. Other than the subsequent appointment as an agent to New York, very little is known of this Associator, and his life after 1692 is a mystery.[4]

He did go to England in the summer of 1692 bearing letters from the new governor to English officials.[5]

DR. JOHN BROOKE
?–1693

John Brooke was the son of Michael Brooke who entered headright demands for himself, his wife, and two servants in Maryland in 1654. The father served as a justice and burgess for Calvert County before his death in 1663. His widow soon thereafter married Henry Trippe of Dorchester County and moved there with her son.

John Brooke was undoubtedly born prior to his parents' arrival in Maryland, and it remains unknown why he was not included in the headright claim. In 1667 he acknowledged a receipt from Trippe for full satisfaction for two-thirds of his father's estate. He was also a justice of Dorchester by 1671, a

---

History of the State of New York, 15 vols. (Albany, 1856–1887), III, 788–89; *Randolph Letters,* VII, 392.

[3] Baltimore County Rent Roll (1658–1723), f. 115 (Calvert Papers, mss., MHS); Cecil County Rent Roll (1658–1724), ff. 110, 112, 124 (Calvert Papers, mss., MHS).

[4] *Md. Archives,* XIII, 247. He was a witness at the trial for the men charged with Payne's murder, and a "William Blakiston" was a justice in St. Mary's in June of 1692 (VIII, 247; XIII, 338).

[5] Lionel Copley to Wm. Blathwayt, June 20, 1692, and July 30, 1692, Blathwayt Papers, XVIII, Research Library, Colonial Williamsburg, Inc.

position he would have been too young to hold had he been born after 1654.[1]

Brooke was often identified as a "chirurgeon." He played a prominent role in the county and inherited considerable status through both his father and his stepfather. Brooke sat as a justice from 1671 to 1674 and from 1676 until his death in 1693. He represented Dorchester in the lower house from 1681 until his death, serving under the proprietor, the Associators, and the crown. Between 1689 and 1692 he saw further service as a member of the Grand Committee and the Provincial Court.[2]

Through the marriages of his mother and his daughters, Brooke was related to the major political figures of the county during this period, including two of the other delegates to the Associators' Convention. His stepfather was a burgess for the years 1671–75, 1681–82, and 1689–93. Brooke's daughters married Thomas Cooke and Joseph Ennalls. Cooke became sheriff in 1691 and still held the office at his death in 1692/93. Ennalls was a prominent burgess in the royal period. Brooke had no sons. He left an estate of more than 1,000 acres at his death.[3] There is no record of an inventory of his personal estate.

DAVID BROWNE
?–1697

David Browne, a native of Glasgow, Scotland, had migrated to Maryland by April of 1670. Within two years he had married the widow of Captain William Thorne and succeeded to the estate of "Thornton."

---

[1] Elias Jones, *History of Dorchester County, Maryland* (Baltimore, 1902), 272–73.

[2] Dor. Land Rec., O no. 1, f. 29; *Md. Archives*, XV, 38, 254, 326; XVII, 43, 381; V, 355; VII, 227; XIII, 20, 153; VIII, 199, 245.

[3] Jones, *Dorchester*, 272–74; Wills 7, f. 26. See the biographies of Trippe and Cooke.

Browne may have studied at the college in Glasgow before he sailed to Maryland; in his will he left a bequest to that "famous College." Upon migrating, he established trade relations between Chesapeake planters and the Scottish merchants, an enterprise in which he became very successful. He settled in Somerset County and conducted an extensive trade on the Manokin River. By 1690 he had accumulated 1,690 acres.[1]

Browne's success brought him to the attention of the proprietor, who responded with an appointment to the county court in 1672/73. Browne became a justice of the quorum in 1679/80 and continued to sit on the court through the revolution. He also acquired a militia captaincy in 1679/80.[2]

Under the Associators, Browne's rise became more dramatic. He sat on the Grand Committee and by August of 1690 was "Coll David Browne." A Presbyterian, Browne was the only non-Anglican on the first royal council. Although Edward Randolph recommended that Browne "be turned out of the council" in 1692 for his trading with Scotland, he sat on the council until his death in 1697, and served briefly on the Provincial Court (1693–94).[3]

There is no record of any children. Browne left an estate of 980 acres and £1,838.1.6.[4]

[1] *Randolph Letters*, VII, 377; *Old Somerset*, 212–13, 292, 363. Torrence incorrectly read "famous college" to be "former college." See Wills 6, ff. 150–53.

[2] *Old Somerset*, 364; *Md. Archives*, XV, 77, 216, 275, 328; LIV, 775; Som. Jud. Rec., 1687–89, ff. 1–3; Chancery Record CD, f. 85.

[3] Som. Jud. Rec., 1689–90, f. 147; *Md. Archives*, VIII, 199; Prov. Ct. Judg., DSC, ff. 323–25; TL no. 1, f. 1; "Royal Period," 62–66; Wills 6, ff. 151–53; *Randolph Letters*, VII, 381–82.

[4] Wills 6, f. 150; I&A 16, ff. 221–23; 20, f. 106; 33A, f. 15.

JOHN CAMBELL
?–1695/96

John Cambell arrived in Maryland sometime between 1649 and 1653 as an indentured servant and completed his service for Dr. John Wade in 1656.[1] Cambell settled in St. Mary's County, where he became a planter and by 1670 had his own servant. He patented 100 acres there in 1662, added 50 more in 1666 and another 100 acres in 1685. At the time of his death, he held more than 500 acres.[2]

Cambell saw service as a petty juror in 1660's and a grand juror in 1671. He received appointment as a militia captain by 1681. By the eve of the revolution, he had been promoted to major. That he was illiterate and had been a servant were double barriers to any advancement in the civil sphere of government. Cambell is the only Associator for whom illiteracy in 1689 can be definitely established.[3]

One of the initial leaders of the revolt, Cambell may have established a friendship with John Coode while both were militia officers. His name was one of the few affixed to the declaration of July 25, 1689, and the articles of surrender. He acquired his first appointive civil office when his fellow Associators made him a justice in 1689. He continued in his militia office until 1694 at least, and represented St. Mary's again in the first royal assembly. There is no proof he remained on the bench, and quite likely he lost that commission because he was illiterate. He did serve on his local vestry.[4]

Cambell died in 1695/96, survived by three sons and two daughters. His sons did not attain any notable prominence. In

---

[1] Patents Q, ff. 189, 479; 4, f. 19.

[2] *Md. Archives*, LVII, 547; St. Mary's County Rent Roll, 1639–1724, ff. 20, 21, 22 (Calvert Papers, mss., MHS); Wills 7, ff. 190–92.

[3] Wills *loc cit.*; *Md. Archives*, LXV, 2; LVII, 123; VII, 148; VIII, 156.

[4] *Md. Archives*, VIII, 107, 108; XIII, 241, 350; XX, 106; XXIII, 17.

addition to his landed estate, his personal belongings were valued at £198.14.5, including two servants.[5]

KENELM CHESELDYNE
1640–1708

Kenelm Cheseldyne was the second son of Kenelm Cheseldyne, an Anglican minister and vicar of Blaxham in Lincolnshire. The son was educated in England where he also practiced law for some years. After the death of his father and the sale of the family's manor lands in 1667, he came to Maryland.[1]

Cheseldyne settled originally on the Eastern Shore in 1669 and there married Bridget Faulkner. She evidently did not live very long. By 1677 he had married Mary Gerard, daughter of the wealthy Catholic Thomas Gerard. Cheseldyne himself had patented 1,300 acres by 1689 and with his wife's inheritance was quite a prosperous resident of St. Mary's, where he had moved and settled.[2]

Cheseldyne was one of the most active attorneys in the colony. He became Lord Baltimore's attorney general in 1676, but lost that post in 1681.[3] Perhaps Cheseldyne lost the proprietor's favor because of family involvement in the abortive coup of that year; however, he was later appointed a justice in 1686. He represented St. Mary's City as a burgess in 1676–82 and 1686–88, serving as speaker in the latter assembly.[4]

With his brothers-in-law Coode and Blakiston, Cheseldyne was an active opponent of the proprietor in the late 1680's, and he was a prominent figure in the revolution. He accompanied

[5] Wills 7, ff. 190–92; I&A 13B, ff. 28–30, 108; I&A 15, f. 325.

---

[1] Edwin W. Beitzell, "The Cheseldine Family" (revised ms., Washington, D.C., 1949; copy in MHS).

[2] *Ibid.*; Patents 14, ff. 240, 477; 18, f. 231; 19, f. 375.

[3] *Md. Archives*, LXVIII, xiii; *HLP*, 133.

[4] *Md. Archives*, VII, 6; XIII, 163; V, 462.

Coode to England in 1690 and strangely plays a secondary role thereafter. He was not appointed to the first royal council.[5] He did continue to sit in the assembly (1692–97 and 1701–4), and served as its speaker in 1692–93 and 1696–97. His legal training and expertise led to his appointment as commissary general in 1693, but he was dismissed temporarily for drunkenness and negligence in 1697. During much of this period he was also chief justice of St. Mary's County and enjoyed a brief appointment to the Provincial Court in 1708, the year of his death. Cheseldyne finally obtained appointment to the council on March 11, 1702/03. He took his oaths in 1704 and sat until his death.[6]

Cheseldyne's son, also named Kenelm, was sheriff of St. Mary's County in 1709–11 and sat as a burgess for one term in 1712–14. A personal scandal and repercussions of a verbal attack on the restored proprietor probably account for his failure to be re-elected to the assembly. He died in 1718. The daughters of the elder Cheseldyne all married into prominent local families. Two sons-in-law, Thomas Truman Greenfield and Henry Peregrine Jowles, also sat as burgesses for the county.[7]

Cheseldyne left an estate of 1,308 acres, and personalty valued at £259.9.6,[8] including twelve slaves.

GILBERT CLARKE
c. 1654–1700

Gilbert Clarke was one of only three native Marylanders and the only third-generation colonist to sit in the Associators'

[5] See pp. 167–68 above.

[6] "Royal Period," *passim*, especially 356, 357, 359; *HLP*, 130; *Md. Archives*, XX, 190, 465; XXII, 159; XXIII, 111, 128; Prov. Ct. Judg., WT no. 3, 548; PL no. 2, 129, 252; *Cal. S. P., Col., 1702–3*, no. 434. Cheseldyne was also a vestryman (*Md. Archives*, XXIII, 17).

[7] Prov. Ct. Judg., PL no. 3, f. 18 and *passim;* VD no. 1, f. 619; VD no. 2, f. 367; Wills 14, f. 728; *Md. Archives*, XXIX, 125.

[8] Wills 12A, f. 307; Rent Roll 44, f. 33; I&A 29, ff. 139–41.

Convention. He was a grandson of Robert Clarke, a Catholic who immigrated in 1637 and became a Provincial clerk, surveyor, and even briefly a member of the council, before dying in 1664 as a relatively poor man. Gilbert's father, John Clarke, never held high office, and although he accumulated at one time about 1,500 acres, he had lost it by the time he died in 1698.[1]

Some uncertainty exists over Gilbert Clarke's birthdate. A deposition taken in 1692 gave his age as thirty-eight, while another deposition taken in 1684 identified him as being twenty-seven. In that year, he was termed "Gilbert Clarke of St. Mary's County gentl." It is known that he also held land in other counties, particularly Charles, where he had patented 828 acres by 1689.[2]

Clarke served as a messenger for the council in the 1680's and was a councilman of St. Mary's City in 1685. The following year he was convicted of perjury, which probably affected his political career.[3] He did not hold any office again until after the revolution. His name was frequently mentioned, however, in connection with rumors of a Catholic-Indian conspiracy in 1689. His reward for services rendered during the overthrow was appointment as sheriff of Charles County. As a leading member of the Associators' Convention, he also sat on the powerful Committee of Secrecy and the committee which assessed the levy.[4]

Clarke lost his sheriff's commission in 1691 under charges of extortion, for which he was later found guilty. He held no office

[1] Patents 2, f. 425; 8, f. 420; 9, f. 228; *HLP*, 135, 171; *Md. Archives*, I, 276, 279; III, 299–300, 342; Test. Pro. 1E, 74–75; Wills 2, f. 169; 6, f. 177; Ch. Ct. and Land Rec. A no. 1, ff. 189–90; B no. 1, ff. 205–6; D no. 1, ff. 14–15; I No. 1, ff. 225–26.

[2] *Md. Archives*, VIII, 434; XVII, 266, 306; Rent Roll 8, f. 110; Prov. Ct. Judg., WRC no. 1, ff. 337–39; see also Baltimore County Rent Roll, 1658–23, 225 (Calvert Papers, mss., MHS).

[3] *Md. Archives*, XVII, 266, 410, 418; Prov. Ct. Judg., TG, ff. 76–78. Clarke was found guilty of changing figures on a writ and a failure to execute properly his oath of office.

[4] *Md. Archives*, VIII, 87, 93–94, 160–61; XIII, 243, 247.

thereafter, except service in the post of vestryman for Nanjemy parish in Charles County.[5]

Clarke died in late 1700. He left a personal estate of £84.5.0, including four servants. Clarke apparently had no will, and his land ownings in 1700 are uncertain.[6]

JOHN COODE
1648–1708/09

John Coode had perhaps the most colorful and tempestuous career of any figure in Maryland's history. The 1689 revolution, sometimes known as Coode's Rebellion, was but one of several uprisings in which he played a significant role.

Coode was born at Penryn, Cornwall, in 1648. The son of an attorney, Coode matriculated at Exeter College, Oxford, at the age of sixteen. He was later ordained a deacon and returned to Penryn, where he was "turned out" of the ministry sometime before his immigration to Maryland. Coode served briefly as a minister in the colony, but clearly he was not suited by religious beliefs or temperament for the clerical profession.[1]

Coode was in Maryland by the spring of 1672, and he quickly assumed the title and role of a colonial "Gent." By the fall of 1674, he had married Susanna Slye, a wealthy forty-year-old widow; Coode was about twenty-four years of age at the time.

[5] Prov. Ct. Judg., DSC, ff. 150–52; *Md. Archives*, XX, 543. Clarke was fined 2,500 pounds of tobacco in 1697, one of the rare occasions his name appears in the records after 1691. (CO5/749/I, no. 19).

[6] I&A 20, ff. 171, 261–62.

---

[1] Nelson Waite Rightmyer, *Maryland's Established Church* (Lebanon, Pa., 1956), 174; *Md. Archives*, XIX, 469, 479; Chancery Records, PC, f. 548; Rev. Columba J. Devlin, "John Coode and the Maryland Revolution of 1689" (M.A. thesis, Catholic University, 1952), 5–15. The most complete account of Coode's life is found in Gene Perkins Thornton, "The Life and Opinions of Captain John Coode, Gentleman" (M.A. thesis, Columbia University, 1953).

Mrs. Coode was the daughter of Thomas Gerard, a prominent Catholic and former councillor. Coode immediately became involved in extensive litigation over her property.[2] The wealth and status which this marriage conferred upon Coode led to his appointment as a militia captain in 1676 and his election that year to the assembly. By 1677 he was a quorum justice of St. Mary's County and had probably been on the commission before that date.[3]

Coode was never able to function very cooperatively and effectively within governments. His first involvement with opposition came in the so-called rebellion of 1681. His precise role in that is uncertain, but it completely estranged him from the proprietary regime. Coode was temporarily deprived of his seat in the assembly, but he did return to represent St. Mary's in 1682. He held no other public office until his election as a burgess in 1688, but throughout this period he was a leading opponent of Lord Baltimore and his Catholic government. He later boasted that he led the revolution in 1689 as a matter of revenge.[4]

Coode was clearly the military leader of the revolt. He styled himself commander in chief, although he had no special powers outside St. Mary's County until his appointment in the spring of 1690 as leader of the Grand Committee of Twenty. Later that summer he sailed for England as agent for the Associators. While defending the revolt, Coode registered an unfavorable impression on English officials. Despite Governor Copley's initial recommendation, Coode did not receive an appointment to the council.[5]

[2] *Md. Archives*, LXV, xxxviii, 393–94, 395–96, 399–400, 409–11; Edwin W. Beitzell, "Thomas Gerard and His Sons-in-Law," *MHM*, XLVI (1951), 189–206.

[3] *Md. Archives*, XV, 119, 153, 255, 388–92, 399; VII, 112–13, 115–16, 135–36, 137–38, 139; V, 332.

[4] *Ibid.*, XV, 388–92, 399, 407; V, 281, 301, 312–34; VIII, 210.

[5] *Ibid.*, XIII, 241–47; VIII, 195–96, 199, 280; William Blathwayt to Lionel Copley, Feb. 28, 1692/93, Blathwayt Papers, XVIII, Research Library, Colonial Williamsburg, Inc.

Coode returned to Maryland in 1692 without any civil office and quite hostile toward his former colleague Nehemiah Blakiston, now the principal figure in the government after Copley. Coode promptly began circulating rumors about Copley's recall and joined forces in the fall of 1692 with Secretary Thomas Lawrence, who was at battle with the governor.[6] After Copley's death and the arrival of Francis Nicholson as governor in 1694, Coode's support of Lawrence was rewarded with appointments as sheriff of St. Mary's and lieutenant colonel of the militia. The freeholders elected him to the assembly in 1696.[7]

Once again, Coode's instincts of opposition arose. He sufficiently alienated Nicholson that the governor revoked Coode's militia commission and successfully sought his expulsion from both the assembly and the parish vestry. Coode's unseemly behavior and blasphemy soon erupted into more outright opposition to the government. Finally he went into exile in Virginia to avoid arrest. Nicholson instituted legal proceedings against him.[8]

Upon Nathaniel Blakiston's assumption of the governorship, Coode returned to Maryland and stood trial. The Provincial Court found him guilty of blasphemy but innocent of the charges of rebellion. Blakiston pardoned Coode "upon Consideration of his Service done in the Revolution." When Coode then represented himself as "very poor" and unable to pay his fines, Blakiston also remitted them.[9]

Coode returned once again to the political arena in 1708, this time to do battle with yet another governor, John Seymour. St. Mary's County elected Coode to the assembly that convened in September 1708, but the lower house ruled he had been unduly elected and brought charges against his son William who had

[6] *Randolph Letters*, VII, 393–94, 452; Copley to Blathwayt, June 20, 1692, Blathwayt Papers, XVIII.

[7] *Md. Archives*, XX, 106, 113, 130; XIX, 435.

[8] *Ibid.*, XX, 489–94, 511, 514, 515, 540, 561–62, 564–65, 579, 583.

[9] *Ibid.*, XXV, 58, 75, 80, 103; Prov. Ct. Judg., WT no. 3, ff. 7, 104–6, 208–13.

conducted the election as sheriff. The freeholders then re-elected Coode. The lower house now ruled Coode was ineligible to be a burgess, since he had once been in holy orders.[10]

Coode died within three months. His will did not list his land-holdings, but his personal estate, including seven slaves, was valued at £259.13.8.[11]

John Coode, Jr., and William Coode both served as sheriff of St. Mary's County during the period 1704–1709, but they never held office on the provincial level.[12]

THOMAS COOKE
?–1692/93

Thomas Cooke belonged to a prominent mercantile family. He was almost certainly the son of Sir Andrew Cooke, the London merchant who patented over 1,000 acres in 1664 and returned to England shortly thereafter.[1] Thomas Cooke of London, merchant, had some dealings with the colony before he settled in Dorchester County temporarily in 1679. That year he claimed headrights for transporting twelve persons.[2] The following year, he returned to London; Cooke gave his brother Edward power of attorney, particularly to oversee his lands on the Blackwater River. Cooke had purchased these tracts in March of 1676/77. While in England, he arranged to lease out part of this land for 1,000 years.[3]

[10] *Md. Archives*, XXVII, 210, 211, 266, 270, 271, 333. This had also been the grounds for Coode's dismissal from the assembly in 1696.

[11] Wills 12A, ff. 341–42; I&A 29, ff. 241–43.

[12] CO5/716/I, no. 20iii and CO5/716/IV, no. 69iii; *Md. Archives*, XXVII, 333; Prov. Ct. Judg., PL no. 2, f. 422.

---

[1] Patents 7, ff. 520–22, 524. For the probable link between Andrew Cooke and the brothers Thomas and Edward Cooke, see Wills 8, ff. 119; 11, f. 404.

[2] Patents WC#2, ff. 86–87. Cooke immediately signed over these rights to Samuel Cooper.

[3] Dor. Land Rec., O no. 4, ff. 7, 9, 181–83; O no. 6, f. 75.

Apparently Cooke had returned to Dorchester by 1683 and settled there permanently. He lived in the town of Cambridge, where he also operated an ordinary. Cooke served at least briefly as county clerk in May 1686 following the illness of the incumbent. By that spring he had also married the daughter of Dr. John Brooke, one of the most influential men in the county and soon to be a fellow Associator.[4]

Cooke's first public office came with his election to the Associators' Convention. He was not appointed to any county office in the September ordinance, probably by choice. He continued to operate his ordinary and he was also active in 1690 as an attorney, an occupation for which a judicial appointment would have rendered him ineligible. In September of 1691, however, he became sheriff of the county, replacing Edward Pindar. Cooke continued in that post after the arrival of Governor Copley.[5]

Cooke died in the winter of 1692/93. He left an estate of at least 500 acres, a house in Cambridge, and personalty valued at £208.7.1, including two slaves and a servant. He was survived by his wife and four infant children.[6]

JOHN COURTS
1655/56–1702/03

John Courts, one of three native Marylanders in the Associators' Convention, was the son of John and Margaret Courts. In 1639, the father had bought his time of service from Fulke Brent, and he similarly purchased his wife's time of service in 1649.[1]

Their son John, born in February of 1655/56, married Charity Henley, the daughter of a Charles County burgess and justice.

---

[4] *Md. Archives*, LXX, 399; Dor. Land Rec., O no. 4½, f. 113; O no. 1, f. 148; O no. 4, ff. 165, 168; *HLP*, 154. See also Brooke's biography.

[5] CO5/719/I, no. 1; Dor. Land Rec., O no. 4½, ff. 23, 108, 113, 114; O no. 4, ff. 108, 110, 130.

[6] Wills 2, ff. 305–7; I&A 13B, ff. 75–76; 20, ff. 224–25.

---

[1] Patents ABH, ff. 23, 44.

Courts earned his livelihood as a planter and owned approximately 1,000 acres in 1689. He was also identified a few years later by Edward Randolph as a "wheelwright."[2]

Courts's first public office came with his appointment as a justice in 1685. He was one of the initial residents of the lower Western Shore to pass the word of a conspiracy against the Protestants in 1689 and became an early adherent of the rebels. The September convention made him a militia captain. Soon thereafter he sat on the Grand Committee of Twenty and became coroner of Charles County.[3]

In 1692 Courts took his oath as one of the original royal councillors. He remained on the council until his death, and he also served as a vestryman during this period.[4]

Courts's brother-in-law, James Keech, was also an Associator. One of his sons, also named John Courts, was later a prominent burgess and militia officer.[5]

John Courts died in March 1702/03. He left an estate of 2,260 acres and £1,815.11.2, including six servants and thirty slaves. He was survived by four sons, two daughters, and his widow.[6]

THOMAS DAVIS

Thomas Davis of Kent County is the least known of the Associators. Men with this not uncommon name are mentioned in the records of various counties, but there is no evidence linking them with the Kent County Associator.

[2] Ch. Ct. and Land Rec., P no. 1, f. 205. James Wade Emison, "Supplement (1962) to the Emison Families, Revised (1954)," 216, copy in MHS; Rent Roll 8, nos. 80, 81, 90, 91, 116, 119; *Randolph Letters*, VII, 377.

[3] *Md. Archives*, XVII, 380; VIII, 87, 93, 199; XIII, 243; Ch. Ct. and Land Rec., R no. 1, f. 275.

[4] *Md. Archives*, VIII, 305; XXIII, 19; Wills 11, ff. 445–50.

[5] See Keech's biography; *Md. Archives*, XXV and XXVI, *passim*; Emison, "Supplement," 266.

[6] Wills 11, ff. 447–50.

The only indisputable information on his background is that he sat as foreman of the Kent grand jury in November of 1686.[1] Davis's activities after the revolutionary period are as mysterious as before that time.

Davis signed the petition to the crown on September 4, 1689. There is no evidence of any further attendance at the convention or of any officeholding on the county level.[2]

No probate records survive in Maryland.

JOHN EDMUNDSON
?–1697

John Edmundson came to Maryland by 1658 as the servant of Captain John Horne, a merchant of London. His migration was by way of Barbados; his connections both there and in England became very important in the extensive mercantile enterprises he soon undertook. Edmundson became a merchant, shipbuilder, realtor, and perhaps the largest land speculator on the Eastern Shore. His Maryland patents totaled at least 40,000 acres and he acquired over 27,000 acres in lower Pennsylvania (now Delaware). Evidently, he built up some of his capital through patenting and selling land.[1]

Edmundson married the daughter of William Parker, a prominent merchant who had helped to found Anne Arundel County before returning to England. The Edmundson family were Quakers, a fact which probably accounts for his not sitting on the county bench during the proprietary period. However, he did serve on the Provincial Court during the reign of the Associators.[2]

[1] Kent Ct. Pro., I, f. 213.
[2] C05/719/I, no. 1.

---

[1] Frank B. Edmundson and Emerson B. Roberts, "John Edmundson—Large Merchant of Tred Haven Creek," *MHM*, L (1955), 219–223.
[2] *Ibid.*, 224; Charles Stein, *A History of Calvert County, Maryland*

Talbot County elected Edmundson to the assembly for the sessions of 1676 to 1682, and again from 1686 to 1688. He became quite active during the period of the revolution, and represented the county on the Grand Committee.[3]

In 1692, when Governor Copley insisted upon oaths rather than affirmations from the burgesses, Edmundson was denied his seat as a delegate. His exclusion created a disturbance in Talbot County. Two years later, during Francis Nicholson's tenure as governor, the county again elected Edmundson, but his continued refusal to take the oath prevented his seating.[4]

Edmundson died in late 1697. He was survived by his wife, four sons, and a daughter. The sons did not enter political life. Edmundson's estate comprised over 5,650 acres and £387.13.3, including twelve slaves.[5]

NICHOLAS GASSAWAY
1634–1691/92

Nicholas Gassaway, son of Thomas Gassaway and Ann Collingwood, was born in London in 1634. Young Gassaway came to Maryland in 1649 or 1650 as a servant of Richard Ewing. He settled on the South River, where he became one of the first merchants in the area and owner of over 1,320 acres by 1689.[1]

(Baltimore, 1960), 299–300; Prov. Ct. Judg., DSC, f. 1. See also Kenneth Carroll, "Talbot County Quakerism in the Colonial Period," *MHM*, LIII (1958) 326–70, and the Minutes of the Third Haven Monthly Meeting (microfilm, Maryland Hall of Records).

[3] *Md. Archives*, II, 478; VII, 123; VIII, 159, 199, 242; Talb. Judg., 1682–85, f. 214.

[4] *Md. Archives*, XIII, 254, 257, 352, 354, 361; XX, 126–28; Talb. Land Rec., NN no. 6, f. 32b (rear).

[5] Talb. Wills, box 8, folder 8, written Oct. 9, 1697, and proved March 7, 1697/98; I&A 16, ff. 26–28, 142–44.

---

[1] Harry Wright Newman, *Anne Arundel Gentry*, rev. ed. (Annapolis, 1970), 148–51; Patents AB&H, f. 174; I&A 11A, ff. 36–37. The dispute on the immigration date reflects a conflict between the headright warrant and Gassaway's later testimony (Patents 4, f. 109; 5, f. 467).

Gassaway's first wife remains unidentified, but by 1672 he had married the daughter of Captain Thomas Besson. He became a justice of Anne Arundel County in 1679 and continued on the bench until his death. In the county militia, he was a captain by 1679, a major by 1685, and was termed "a chief militia officer" in 1687.[2]

Nothing is known about Gassaway's initial response to the revolution. Anne Arundel had no delegates at the first convention. Nonetheless, he was continued as a justice and a militia officer, perhaps in an effort to win his allegiance. He became one of the county's two delegates on the Grand Committee, but it is quite possible he did not serve as an Associator until after the arrival of the royal letter in May 1690. He subsequently received appointment to the Provincial Court and became a colonel.[3]

When Gassaway died in January of 1691/92, he left a large estate consisting of £1,144.14.7½ (including twenty Negroes), 109,898 pounds of tobacco, and well over 1,080 acres of land.[4]

His son Nicholas succeeded to the offices of justice and militia captain, but never rose higher. His son Thomas served as sheriff of Anne Arundel County. None of the other children attained public prominence.[5]

CHRISTOPHER GIST
?–1690/91

No record survives of Christopher Gist's early years. He immigrated to Maryland with his wife by 1679. She was the sister

[2] Newman, *Anne Arundel Gentry*, 149; *Md. Archives*, XV, 253, 323–34; XVII, 379; V, 462, 554; Prov. Ct. Judg., DSA, f. 179.

[3] *Md. Archives*, XIII, 242; VIII, 199, 242.

[4] I&A 11A, ff. 36–43; Wills 2, ff. 228–31.

[5] *Md. Archives*, XX, 107, 138; Newman, *Anne Arundel Gentry*, 152–86.

of Richard Cromwell, with whom Gist purchased several tracts of land in Baltimore County in the 1680's.[1]

Gist was a planter. He served frequently on the county jury in the mid-1680's but held no public office other than overseer prior to the revolution. The convention made him a justice of Baltimore County.[2]

Gist's will was written on February 17, 1690/91, and was proved less than a month later. His infant son Richard later became a justice and burgess.[3]

Gist possessed 581 acres of land at his death.[4] No record of his personal estate survives.

NICHOLAS GREENBERRY
1627–1697

Nicholas Greenberry's exact English origins are obscure, but he obviously had some financial backing. When he came to Maryland in 1674, he brought his wife, two children, and three servants; this entitled him to the rights to 350 acres. In 1680 he purchased a plantation of 450 acres and added another 250 acres in 1685.[1]

Greenberry became a justice of Anne Arundel in 1686. He was titled "Capt. Nicholas Greenberry" in the last proprietary commission, but the Associators' commission in 1689 described him as a militia replacement.[2]

---

[1] Jean Muir and Maxwell Jay Dorsey, *Christopher Gist of Maryland and Some of His Descendants, 1679–1957* (Urbana, Ill., 1958), 1.

[2] Balt. Ct. Pro., D, ff. 49, 359; *Md. Archives*, XIII, 243; Dorseys *Christopher Gist*, 1.

[3] Balt. Land Rec., RM no. HS, f. 331; Dorseys, *Christopher Gist*, 1.

[4] Patents 22, f. 3; Balt. Land Rec., RM no. HS, ff. 279–81; IR no. AM, ff. 179, 193–95.

---

[1] Henry Ridgely Evans, *Founders of the Colonial Families of Ridgely, Dorsey and Greenberry of Maryland* (Washington, D.C., 1935), 41; Patents 20, f. 400; NS#B, f. 513. Edward Randolph referred to Greenberry as a "Highwayman in England" (*Randolph Letters*, VII, 377).

[2] *Md. Archives*, V, 462; XIII, 242.

Like Nicholas Gassaway, Greenberry may not have initially supported the revolution. He was recorded as one of "his Ldshipps justices" on December 14, 1689. It is uncertain whether he and the other Anne Arundel delegates first sat in April or in September of 1690, but he was appointed to the Grand Committee, which was designated at the April session. He served on the Provincial Court upon its reconstitution in 1691, by which time he was also a major.[3]

Greenberry received appointment to the first royal council. After the death of Lionel Copley, he served as president of the council and Maryland's chief executive for a brief period (October 2, 1693–May 1, 1694).[4] Before his death in December 1697, Greenberry also occupied the offices of chancellor and judge of the Admiralty Court and militia colonel.[5]

His son Charles was a burgess for Anne Arundel from 1701/02 until his promotion to the council in 1709. Greenberry's three daughters married prominent men. John Hammond was a burgess and councillor; Robert Goldsborough served Talbot County in the assembly (1704–7) and became chief justice of the Provincial Court (1719–40); Henry Ridgely, wealthy son of a burgess and militia colonel, died early, but his son Henry became a justice and militia colonel and a very large landowner.[6]

Greenberry's landholdings were not listed in his will, but his personal estate was appraised at £1,045.15.3½, including one servant, six slaves, and £363.12.4½ in cash in possession of London merchants.[7]

[3] AA Land Rec., IH no. 2, f. 53; *Md. Archives*, VIII, 199, 242.

[4] "Royal Period," 115–27.

[5] *Md. Archives*, XX, 110; Wills 7, ff. 314–15.

[6] "Royal Period," 354, 371; Hester Dorsey Richardson, *Sidelights on Maryland History*, 2 vols. (Baltimore, 1913), II, 330–39; "County Government," appendix, 351–53.

[7] Wills 7, ff. 314–15; I&A 17, ff. 54–60; 19, f. 64; 20, ff. 244–46; 21, ff. 327–28. Greenberry probably owned slightly more than 600 acres.

HANS HANSON
c. 1647–1703/04

Hans Hanson was born on Tinicum Island, New Sweden, of Swedish parents in approximately 1647. Andrew Hanson, a small planter with no land, had migrated to the Delaware Bay region from Sweden and he later moved to Maryland. Upon his death in 1655, the mother apprenticed the young Hans Hanson to Joseph Wickes of Kent County. He was to serve until age twenty-one. In 1671, Hanson applied to the Maryland assembly for naturalization. Eight years later, he purchased from Charles Vaughan the estate "Kimbolton," where he resided thereafter. It was at this time he married Martha Wells Ward.[1]

Hanson was a planter, and at his death he also owned a grist-mill. His first county office came in 1685 with appointment as a Kent County justice of the peace. The Associators promoted him to justice of the quorum and he continued in that capacity to 1697. He later sat on the Cecil bench.[2]

Hanson represented Kent County in the assembly from 1692 to 1697, and then was a burgess for Cecil County from 1697/98 to 1700. He was a member of the first vestry for St. Paul's parish. A militia captain in 1693, he eventually rose to the rank of colonel.[3]

Hanson died in 1703/04 and left an estate of 1,175 acres and personalty inventoried at £1,066.14.1. Although none of his sons attained his stature, his children married into the prominent Codd, Pearce, and Hynson families.[4]

[1] George Hanson, *Old Kent: The Eastern Shore of Maryland* (Baltimore, 1876), 159; *Md. Archives*, II, 319, 331; LIV, 28–29; St. Paul's Parish Register, f. 31.

[2] Wills 3, ff. 264–68; *Md. Archives*, III, 241; XVII, 379; XXV, 125; Kent Ct. Pro., I, ff. 402–3, 481–82, 592–94, 758–59.

[3] *Md. Archives*, VIII, 363; XIX, 555; XXII, 77; St. Paul's Vestry Minutes 1693–1726, f. 1; Kent Ct. Pro., I, ff. 406, 483.

[4] Hanson, *Old Kent*, 159, 163; Wills 3, ff. 264–68; Cecil Wills AA#1, 121–24; I&A 25, f. 86.

WILLIAM HARRIS
c. 1644–1712

Much of William Harris's early history remains unknown. He was born in approximately 1644, according to a deposition he swore in 1684. No precise arrival date in Maryland can be determined. He may be the William Harris "late of St. Maryes County" involved in a Provincial Court suit in 1675. Apparently this individual sat as a juror in 1672.[1]

William Harris the Associator was definitely in Kent County by 1674. He began actively patenting land in the early 1680's, accumulating 1,900 acres by 1689. He also became a partner with Hans Hanson in a water mill. In 1685, and probably earlier, Harris was engaged in an active legal practice in the Kent court. He delayed slightly his qualifying as a justice in September 1686 in order to complete his current cases. Harris returned briefly to England in 1687, perhaps on business matters. It appears he served as attorney for some English merchants.[2]

Harris won election to the assembly in 1686. Kent County returned him to the Associators' Convention, and by 1690 he was also sitting on the Grand Committee of Twenty. He continued as justice of Kent.[3]

During the royal period, Harris represented first Kent (1692–94) and then Cecil (1697/98–1704) in the assembly; he served as justice in Cecil from 1693 to 1702. He was a vestryman and evidently acquired a militia office as well, for a 1701 reference identifies him as "Maj. Wm. Harris."[4]

[1] *Md. Archives*, XVII, 291; LXV, 47–48, 627.

[2] *Ibid.*, LIV, 331–32; Patents NS#2, ff. 14, 231; IB&IL#C, ff. 46, 313; NS#B, f. 390; CB#2, f. 416; SD#A, f. 202; Kent Ct. Pro., I, ff. 87–92, 116, 157–58, 194, 207, 271, 278, 352. There is a gap in the Kent records for the early 1680's.

[3] *Md. Archives*, X, 495; VIII, 184, 199; XIII, 241.

[4] *Ibid.*, 350; XXIII, 20, 129, 401; XXV, 125; XXII, 77; XXIV, 159; Kent Ct. Pro., ID no. 2, ff. 2, 34; Cecil Judg., 1692–98, ff. 78, 271, 317; 1698–1700, ff. 1, 31.

Harris was recommended for a seat on the council in 1691, 1702, and 1707, but he was never appointed. Although he lived until 1712, he was not active politically after 1704. His son James was a burgess, sheriff, and justice for Kent, and his daughters married into the prominent Tilden and Hynson families.[5]

Harris's will does not list his landholdings, but his personal estate was valued at £960.19.8¾.[6]

HENRY HAWKINS
?–1699

Henry Hawkins claimed land rights in 1666 for transporting himself, his wife, and his son to Maryland. He immediately assigned those rights to Thomas Layne. Hawkins settled in Charles County. By 1682 his first wife had died, and he had married the widow of Francis Wyne.[1]

Hawkins was both a planter and a tanner. He had patented at least 1,400 acres by the eve of the revolution.[2] His economic prosperity brought political advancement as well. Beginning as constable of his hundred in 1670/71, Hawkins became a justice of the peace by 1680 and served on the bench until his death.[3] He won election to the last proprietary assembly in 1688 and continued to represent Charles County in the assembly for the next eleven years. After establishment of the Anglican church,

[5] *Md. Archives*, VIII, 284; XXIV, 218; CO5/324/48, f. 6; Wills 13, ff. 488–90; Kent Ct. Pro., 1707–09, ff. 1, 176; JS no. W, f. 51; Christopher Johnston, "Hynson Family," *MHM*, XVIII (1923), 186–92; "Notes," *MHM*, I (1906) 75.

[6] Wills 13, ff. 488–90; Cecil County Original Inventory, box 2, folder 62.

[1] Patents 9, f. 307; I&A 8, ff. 56, 269–70. She may have been a Holland; a son was later named Henry Holland Hawkins.

[2] *Md. Archives*, LX, 145; Patents NS#2, ff. 293, 470; NS#B, ff. 591, 596.

[3] *Md. Archives*, LX, xix; XV, 327; XVII, 380; VIII, 8, 565; XX, 466; XXIII, 128, 469; Ch. Ct. and Land Rec., S no. 1, f. 1; V no. 1, ff. 205–6.

he sat as chief vestryman of his parish. During the royal period Hawkins also acquired the rank of captain in the militia.[4]

Hawkins did not lend active support to the Associators until after the arrival of the royal letter of approval in May of 1690. He apparently did not attend either the second or third sessions of the convention, although he was present at both sessions in 1691. Like his fellow delegate and justice John Stone, Hawkins did not participate in Charles County court proceedings during the period from September 1689 to June 1690. His reservations about serving, as well as Stone's, help account for the rapid rise of John Courts and John Addison.[5]

Hawkins died in 1699. He bequeathed approximately 2,800 acres and a personal estate valued at £327.18.8.[6]

SAMUEL HOPKINS
?–1711/12

Samuel Hopkins migrated to Maryland with his wife and four children in 1680. Nothing is known about his origins or his life prior to that date.[1]

In all probability, Hopkins was a factor, for he served as an attorney for a London mariner in 1690. At his death, he left an estate of 1,450 acres and modest personal property.[2]

Hopkins was a member of the active band of Presbyterians in Somerset County. His sole public office prior to the revolution was a justiceship, which he held from 1687 until 1700/01. He never sat again in the assembly after the Associators' regime, but

[4] *Md. Archives*, XIII, 157, 243; XX, 130; XXIII, 19; VIII, 363; XIX, 555; XXII, 77, 368; Ch. Ct. and Land Rec., R no. 1, f. 502.
[5] Ch. Ct. and Land Rec., R no. 1, ff. 129, 332; P no. 1, f. 185; Q no. 1, f. 8
[6] Wills 6, f. 311; Charles Inv. 1677–1711, ff. 120–23.

[1] Patents, WC#2, f. 321.
[2] Som. Jud. Rec., AW, f. 21; Wills 13, ff. 417–30. £ 77.10.17, including two Negroes, comprised his personal estate (I&A, 33B, ff. 203–4).

he did serve as a deputy commissary from 1692 to 1699. Hopkins's absence from public life after 1701 was undoubtedly a result of his indictment in 1700 for extortion and malfeasance while serving as deputy commissary in 1694 and 1695. The case was "quasht" in 1701 on a technicality.[3]

Hopkins was survived by his son Samuel who later represented the county in the assembly. One of his daughters married William Whittington, a burgess and later councillor.[4]

WILLIAM HOPKINS
?–1702

William Hopkins of Anne Arundel County came to Maryland as a servant before 1658 and patented his first land in 1659. He added several other tracts of land in the 1660's. Hopkins married the widow of Thomas Browne sometime after the latter's death in 1673. Hopkins's stepson, Thomas Browne, was married to the daughter of a fellow Associator, William Harris.[1]

Hopkins was foreman of the Provincial Court jury in 1678 and served jury duty frequently in the following decade. There is no record of any other officeholding before 1689. He became a justice in the ordinance of April 1690, perhaps as a result of his election and probable attendance at that session of the convention.[2]

Hopkins was not reappointed as a justice in 1692 and never served in that office after the beginning of royal government,

---

[3] Som. Jud. Rec., 1687–89, ff. 1–3; 1698–1701, ff. 409, 486, 500, 509; Wills 6, ff. 159 and *passim; Old Somerset*, 395, 468.

[4] *Md. Archives*, XXX, 97; Wills 13, ff. 417–20; *Old Somerset*, 379–81.

---

[1] Patents Q, f. 72; 4, f. 454; 7, ff. 272, 273. James Wade Emison, "Supplement (1962) to the Emison families, Revised (1954)," 164, copy in MHS; Wills 11, ff. 236–40.

[2] *Md. Archives*, LXVII, 346; Prov. Ct. Judg., DSA, f. 523; AA Land Rec., WH no. 4, f. 51.

perhaps because of his servant origin. He was literate. In his only proven office after 1692, Hopkins served as a vestryman.[3]

Hopkins died in the summer of 1702. Most of his holdings, over 1,000 acres, went to the children of John and Ann Jobson. She was probably his daughter; she was made executrix of the will and retained use of the home plantation. The personal estate was inventoried as £405.3.5 including two servants and one slave.[4]

CHARLES HUTCHINS
?–1700

Charles Hutchins immigrated to Maryland in 1672 and assigned his headright claim to Francis Hutchins, a Calvert County planter who may have been a relation.[1] Charles Hutchins was married and had a son in England, but he apparently came alone to the colony. From a suit arising over the settlement of Hutchins's estate, it appears that his wife Dorothy left him, had a bastard child, and then later lived with another man by whom she had several children. It is unclear whether the desertion came before or after Hutchins's departure from England.[2]

Hutchins settled in Dorchester County, where he earned his livelihood as both a planter and a carpenter. By 1689, he had patented or purchased approximately 5,000 acres. He remarried, but the precise identity of his second wife is uncertain.[3]

[3] Wills 11, ff. 212–14. For vestry service, see *Md. Archives*, XXIII, 20.
[4] Wills 11, ff. 236–40; I&A 23, ff. 152–56; 24, f. 52.

---

[1] Patents 4, f. 140. Francis Hutchins was a justice and burgess for Calvert and initially opposed the 1689 revolution (*Md. Archives*, VIII, 131–32).

[2] Test. Pro. 20, f. 43a. Dorothy Hutchins's suit for one-third of Charles Hutchins's estate was denied.

[3] Dor. Land Rec., O no. 1, f. 101; O no. 3, f. 62. In 1692, Edward Randolph called Hutchins a "broken London carpenter" (*Randolph Letters*, VII, 377). For Hutchins's land, see Patents 15, ff. 17, 117, 137; 20, ff. 333, 334; SD#A, ff. 83, 165, 169, 358, 365, 366; NS#2, ff. 460,

In 1674 Hutchins received an appointment to the county bench, and he served as a justice until 1692.[4] He rose rapidly in importance during the Associators' regime. By the spring of 1690 he was a colonel of the militia, although he had not been commissioned in the first ordinance. His militia office and his appointment to the first royal council are particularly surprising, because he was not a member of the Grand Committee of Twenty, and he was probably the only Dorchester delegate to the convention not related to John Brooke, the most powerful figure in the county.[5]

Hutchins sat on the council until his death in 1700. The bulk of his estate went to an infant grandson. His will did not list landholdings. His personal estate was inventoried at £1,058.8.7¼, including six servants and eighteen slaves.[6]

CHARLES JAMES
?–1698

Charles James, formerly a merchant in London, came to Maryland in 1661, bringing five other immigrants with him. By the end of the decade, he had married the daughter of Leonard Strong of Anne Arundel County.[1]

James continued his occupation as a merchant in Cecil County. He was soon filling several offices on the local level, serving as coroner of both Cecil and Baltimore counties in the 1670's. Appointed sheriff of Cecil in 1676, he was impeached after only five months for perjury, suborning to perjury, and false impris-

---

553; Dor. Land Rec., O no. 3, ff. 62, 144; O no. 5, f. 149. His new wife's first name was Ann (Dor. Land Rec., O no. 1, f. 101).

[4] *Md. Archives,* XV, 38, 254, 326; XVII, 381; XIII, 244.
[5] Dor. Land Rec., O no. 4½, ff. 9, 195; *Md. Archives,* VIII, 199, 271.
[6] Wills 11, ff. 134–36; I&A 20, ff. 218–24.

---

[1] Patents 4, f. 454; 14, f. 40; *Md. Archives,* LXV, 606; XLIX, 180.

onment. The lower house of the assembly subsequently ruled that he not be allowed to hold public office again.[2]

This injunction held until the revolution, when James stepped forth as a rebel and a person around whom opponents of the proprietor could gather. After election to the Associators' Convention, James was appointed a militia captain in September 1689 and a justice of the peace the following spring. During the ensuing months, he was involved in countless disputes with his fellow commissioners, disputes which eventually had to be handled by the convention and the Grand Committee. Due to his support of the revolution and his seat on the Grand Committee, James had some basis of power for contending with his opponents.[3]

With the initiation of royal government, James continued as a justice. He lost that position, however, upon the arrival of Governor Francis Nicholson, who sought to impose higher standards for justices and to disregard 1689 allegiances in making appointments. James held no public office thereafter.[4]

James died in 1698. No will survives, but the inventory of his personal estate totaled £213.14.9, including one servant and one slave.[5]

FRANCIS JENKINS
c. 1650–1710

Francis Jenkins, born in approximately 1650, did not come to Maryland until 1671. The following year he married the widow

[2] *Md. Archives*, LXVIII, 93; LXVII, xxxiii; LXV, 605–8; II, 480, 491, 496, 499; Cecil Judg., 1683–92, f. 117.

[3] *Md. Archives*, XIII, 244; Cecil Judg., 1683–92, ff. 84a–84b. See pp. 125–27 above.

[4] Cecil Judg., 1683–92, f. 121. On Nicholson's reforms, see "Royal Period," 131–200.

[5] Cecil County Original Inventory, box 1, folder 40; I&A 16, ff. 121–23; 23, ff. 98–99.

of James Weeden, a prominent merchant. Jenkins survived this wife, as well as a second. His third marriage was to the daughter of Major Robert King, a fellow Associator.[1]

Jenkins settled on the Pokomoke River in Somerset County. By 1689 he had patented 6,850 acres and was a prosperous merchant.[2]

Jenkins first received an appointment to the bench in 1676. He stepped down temporarily in 1683 to become sheriff, a post he held until the revolution. In 1689 Peter Sayer referred to "Little Jenkins" as the chief of the Somerset delegation to the convention. Interestingly, he did not become one of the county's representatives on the Grand Committee of Twenty.[3]

During the royal period, Jenkins continued on the county bench until his promotion to the Provincial Court in 1697. Two years later he replaced the deceased David Browne as the Somerset member of the royal council. Ordinarily, as senior member of the council he would have become president at the death of Governor John Seymour in 1709; however, he was denied that position by the other councillors who accused him of "not taking any notice of the Government after the Governor's Death."[4]

Jenkins was a vestryman in the newly established Anglican church, but he personally leaned strongly to the Presbyterian faith. There is circumstantial evidence that he was a member of Francis Makemie's congregation; in any case, he was the guardian of Makemie's children.[5]

Jenkins died in 1710 without a male heir. His estate exceeded 4,500 acres and £4,006.14.10, including twenty-two slaves.[6]

---

[1] *Old Somerset*, 373–74; Patents 16, f. 370.

[2] Patents 15, f. 491; 17, f. 89; 19, f. 623; NS#B, ff. 272, 277, 285, 504; NS#2, ff. 176, 196, 194, 173, 174; CB#2, f. 162; CB#3, ff. 65, 167.

[3] *Old Somerset*, 373; *Md. Archives*, V, 470, 545; XIII, 225; VIII, 22, 160, 199.

[4] Som. Jud. Rec., 1690–92, ff. 221–22; *Md. Archives*, XXIII, 126, 234, 256; XXII, 294; XXVII, 377–78.

[5] *Old Somerset*, 374; *Md. Archives*, XXIII, 22.

[6] Wills 13, f. 65; I&A 34, ff. 93, 95; 32B, f. 70; 32C, f. 156.

EDWARD JONES
?–1697

Edward Jones had migrated to Maryland and settled in Cecil County by 1661. Sometime thereafter, he married the widow of William Brockhurst.[1]

Little is known about the early years of his life in the colony. He did serve as a deputy surveyor of Cecil in the late 1670's. In 1685, Jones was appointed to the county bench, but he was dropped from the commission two years later due to "factious and turbulent spiritts." At the same time he lost his commission as coroner. Jones had the support of Colonel Henry Coursey, a powerful figure in the colony, and once again obtained an appointment as justice in October of 1688. He probably represented Cecil County in the last proprietary assembly.[2]

Jones's role in the revolutionary period is very unclear. He sat in the convention and on the Grand Committee, but he was also involved in the complicated problems plaguing Cecil County in ways which throw some doubt on his allegiances.[3]

Governor Copley, significantly, did not name Jones on his commission for Cecil in 1692, but he was sitting as a justice at Governor Nicholson's arrival in 1694. Nicholson also appointed Jones to the Provincial Court later that year, where he served until his death. Nicholson's pattern of appointments elsewhere suggests he returned to office men who had opposed the revolution and suffered political losses thereafter.[4]

Jones represented Cecil in the first royal assembly, and he was the county's only delegate not expelled from that body. Perhaps

[1] Patents 4, f. 578; I&A 8, f. 271.

[2] 1678/79 survey certificate, found in the Corner Collection, MHS; *Md. Archives*, XVII, 381; V, 545–46; VIII, 32–34, 49; XIII, 170.

[3] See pp. 123–27 above.

[4] *Md. Archives*, XX, 111, 137, 466. On Nicholson, see "Royal Period," 131–200.

his moderation left him unwelcome in both opposing camps. He served as a vestryman from 1693 until his death.[5]

Jones died in 1697. His heirs were a wife and daughter. Should they die, his will provided that his estate go to a free school for the use of poor children in his area. His personal estate totaled £420.9.8, including six slaves, plus 13,533 pounds of tobacco. His landed estate was not listed in the will.[6]

HENRY JOWLES
c. 1640–1700

Henry Jowles was the son of John Jowles Esq. of Newington Butts, Surrey. Young Jowles matriculated at Queen's College, Oxford, in 1656/57 and subsequently entered Gray's Inn for legal training in 1663. Designated "Henry Jowles of Chartham in Com. Kent, g'" he was also noted in 1663 as married to Rebecca, the daughter of John Allen of Chartham. Jowles had a son John and perhaps a daughter by this marriage.[1]

There is no evidence that Rebecca Jowles accompanied her husband to Maryland, where he was living in 1672. Perhaps she had died. By 1678, Jowles was married to the recent widow of William Groome, a Calvert County planter.[2]

It does not appear that Jowles ever practiced law in the colony. Nevertheless, the connection between the Henry Jowles

---

[5] *Md. Archives*, XIII, 351, 354, 359–60, 364–68; North Sassafras Parish Vestry Minutes 1693–1726, ff. 1–16 (microfilm in the Maryland Hall of Records.)

[6] Wills 7, f. 316; I&A 17, ff. 44–51.

---

[1] Joseph Foster, ed., *Alumni Oxoniensis: The Members of the University of Oxford, 1500–1714*, 4 vols. (London, 1891–92), II, 834; Sir George J. Armytage, ed., "A Visitation of the County of Kent," *The Publications of the Harleian Society*, LIV (London, 1906), 5, 89; Joseph Foster, ed., *The Register of Admissions to Gray's Inn, 1521–1889* (London, 1889), 295.

[2] *Md. Archives*, LXVI, 258; LXVIII, 52; LI, 224. Jowles claimed a headright only for himself (Patents WC#2, ff. 144–45).

of Gray's Inn and the Associator seems indisputable. Governor Francis Nicholson, for example, showed obvious respect for Jowles's education and legal knowledge in the 1690's; furthermore, Jowles's will makes mention of his son John "now living in England" and a daughter Rebecca.[3]

Jowles acquired at least 1,700 acres of land before 1689, in addition to the property which Sybil Groome brought to their marriage. He apparently earned his primary income as a large planter. Edward Randolph makes a reference to Jowles in 1692 as a "Surgeon," but there is no other evidence of this occupation.[4]

Lord Baltimore early showed his pleasure with Jowles by commissioning him a militia officer. He was a major by 1676 and a colonel three years later. Jowles served as a justice of Calvert County from at least 1679, and perhaps earlier, since he was named second in the commission of that year. He left the bench briefly from 1681 to 1685 when he became sheriff of Calvert.[5]

The freeholders elected Jowles in 1685 to sit in the last proprietary assembly. With the exception of Councillor Henry Darnall, Jowles was perhaps the most important figure in the county in 1689. It was he who led a group of disgruntled planters to St. Mary's City in March of 1688/89 to seek an explanation of the council's recent policies. During the later uprising, the council appealed to him with an offer to become commander in chief of the militia. Nonetheless, Jowles joined with the Associators and was very important in rallying support and providing leadership. He personally called and conducted the election in Calvert when other officials hesitated to comply. Jowles's name was usually listed immediately after Coode's on all important documents. He

---

[3] Carroll T. Bond, ed., *Proceedings of the Maryland Court of Appeals, 1695–1729* (Washington, D.C., 1933), xviii; Wills 6, ff. 400–402.

[4] Patents NS#A, ff. 58, 91; NS#B, f. 142; SD#A, f. 22. For the Groome lands, see Wills 5, ff. 191–93; for Randolph's reference, *Randolph Letters*, VII, 376.

[5] *Md. Archives*, XV, 99, 268, 327, 395; XVII, 117, 142, 379.

sat on the Grand Committee of Twenty and the Provincial Court during the interim regime.[6]

Jowles received an appointment to the first royal council, where he was soon at odds with Nehemiah Blakiston and Governor Lionel Copley. Jowles aligned himself with Secretary Thomas Lawrence, whom he may have known from his student days in England. That alignment brought Jowles's dismissal from the council and his militia office in November 1692. After Francis Nicholson became governor in 1694, Jowles was reinstated to the council and favored with considerable patronage. Among his new posts were the offices of chancellor and judge of the Admiralty Court.[7]

Jowles died in 1700. He left an estate of 2,100 acres, 22,220 pounds of tobacco, and personalty worth £426.14.10.[8]

His son Henry Peregrine Jowles, who married Kenelm Cheseldyne's daughter, represented St. Mary's County in the assembly from 1708 to 1714 and again from 1716 until his death in 1720.[9]

JAMES KEECH
c. 1651–1708

James Keech was born in approximately 1651 and had immigrated to Maryland by 1671 when he claimed his fifty-acre headright and patented "Trent Fort" in Calvert County with John Burroughs. At that time, Keech was identified as a planter. He later patented land in St. Mary's County also. Keech married

[6] *Ibid.*, XIII, 147; VIII, 107, 108, 117, 119–20, 154, 155–56, 199, 242; "Mariland's Grevances," 405.

[7] "Royal Period," 110–13, 143; *HLP* 123–24. Lawrence appointed Jowles clerk of Calvert County, and in turn Jowles supported Lawrence in the latter's struggles with Copley.

[8] Wills 6, ff. 400–402; I&A 20, ff. 214–15.

[9] *Md. Archives*, XXVII, 202, 267; XXIX, 125, 467; XXIII, 566; Wills 14, ff. 748–49.

Elizabeth Courts, the sister of John Courts of Charles County who also became an Associator.[1]

There is no evidence that Keech held any office before the revolution. He was an ensign in Coode's army in 1689 and was one of Henry Jowles's militiamen to be elected in the disputed Calvert County selection of delegates to the 1689 convention. That body made him a justice of Calvert, a position he maintained through at least 1694. Shortly thereafter, he moved to St. Mary's County where he appears as a justice of the quorum in 1696. Keech received an appointment as justice of the Provincial Court in 1698 and served there until 1704. He was also a vestryman during most of the early royal period.[2]

Keech died in 1708, leaving a widow and four children. His estate included 1,694 acres of land and personalty valued at £654.16.5. Keech's sons did not achieve his prominence.[3]

ROBERT KING I
?–1696

Robert King moved to Maryland in 1666 with his wife Susannah and daughter Mary. There is no information on his life prior to that year. King eventually settled in Somerset County where he purchased 300 acres in 1682. He was also a merchant and ran a store there. In 1692, Edward Randolph called King "a Scotch Irish Man" and a chief supporter of the Scots trade.[1]

King became a justice in 1687. He was evidently an active

[1] *Md. Archives*, VIII, 558–59; Patents 16, ff. 456–58; St. Mary's County Rent Rolls, 1639–1724, ff. 52, 55, 58, 59, 63, 66 (Calvert Papers, mss., MHS). Wills 12A, ff. 215–16; Ch. Ct. and Land Rec., P no. 1, f. 205.

[2] *Md. Archives*, VIII, 117, 474; XIII, 242; XX, 465; XXII, 18; XXIII, 121, 128; Prov. Ct. Judg., IL, f. 51; WT no. 3, ff. 1–3, 612–14; WT no. 4, ff. 3–4, 165–67; TL no. 3, ff. 258–59.

[3] Wills 12A, ff. 215–16; I&A 29, ff. 305–6; 35B, f. 41.

[1] Patents 9, f. 311; I&A 19, ff. 62–63; *Old Somerset*, 365; *Randolph Letters*, VII, 361, 378.

supporter of the revolution, for his career prospered significantly after the overthrow. The Associators' Convention continued him as a justice and also appointed him a militia captain and a naval officer. In the spring of 1690, King became an original member of the Grand Committee of Twenty. He was supposed to accompany Coode and Cheseldyne to London, but for unexplained reasons he apparently journeyed with them no farther than Plymouth. The following spring the convention named him to the reconstituted Provincial Court. By this time he had become "Major King."[2]

King continued to serve as a Provincial Court justice and as a naval officer until his death in 1696. His daughter Mary was married to Francis Jenkins, a fellow Associator, a burgess, and later a councillor.[3]

The Kings were Presbyterians. His personal estate was valued at his death in 1696 at £629.10. This included four servants, four slaves, a sloop, and one-eighteenth part of a brigantine.[4]

ROBERT MASON
1653–1700/01

Robert Mason is the only Associator, other than the Anne Arundel delegates, known to have been elected after the first session of the convention. He replaced either Cheseldyne, Coode, or Clarke and definitely sat in the convention in the spring of 1691.[1]

Mason immigrated to Maryland in 1677 with his wife Susan

[2] Som. Jud. Rec., 1687–89, ff. 1–3; *Md. Archives*, XIII, 244, 246; VIII, 195, 199, 242; *Randolph Letters*, VII, 379.

[3] Prov. Ct. Judg., DSC, ff. 38–40, 49–50, 323–25; TL no. 1, ff. 1, 120–21; *Md. Archives*, XX, 465–66; XXIII, 126. See biography of Jenkins.

[4] *Old Somerset*, 213; I&A 19, ff. 62–63.

---

[1] *Md. Archives*, VIII, 250. Mason may have been elected prior to the convention meeting in the fall of 1690.

and nine other people. He proceeded to establish himself as an attorney and merchant and eventually became part owner of at least two ships.[2]

Little is known of Mason's activities prior to 1689. He did not sign the St. Mary's County petition in November of that year, but he was undoubtedly warm to the cause of the rebels. The first session of the convention made him an alderman of St. Mary's City.[3]

Mason assumed a leading role shortly after joining the convention. He received appointment to the Provincial Court in 1691 and sat as a justice until he became sheriff of St. Mary's the following year. Following a two-year tenure in that office, he regained a seat on the Provincial Court bench as the second ranking justice in October of 1694. He resigned once again to become sheriff in 1696.[4]

Mason's two stints as county sheriff also necessitated resignations from the assembly. He served as a St. Mary's City burgess at the May-June 1692 session and represented the county from 1694 to July 1696. In addition, he served as treasurer of the Western Shore from October 1695 until 1698, when he was suspended both as treasurer and sheriff. A number of matters had drawn the ire of Governor Francis Nicholson. Mason had breached his oath as a vestryman, had committed illegal acts as treasurer, and was accused of conspiracy with John Coode, then in forced exile in Virginia. He lost his posts, but a confession of his role in the conspiracy brought only a fine for contempt. The assembly reinstated Mason as treasurer in 1699. He was again discharged eleven months later; on this occasion, however, it was for living too far from the new capital at Annapolis. Mason's tenure in several lucrative offices was probably a significant factor in his accumulation of a large fortune.[5]

² Patents 15, f. 433; *Md. Archives*, XX, 386; I&A 27, ff. 155–60, 169.

³ *Md. Archives*, VIII, 145–47; XIII, 245.

⁴*Ibid.*, VIII, 244, 306–7, 405; XX, 137, 466; Prov. Ct. Judg., DSC, ff. 38–40.

⁵ *Md. Archives*, XIII, 350; XIX, 4, 30, 127, 171, 320, 404; XX, 183;

Mason died in 1701. He left an estate of 1,923 acres, £1,303.-0.5, including nine slaves and four servants, plus 105,561 pounds of tobacco. Before the end of the royal period, his son Matthew served as a delegate from St. Mary's.[6]

MICHAEL MILLER
c. 1644–1700

Michael Miller was probably the son of the Michael Miller who attended St. John's College, Oxford, in 1635. The former migrated to Maryland and had settled in Kent County in 1670. He apparently married at least twice. The mother of his son Michael, born in 1675, was Alice Stevens, the widow of John Stevens. By 1678, it appears he had married the widow of Robert Hood.[1]

Miller had patented over 2,300 acres by 1689. He practiced law as well as earning a livelihood as a large planter. In 1685 he made a voyage to Barbados for unknown reasons, although there are other suggestions he may have been a factor.[2] Miller's career encompasses a stormy role in local politics. He served twice as a sheriff (1678, 1680–82) and was the ranking justice until his removal from the commission in 1683 for allegedly seizing the estate of another planter unjustly without proper condemnation procedures. He probably held no other appointive office before the revolution. However, Kent voters in 1685 did send him to the last proprietary assembly.[3]

XXII, 319; *Cal. S. P., Col., 1697–98*, no. 782; "Royal Period," 184–96; *HLP*, 157.

[6] Wills 11, ff. 151–54; I&A 29, f. 157; 26, f. 275; 32B, f. 241; *Md. Archives*, XXX, 96.

---

[1] Anna Catherine Pabst, *Nashes of Ireland* (Delaware, Ohio, 1963), 393–97. His second wife's name was Anne (Kent Ct. Pro., I, f. 286).

[2] Patents CB#2, ff. 159, 524; SD#A, f. 477; NS#B, f. 127; Kent Ct. Pro., 1676–98, f. 130; I&A 23, ff. 82–83.

[3] Kent Ct. Pro., I, f. 496; Owings, "Private Manors: An Edited List," *MHM*, XXXIII (1938), 327; *Md. Archives*, XVII, 93, 171–72; XV, 328;

The Associators' Convention rewarded Miller with appointment as clerk of the county. He also sat on the Grand Committee of Twenty. He did not continue as clerk after the institution of royal government, and apparently he held no appointive office after 1692. Miller again served as a burgess from 1697/98 until his death, and was also a member of his local vestry.[4]

There is evidence that Miller was at least sympathetic to, if not more intimately involved in, the John Coode–Philip Clarke conspiracy against Governor Francis Nicholson in 1698. His descendants did not enjoy political success.[5]

Miller died in 1700. His estate included 2,000 acres of land and approximately £1,121.7.5, including ten servants and nine slaves.[6]

HENRY MITCHELL
?–1701

Henry Mitchell had come to Maryland by 1658 and settled in Calvert County. He was a planter and probably engaged in some trading ventures as well. He eloped in 1659 with the young stepdaughter of William Parker, a wealthy merchant planter. In 1673, he was identified as "Henry Mitchell of the Clifts, gentl." Mitchell was illiterate in 1665 but had perhaps become literate by 1693, when he signed a will as witness.[1]

I, 122. Either Miller or his son—quite likely it was the latter—became clerk of indictments for Kent in March 1686/87 (Kent Ct. Pro., I, f. 259).

[4] *Md. Archives*, XIII, 242; VIII, 184, 199; XXII, 77, 213, 367; XXIV, 35; XXIII, 21; *HLP*, 146.

[5] *Md. Archives*, XXV, 31–32; "Royal Period," 187; Pabst, *Nashes*, 396–97.

[6] Kent Wills II, f. 794; I&A 1, ff. 660–67; 23, ff. 82–83.

[1] *Md. Archives*, LXV, 92, 169; XLI, 336–38; XLIX, 565; Wills 2, f. 305; Patents Q, f. 317; St. George's Parish Register, 1681–1741, f. 10. The assumption here is that Mitchell is the same person of that name who

The court records reveal that Mitchell was a man of vicious character. He, Coode, Gilbert Clarke, and Charles James were probably the persons most often in mind when the anti-Associators labeled the rebels as disreputable men. Mitchell was brought before the Provincial Court in 1670 as a common barretor, a rarely used legal term which was applied to troublemakers who repeatedly stirred up quarrels. He was also accused at various times of assault and hog-stealing. Mitchell was involved in several debts cases brought to the Provincial Court in the 1670's. Some of these judicial matters necessitated his being kept in the custody of the county sheriff. During the early 1680's, he served as a Provincial Court juror.[2]

Peter Sayer described Mitchell as a captain in Coode's army during the rebellion. It is unlikely Mitchell had held a militia appointment under Lord Baltimore. In any event, the Associators' Convention made him a captain in 1689. Mitchell was one of Henry Jowles's military associates chosen for the convention in the disputed Calvert County election. In 1690, Mitchell received an appointment as justice of the peace.[3]

Mitchell continued to serve on the bench and as a militia officer during the early royal period, and he eventually attained the rank of colonel. He sat in the first royal assembly, 1692–94, but after 1694 there is no evidence of his holding any elective or appointive office other than his militia commission. His earlier unsavory record probably explains his inactivity in the civil sphere, especially under Governor Nicholson.[4]

Mitchell died in 1701, but left no will. His personal estate was

---

patented several hundred acres of land in Talbot County in the 1660's (Patents 7, ff. 333; 9, f. 334; *Md. Archives*, LXV, 288–89, 93).

[2] *Md. Archives*, LVII, xxxii–xxxiii, 109; XLI, 336–38; LXV, 93–94, 169–70, 548, 559–60; LXVI, *passim.*; LXX, 239, 256.

[3] *Ibid.*, VIII, 117, 148; XIII, 242; Test Pro. 16, f. 23; Prov. Ct. Judg., DSC, f. 133. Since Mitchell's militia appointment in 1689 was "in the roome of Captain Richard Ladd," it is unlikely he held a commission under the proprietor. See also *Md. Archives*, VIII, 148.

[4] *Md. Archives*, XX, 76, 108, 465, 543; XIII, 351; XXIII, 486.

valued at £894.19.1, including twelve slaves and eleven servants, plus 12,128 pounds of tobacco.[5]

GEORGE ROBOTHAM
?–1698

George Robotham had migrated to Maryland by 1669. After first settling in Calvert County, he moved to Dorchester and finally to Talbot County by 1679.[1]

During his first decade in the colony, Robotham was identified as the partner of a Western Shore bricklayer and as attorney for a non-resident merchant. Robotham himself gradually acquired at least 2,300 acres by 1689 and was active in a number of business enterprises.[2]

Robotham first obtained public office in 1681 when he was elected to the assembly and appointed to the Talbot bench. He rose steadily in the judicial commission and by 1685 was a quorum justice. The assembly journals indicate he was a very active burgess during the sessions of 1681–82 and again in 1688.[3]

Robotham's actions in the initial stages of the revolution reflect some reluctance to commit himself wholeheartedly to the rebel cause. He sat with three fellow justices in the proprietor's name at the September court. However, he signed the county petition requesting a royal government two months later. One contemporary account suggests Robotham was attempting to steer a middle course between the people's "humor" and rebel

---

[5] I&A 20, ff. 247–49; 23, ff. 70–71.

[1] Patents 16, f. 431. In March 1669/70, George Robotham of Calvert County received power of attorney in the Provincial Court (*Md. Archives,* LVII, 496; LXVIII, 243).

[2] *Md. Archives,* LXV, 138; LXVI, 198. Robotham also practiced in the county courts (LIV, 598–99). Patents 17, f. 108; CB#2, ff. 58, 407; CB#3, f. 343; NS#B, f. 165; NS#2, 213; IB&IL#C, f. 251.

[3] *Md. Archives,* XV, 346; XVII, 381; VII, 317; XIII, 157, 158, 183.

pressures on the one hand and concerns for stability and obligations to Lord Baltimore on the other. By the following spring,
Robotham had made his commitment. He became a member of
the Grand Committee of Twenty, was speaker of the third session of the convention, and was appointed to the Provincial
Court in early 1691. Furthermore, he was by now a militia
colonel.[4]

The king commissioned Robotham as one of the original royal
councillors. Robotham sat regularly with the council until his
death, with the exception of a two-year period, from the fall of
1692 to the summer of 1694, when he was in England.[5]

There is some question about Robotham's religious allegiances.
Edward Randolph called him a "halfe faced Quaker" in 1692,
but Copley certainly made no move against him as he did against
other Quakers. However, there is no record of vestry service
or activity with the Anglican church, and Robotham's will did
provide 10,000 pounds of tobacco to enlarge the Quaker meeting
house between Tuckahoe and King's Creek in Talbot County.[6]

Robotham died in 1698 and left no heirs in Maryland. His
substantial estate, over £1,000 and 1,750 acres, went primarily
to three nieces in England.[7]

[4] Talb. Land Rec., NN no. 6, f. 315; KK no. 5, *passim; Md. Archives,*
VIII, 143–44, 158, 199, 242; XIII, 243. Thomas Bacon, *Laws of Maryland
with Proper Indexes* (Annapolis, 1765), chapter XI. It is unknown why
Blakiston subsequently replaced Robotham as speaker; the latter does not
appear to have been present at the April 1691 sssion (*Md. Archivs*, VIII,
250).

[5] *Md. Archives,* VIII, 310; XX, 126. On council attendance, see vols.
VIII and XX.

[6] *Randolph Letters*, VII, 376; Wills 7, ff. 358–60. See Kenneth Carroll,
"Talbot County Quakerism in the Colonial Period," *MHM*, LIII (1958),
326–70. Robotham's name does not appear in any of the Quaker minutes.

[7] Wills 7, ff. 358–60; I&A 16, ff. 77–85; 19½, ff. 67–68; 19½B, ff. 63–64.

WILLIAM SHARPE
1655–1699

William Sharpe was born in Maryland about 1655, the son of Dr. Peter Sharpe, a "chirugeon." The senior Sharpe had immigrated to the colony in 1650 and shortly thereafter had married the widow of John Gary. William Sharpe is therefore one of three native Marylanders to sit in the Associators' Convention.[1]

Peter Sharpe settled in Calvert County, but he also patented land on the Eastern Shore. By his death in 1672, he owned at least 2,100 acres. William, who settled in Talbot County after his marriage in 1673 to the daughter of Thomas Thomas, inherited approximately 1,400 acres from his father.[2]

Both Peter and William Sharpe were active, eminent Quakers. William's religious beliefs prevented his acceptance of an appointment to the Talbot bench in 1685. There is no record he ever served in an appointive or elective office other than overseer of the highways prior to 1689. After 1692, the prohibitions against Quakers rendered him ineligible for such offices. The Associators' Convention did not appoint him to any office.[3]

In 1675, while still legally a minor, Sharpe was called a planter, but in later years he was engaged in mercantile activities as well. It was perhaps in conjunction with the latter that he returned briefly to England in 1680 for business matters.[4]

Sharpe died in 1699 and was survived by two sons and a

[1] Talb. Land Rec., GG no. 3, f. 28; A no. 1, ff. 348–54; Patents Q, f. 28; Emerson B. Roberts, "Some Friends of Ye Friends in Ye Ministry," *MHM*, XXXVII (1942), 325.

[2] Roberts, "Some Friends," 324–25; Wills 1, ff. 494–95; *Md. Archives*, LIV, 603–4.

[3] Third Haven Monthly Meeting Minutes, 1676–1746, f. 2 and *passim* (microfilm in the Maryland Hall of Records); *Md. Archives*, XVII, 380; V, 565; XIII, 243–44; Talb. Ct. Pro., 1685–1689, f. 144.

[4] Talb. Land Rec., A no. 1, f. 348; *Md. Archives*, VIII, 445; Third Haven Minutes, ff. 31–32.

daughter. The latter had married a son of Sharpe's fellow Quaker and Associator John Edmundson. Sharpe's will did not list his landholdings, but he patented at least 1,324 acres, while selling some of his own inheritance. His personal estate was inventoried as worth £646.4.3, including a servant and fourteen slaves.[5]

ROBERT SMITH
?–1706/07

Robert Smith the Associator cannot be precisely identified. Two men are clear possibilities, or the two may be the same individual. In 1677 a Robert Smith was a tenant of Hinson's Addition, and three years later a Robert Smith married Ann, the widow of Thomas Hinson.[1] This is probably the Robert Smith of Chester River who owned the ship "Robert and Ann" which was ordered seized in 1695 for violation of the Navigation Acts.[2] The Robert Smith who qualified as an attorney of the Kent County Court on November 27, 1677, is perhaps a different individual. It seems most likely that he became an Associator and then went on to a distinguished legal career in the colony.[3] Robert Smith the lawyer was definitely a native of England; he testified in 1696 that he had known John Coode in Penryn, Cornwall. He may have been the Robert Smith who received a degree from Cambridge in 1672.[4]

Much of the reasoning for identifying the Associator as Robert Smith the lawyer rests upon two points. First, the convention

[5] Wills 6, ff. 289–91; I&A 19½, ff. 132–34. For Sharpe's landholdings, see Talb. Land Rec., GG no. 3, ff. 28, 114–15, 118–19; Patents 17, ff. 182, 390; 21, ff. 1, 2; NS#B, f. 481; BB#3, ff. 324, 330, 508, 509.

[1] *Md. Archives*, LXVII, 231; Christopher Johnston, "Hynson and Smith Families," *MHM*, XVIII (1923), 186–90. I&A 7A, f. 327.

[2] *Md. Archives*, XX, 309.

[3] Kent Ct. Pro., I, f. 33.

[4] *Md. Archives*, XIX, 469; *Graduati Cantabrigiensis 1659–1823* (Cambridge, 1823), 433.

did not appoint Smith to a civil office. An appointment to a justiceship would have ended his lucrative practice as an attorney. This would also explain the absence of any office prior to the convention. Indeed, it was not until 1692 that Smith became a justice, when significantly, he joined the Talbot bench as a quorum justice.[5] Secondly, Governor Francis Nicholson, who diligently sought expertise and quality in his appointments, made Smith chief justice of the Provincial Court where he presided until 1699, and surveyor general of the colony. It seems highly unlikely that Nicholson would have continued in that post a man found guilty of violating the Navigation Acts which the governor was so busily prosecuting. Nicholson was quick to revoke commissions for much lesser offenses.[6]

Smith represented Talbot County in the assembly from 1692 until 1697, serving as speaker of the lower house in 1694–95. Nicholson recommended him for the council, to which an appointment finally came in 1699. Smith continued to sit on the council until his death in 1706/07.[7]

Smith left the bulk of his estate to his brother's children in England, to his brother Renatus Smith, and to his own daughter in Maryland, who had probably married Anthony Ivy. His estate consisted of several thousand acres of land, and personalty valued at £1,067.3.1½.[8]

[5] Talb. Land Rec., NN no. 6, f. 32 (in rear). Smith maintained his practice during the period 1689–92 (Talb. Test. Pro., 1689–1692, *passim*).

[6] *Md. Archives*, XX, 135, 137, 254, 365, 466; XXIII, 128. Nicholson found Smith irreplaceable as chief justice (Nicholson to Lords of Trade, March 27, 1697, CO5/714/I).

[7] *Md. Archives*, XIII, 350; XIX, 3, 96, 171, 242, 329, 403, 555; XXIII, 418–19; XXV, 72.

[8] Wills 12A, ff. 90–92; I&A 29, ff. 13–16; 31, ff. 71–72, 113; 36C, ff. 135–38.

THOMAS STALEY
?–1700

Little information is available on Thomas Staley of Baltimore County. He first appears in the surviving public records as an Associator in 1689. It is known that he earned his livelihood as a planter.[1]

The Associators' Convention made Staley a justice, and he also later represented Baltimore on the Grand Committee. He does not appear on the Baltimore bench during the administration of Governor Copley, but he was reappointed a justice by Governor Nicholson in October of 1694. He sat for two years, at which time he was promoted by Nicholson to the Provincial Court.[2]

Staley sat in the assembly from 1692 to 1694 and again from 1697/98 to 1700, when he resigned his seat to accept a commission as sheriff. He served only a few months before his death. During the 1690's, Staley was also active as a vestryman.[3]

Staley's estate included at least 165 acres, 29,816 pounds of tobacco, and personal belongings, including two servants, valued at £189.13.10, before the payment of debts. His son-in-law James Dunham and two grandchildren were the heirs.[4]

[1] Balt. Ct. Pro., F no. 1, f. 372.

[2] *Md. Archives*, XIII, 243; VIII, 196; XX, 138, 466; XXIII, 128; Balt. Ct. Pro., G no. 1, ff. 132, 320–31, 658; Prov. Ct. Judg., WT no. 3, ff. 1–3, *passim*. Staley served as a jury foreman during Copley's tenure.

[3] *Md. Archives*, XIII, 350; XIX, 3, 30; XXII, 77, 210, 368; XXIV, 41; I&A 20 ff. 79–80; Balt. Ct. Pro., F no. 1, f. 410.

[4] Wills 11, ff. 25–27; I&A 20, ff. 79–80; 23, ff. 79–81.

JOHN STONE
1648–1697

John Stone was the son of William Stone, who had settled in Accomac, Virginia, in 1633. From a well-to-do London merchant family, William Stone had brought thirty-four servants with him to the New World. During the troubled period after the Puritan revolution, Lord Baltimore appointed Stone, a Protestant, as governor of Maryland in a distinctly political gesture. Stone received Poynton Manor and numerous other lands. His daughter married the son of Leonard Calvert.[1]

John Stone came to Maryland with his father shortly after his birth and grew up in Charles County. The first of Stone's three marriages was to Elizabeth Warren.[2]

In 1670, at the age of twenty-two, Stone became a justice of Charles County. He headed the commission on the eve of the revolution. He also had represented the county twice in the assembly, 1678–82 and 1686–88.[3]

Stone appears to have been one of the most reluctant members of the convention in his support of the revolution and establishment of a new government. He declined to sit on the county bench until after the arrival of the royal letter in May of 1690. Two "newcomers" in the county delegation, John Addison and John Courts, surpassed him in influence during this period.[4]

Stone presided over the county bench in the early royal period. He sat as a justice from 1692 to 1694 and again appeared

---

[1] Harry Wright Newman, *The Stones of Poynton Manor* (Washington, D.C., 1937), 4, 12, 7–9.

[2] Patents ABH, f. 150; *Md. Archives*, XVII, 11; Newman, *Stones*, 12. The second wife's name is unknown, but the third marriage was to the daughter of Walter Bayne.

[3] *Md. Archives*, XV, 327; XVII, 380; V, 565; VII, 4, 125, 263; XIII, 161.

[4] Ch. Ct. and Land Rec., P no. 1, ff. 185–201; Q no. 1, 1–8.

on the commission in 1697. During the interim, he had been sheriff of the county. He was also an active vestryman.[5]

Stone died in late 1697. His estate consisted of 1,384 acres and personalty worth £274.6.7 including three servants and a slave. He had four sons; Thomas Stone served later as a burgess from Charles County.[6]

THOMAS TENCH
?–1708

Thomas Tench first appears in the Maryland records in 1675, when he began the importation of at least eighty-one settlers into the colony. Tench was a merchant in London.[1] He may have been related to John Tench, the mariner from Bristol who was also actively importing individuals and trading with Maryland in the late seventeenth century,[2] but no definite connection has been established between the two. Thomas Tench may have been the same individual who matriculated at Brasenose College, Oxford in 1673 at the age of eighteen. That student was the son of John Tench of Nantwich, Cheshire, gentleman, and brother of another Oxford alumnus named John Tench. The latter became a member of Parliament from Ireland. In that regard, it is interesting that Edward Randolph called Thomas Tench an "Irish Merchant" in 1692.[3]

Tench evidently did not migrate to Maryland until 1684,

---

[5] *Ibid.*, S no. 1, ff. 1–128; V no. 1, ff. 205–6; *Md. Archives*, XXIII, 128; XX, 77; XXII, 19.

[6] Wills, 6, f. 153; I&A 17, ff. 11–18; *Md. Archives*, XXX, 96; Newman, *Stones*, 4.

---

[1] Patents WC#2, ff. 380–81. Tench transported at least fifteen indentured servants in 1684 alone (Michael Ghirelli, *A List of Emigrants from England to America, 1682–1692* [Baltimore, 1968], 2, 17, 18, and *passim*).

[2] See, for example, Dor. Land Rec., O no. 3, f. 201, and CO5/749/I, f. 72.

[3] Joseph Foster, ed., *Alumni Oxonienses: The Members of the University of Oxford, 1500–1714*, 4 vols. (London, 1891–92), IV, 5; *Randolph Letters*, VII, 376.

when he settled in Anne Arundel County and within a few months had married the widow of Nathan Smith. Tench prospered as a merchant and large landowner. During this period he maintained quite close connections with the sizable Quaker community in the county. His wife was probably a Friend, and Tench himself may have briefly been affiliated with that religious group. However, he did swear an oath upon his appointment as justice of the peace in 1685, a position he still occupied in 1689, and he served in the 1690's as an Anglican vestryman.[4]

Nothing is known about Tench's initial reaction to the revolution. His brother-in-law by marriage, Francis Hutchins, opposed the Associators. Nonetheless, the first convention, in which Tench did not sit, appointed him a justice and coroner. Anne Arundel elected him to the convention in 1690, but there is no evidence of definite allegiance to the rebels until the following year, when he became a justice of the quorum for the newly constituted Provincial Court. Thereafter, his rise was rapid. He received a commission as one of the original royal councillors. Tench served on the council from 1692 to 1708 with the exception of a brief period while he was regulating the affairs of the deceased Governor Copley. During the initial months of the royal government, Tench became an intimate associate of the governor and Blakiston.[5]

Tench's trading activities posed some troubles and brought him into conflict with Edward Randolph, the customs collector,

---

[4] Wills 4, ff. 49–51; 7, ff. 16–17; AA Land Rec., IH no. 2, ff. 63–67; IH no. 1, ff. 312–18; *Md. Archives*, XIX, 359. Tench owned a mill and several ships (XX, 412, 155, 326). On the possible Quaker ties, see Monthly Meeting at the Clifts, Marriages, 1682–1824, ff. 4, 17, 19 (microfilm in the Maryland Hall of Records); the wills cited above; Charles Stein, *A History of Calvert County, Maryland* (Baltimore, 1960), 49, 239, 314–15. On Tench's judicial and vestry service, see *Md. Archives*, XVII, 379; V, 42; XIII, 242, and St. James Vestry Minutes 1695–1793, 1–43, 44, 61.

[5] Patents WT no. 2, ff. 276–81; *Md. Archives*, XIII, 242; VIII, 248–50, 245, 305; XX, 326; Prov. Ct. Judg., DSC, f. 11; *Randolph Letters*, VII, 397.

during the 1690's. One of Tench's ships, the "Ann," was seized in 1694 for violating the Navigation Acts.[6]

Tench's first wife died in 1694; he remarried, but the identity of his second wife is unknown. Both women were named Margaret. Tench himself died in 1708 with no direct heirs. His estate went to his first wife's grandson. While the will did not list his landholdings, they probably amounted to approximately 1,500 acres, the land listed in his possession by the rent rolls of 1707. The personal estate was inventoried at £562.0.3, including six slaves and one servant, plus 3,600 pounds of tobacco.[7]

JOHN THOMAS
?–1717/18

Several men named John Thomas lived in Maryland in the late seventeenth century. It appears likely, however, that the Associator was the John Thomas of Baltimore County who on May 30, 1681, demanded his rights to fifty acres "for his time of service performed within the province."[1]

Thomas had completed his indenture by early 1680 when he became administrator for two estates, for one of which he was the principal creditor.[2] Thomas was a carpenter, which may explain his seemingly rapid rise from indentured status. By 1689 he had accumlated at least 365 acres and was filling such county positions as overseer of the highways (1683 and 1685) and foreman of the county grand jury (1683/84).[3]

The Associators' Convention made Thomas a justice of the

[6] *Md. Archives*, XX, 155; Carroll T. Bond, ed., *Proceedings of the Maryland Court of Appeals, 1695–1729* (Washington, D.C., 1933), 7–12.

[7] Wills 7, ff. 16–17; 12A, ff. 232–33; Patents WT no. 1, ff. 59–63; WT no. 2, f. 459; I&A 29, ff. 21–23; 32A, ff. 82–83.

[1] Warrants 5, f. 17.

[2] Test. Pro. 11, ff. 338–39; 12A, ff. 48, 55.

[3] Balt. Ct. Pro., D, ff. 102, 129, 342, 359; Baltimore County Rent Roll, ff. 180, 185 (Calvert Papers, mss., MHS).

Baltimore court and a militia captain. In 1690, he became a member of the Grand Committee of Twenty.[4]

During the royal period, Thomas sat on the Baltimore bench from 1692 to 1694 and again from 1696 until his removal in 1700 for his "late irregularitys," which remain unidentified. During the intervening years he served as sheriff. He continued as a militia officer throughout the 1690's; promoted to major in 1690, Thomas was a colonel by 1695.[5]

Following his dismissal from the bench in 1700, Thomas was apparently inactive in public affairs. He prepared his will in September of 1717 and the estate was inventoried March 31, 1718. At that time, it included more than 349 acres of land and personalty worth £50.12.0. He had previously disposed of much of his landholdings. Thomas asked the St. Paul's vestry to assist his wife Sarah as executors.[6]

John Thomas, his son, held no provincial office.

THOMAS THURSTON
c. 1622–1693

Thomas Thurston is one of the more intriguing and controversial figures of early Maryland history. Indeed, his adventures find a place in the history of other colonies as well. Thurston was born in Gloucestershire in about 1622. Sometime before 1656, he became a Quaker. In that year he set out on his first religious journey to New England.[1]

---

[4] *Md. Archives*, XIII, 243; VIII, 196, 199.

[5] *Ibid.*, XX, 77, 466; XXV, 108; Balt. Ct. Pro., F. no. 1, ff. 233–34; G no. 1, ff. 320–21, 422.

[6] Original Wills, box T, folder 17; Inv 1, ff. 19–20. On earlier transfers of land, see Balt. Land Rec., HW no. 2, ff. 171, 174, 229; TR no. A, ff. 247, 445, 454.

---

[1] An excellent account of Thurston's life is available in Kenneth L. Carroll, "Thomas Thurston, Renegade Maryland Quaker," *MHM*,

LXII (1967), 170–92. See especially pp. 170–72 for his early years in England.

Thurston's missionary efforts received the customary treatment accorded to Quakers. He was imprisoned and then deported. He returned to England and migrated the following year to Virginia, where he also met imprisonment. Early in 1658 he first appeared in Maryland, and the council issued a warrant for his arrest. He was later freed upon the condition of leaving the colony. After renewed troubles in New Amsterdam and New England, Thurston was again briefly imprisoned in Maryland in 1659. Another two transatlantic trips came during the interval before his eventual settlement in Maryland with his wife, two daughters, and twenty servants in 1663.[2]

Thurston became a "disruptive spirit" in Maryland Quakerism, with involvement in both the John Perrot schism and the Lynam controversy, two doctrinal disputes which divided Quakers in the colony. George Fox, on a colonial visit, received a special repentance from Thurston, but it is clear Thurston never adhered closely to traditional beliefs.[3] In 1685, the residents of Baltimore County elected him to what became the last proprietary assembly. Thurston served although he did refuse to subscribe the customary oaths. During this period, there were frequent testimonies against him by Maryland Friends.[4]

A more definite estrangement came in the aftermath of the revolution. The records of Baltimore County are not very complete for the period 1689 to 1692, but it is clear that Thurston assumed a militia office. In the fall of 1692, Thurston, styled the

[2] *Ibid.*, 171–84; J. Reaney Kelly, *Quakers in the Founding of Anne Arundel County* (Baltimore, 1963), 29–33.

[3] Carroll, "Thurston," 184–85, 187–88, 190. See also the same author's "The Anatomy of a Separation: The Lynam Controversy," *Quaker History*, LV (1966), 67–78.

[4] Balt. Ct. Pro., D, f. 359; *Md. Archives*, XIII, 163; Carroll, "Thurston," 191. Thurston's prominent role in the county is seen in *Md. Archives*, V, 473.

"late principal Military Officer in Baltimore," came before the council to answer charges of "unruly and disorderly actions and behaviour," for which he was acquitted. It is likely that he received his first militia appointment in 1690. There is some evidence he was completely disowned as a Quaker for these activities.[5]

The prohibitions against Quakers holding public office, which were strictly enforced by Governor Copley, undoubtedly account for Thurston's surrendering his militia colonelcy. He died soon after the institution of royal government. Thurston's will disinherited one daughter who was an active Quaker. His children had married into the prominent Gibson, Skipworth, Coale, and Chew families. He left a young son and daughter, children by his second wife.[6]

Thurston owned six plantations in Baltimore County or on the Eastern Shore. In addition to his landed income, Thurston is referred to in the records as both a trader and a cordwainer. His personal estate was valued at £194.19.2.[7]

HENRY TRIPPE
1632–1698

Henry Trippe was born in Canterbury in 1632, the youngest son of the Reverend Thomas Trippe. He fought in Flanders be-

---

[5] *Md. Archives*, VIII, 338, 378; Christopher Johnston, "Duval-Johnson Families of Maryland," 93 (ms copy in MHS). Thurston was not appointed a justice or militia officer in September 1689, but he was the "principal Military Officer" in Baltimore by 1692 and was called "colonel" at his death (*Md. Archives*, VIII, 378; I&A 13B, f. 86).

[6] Carroll, "Thurston," 192; Johnston, "Duval-Johnson Families," 94–95; Wills 6, ff. 22–23.

[7] Carroll, "Thurston," 184; Kelly, *Anne Arundel Quakers*, 29–33; I&A 10, ff. 282–84; 13, ff. 317–19; Raphael Semmes, *Captains and Mariners of Early Maryland* (Baltimore, 1937), 729.

fore migrating to Maryland in 1663, bringing with him three fellow soldiers. Trippe settled in Dorchester County.[1]

Soon after his arrival, Trippe married the widow of Michael Brooke. His stepson was John Brooke, a fellow Associator in 1689. By the eve of the revolution, Trippe had patented 1,400 acres.[2]

Trippe became a justice of the peace in 1669 and served intermittently on the bench until the revolution. He represented the county in the assembly for the sessions of 1671–75 and 1681–82. During this period, Trippe was also a militia captain.[3]

The Associators' Convention made Trippe a major of the militia and head of the Dorchester court commission. The following spring he took a seat as member of the Grand Committee of Twenty.[4]

Trippe was a delegate to the first royal assembly and served as a justice until September of 1693 when he traveled to England. It is uncertain when, if ever, he returned. His will, drawn up before his departure, was proved in March 1697/98, but there is no mention of him in the Maryland records after 1693. Trippe's personal estate was appraised in 1698 at £307.14.3 with two servants and seven slaves.[5]

Trippe's son Henry was later a burgess and a justice for Dorchester County.[6]

---

[1] Richard Henry Spencer, *Thomas Family of Talbot County, Maryland, and Allied Families* (Baltimore, 1914), 139–40.

[2] Elias Jones, *History of Dorchester County, Maryland* (Baltimore, 1902), 272; Patents 14, f. 146; 13, f. 21; 16, f. 257; IB&IL#C, ff. 106, 109; NS#B, f. 158; NS#2, ff. 210, 212; SD#A, f. 371.

[3] Trippe appears to have been a justice for the years 1669–71, 1674–76, 1681–89 (*Md. Archives*, XV, 254, 326; XVII, 44–45, 381; II, 239, 345, 422; VII, 151, 229, 266; XIII, 244; LI, 365).

[4] *Ibid.*, XIII, 244; VIII, 199.

[5] *Ibid.*, XIX, 7; XX, 67; Wills 7, ff. 324–37; I&A 16, ff. 9–11; 18, f. 147.

[6] The son first sat as a burgess in 1712 (*Md. Archives*, XXIX, 131).

Membership of the Proprietary Assemblies, 1676–1688, by Counties

The following charts indicate membership in the three assemblies elected between 1676 and 1689. Unless otherwise noted, documentation for membership may be found in the journals of the respective assemblies. The charts do not attempt to indicate attendance. Three additional tables are on file at the Hall of Records, Annapolis: Members of the Assemblies, 1676–1688, Religion; Assembly, 1676–1688, Members Alive in July 1689, Attitudes to Revolution; Members of the Assembly, 1676–1688, Dead by July 1689. Xerox copies may be obtained at cost. The information is summarized in Table 3, Chapter VI.

Explanation of Symbols

[+2] = died after second session
[E-3] = elected to assembly for third session
[S-2] = became sheriff after second session
[C-5] = appointed to council after fifth session

Proprietary Assembly, 1676–1682

First session: May 15–June 15, 1676
Second session: October 20–November 14, 1678
Third session: August 16–September 17, 1681
Fourth session: November 1–12, 1681
Fifth session: April 25–May 13, 1682

St. Mary's City	*St. Mary's*	*Kent*
Kenelm Cheseldyne	John Coode	Joseph Wickes
Robert Carvile	Walter Hall [+2]	Thomas Marsh [+2]
	William Hatton	Henry Hosier

Clement Hill*
Richard Gardiner [E-3]

Samuel Tovey
John Hinson [E-3]
?Thomas Smith

Anne Arundel

William Burgess [C-5]
James Rigby [+2]
John Homewood
William Richardson
Richard Hill [E-3]

Calvert

Thomas Brooke [+1]
Richard Hall
Richard Ladd
Christopher Rousby
Francis Billingsley

Charles†

John Allen [+1]
John Douglas [+2]
Robert Henly
Henry Adams
John Stone [E-2]
Randolph Brandt [E-3]

Baltimore

George Wells
John Stansby [S-2]
John Waterton
John Scott
James Mills‡

Talbot

Philemon Lloyd
John Edmundson
Richard Wolman [+2]
Winlock Christison [+2]
George Robotham [E-3]
John Rousby [E-3]

Somerset

William Stevens [C-2]
Roger Woolford
James Dashiel
John White [S-2]
John Goddin [E-3]
Henry Smith [E-3]

Dorchester

John Stevens
William Ford [+2]
Bartholomew Ennalls
John Hudson [+1]
Anthony Tall [E-2] [+2]
John Brooke [E-3]
Henry Trippe [E-3]

Cecil

James Frisby
Jonathan Sybrey
William Pearce
Nathaniel Garratt

* Clement Hill was serving as sheriff during the first session; there is no evidence
to suggest whom he replaced (*Md. Archives*, II, 495; VII, 6).
† In 1678, Josias Fendall was ruled ineligible as a candidate to replace Allen (*ibid.*,
XV, 192–93).
‡ *Ibid.*, V, 355.

Proprietary Assembly, 1682–1684

First session: October 26–November 17, 1682
Second session: October 2–November 6, 1683
Third session: April 1–26, 1684

St. Mary's City

Robert Carvile
Leonard Green

St. Mary's

William Hatton
Clement Hill

Kent

Joseph Wickes
Henry Hosier

Anne Arundel

Richard Hill
William Richardson

*Calvert**

Richard Ladd
Francis Hutchins
Richard Hall

Charles

Henry Adams
Thomas Burford

Baltimore	Talbot	Somerset
Miles Gibson [S-1]	Philemon Lloyd [+3]	Henry Smith
Henry Johnson	John Rousby [+3]	John Osbourne
Thomas Long [E-2]†		

Dorchester	Cecil
Bartholomew Ennalls	James Frisby
John Brooke	William Pearce [S-3]

* For unexplained reasons Calvert clearly had three delegates at the first session of this assembly. Richard Ladd did not attend the two subsequent sessions.
† Long was elected October 11, 1683 (Balt. Ct. Pro., D, f. 85).

Proprietary Assembly, 1686–1688

Elected October 1685
First session: October 27–November 19, 1686
Second session: November 14–December 8, 1688

St. Mary's City	St. Mary's	Kent
Anthony Underwood	Clement Hill*	Henry Hosier†
Kenelm Cheseldyne	Joseph Pile	Michael Miller†
	Richard Gardiner [+1]	William Harris
	John Coode [E-2]	

Anne Arundel‡	Calvert	Charles
Richard Hill	Henry Jowles	John Stone
	George Lingan	Thomas Burford [+1]
		Henry Hawkins [E-2]

Baltimore	Talbot	Somerset
George Wells§	George Robotham	James Round
Thomas Thurston	John Edmundson‖	Stephen Luffe

Dorchester	Cecil
Edward Pindar#	William Dare
John Brooke	(Edward?) Jones
Daniel Clarke [E-1]	

* Promoted to council before first session (*Md. Archives*, V, 495).
† Kent Ct. Pro., I, 1676–98, f. 122; Hosier died before the first session and was replaced by Harris (*Md. Archives*, V, 495).
‡ The second delegate from Anne Arundel has not been identified.
§ Balt. Ct. Pro., D, f. 359.
‖ Talb. Judg., 1682–85, f. 214.
Appointed sheriff prior to the first session (*Md. Archives*, V, 495).

Civil and Military Officers in the Counties, July 1689–April 1692

An additional table, "Service of Civil and Military Officers, July 1689–April 1692," is on file at the Hall of Records, Annapolis. Xerox copies may be obtained at cost.

Table B-1. Justices in July and September 1689

County	Justices July 1689	Appointed Sept. 1689	New appointment Sept. 1689	Reappointed Sept. 1689	Not reappointed Sept. 1689
Anne Arundel	13	12	1	11	2
Baltimore	9	10	3	7	2
Calvert	13	13	5	8	5
Cecil	9	11	2	9	0
Charles	9	9	1	7*	2
Dorchester	9	7	0	7	2
Kent	9	9	2	7	2
St. Mary's	10	9	7	3*	7
Somerset	13	14	1†	13	0
Talbot	10	11	2	9	1
Total	104	105	24	81	23

* William Hatton was reappointed in Charles County from St. Mary's County. He is counted under St. Mary's.

† Francis Jenkins had been sheriff for six years, but was new to the bench since July.

Table B-2. Service of justices, September 1689–April 1692

County	Justices who served			Justices who refused	Service unknown	Died in office	Appointed after Sept. 1689
	Before May 30, 1690	After May 30, 1690	Total				
Anne Arundel	3*	3*	6*	2	4	1	2*
Baltimore	3*	1	4	3	3	2	5
Calvert	7	2	9	4	0	1	4
Cecil	0	9	9	2	0	0	5†
Charles	7	2	9	1	0	0	3
Dorchester	3*	3	6	0	1	0‡	6
Kent	1*	3*	4*	2	3	0	3*
St. Mary's	8	1	9	0	0	0	1*
Somerset	13	1	14	0	0	2	3
Talbot	9§	0	9	4§	0	0	5
Total	54	25	79	18	11	6	37

* Loss of records means information is incomplete.
† Two of these were in office only a few weeks. See above p. 126.
‡ John Woodward's service is listed as unknown, but he died before 1692.
§ Thomas Smithson and Michael Turbutt served until May 1690, then joined protests in Talbot and Kent and were removed. They are counted twice. See above pp. 114–15.

Table B-3. Justices serving in July 1689, still in office in April 1692

| County | Number | Justices in July 1689, Reappointed in September 1689 | | | | Estimated additional justices, April 1692* |
		Dead or service unknown, April 1692	Refused service	Still serving, April 1692	Justices known to have held office, April 1692	
Anne Arundel	11	4	2	5	7	5
Baltimore	7	3	3	1	9	0
Calvert	8	0‡	3‡	5	13	0
Cecil	9	0	2	7	12	0
Charles	8†	0	1	7	10	0
Dorchester	7	1	0(?)	6	12	0
Kent	7	1	2	4	7	2
St. Mary's	2†	0	0	2	2	7
Somerset	13	2	0	11	13	0
Talbot	9	0	4	5	12	0
Total	81	12	17	52	97	14

*Information has survived for all but three counties. Estimates for these are based on number of justices appointed September 1689.

†William Hatton was serving in St. Mary's in July 1689 and was appointed in Charles in September. He is counted in Charles County.

‡Richard Ladd refused service and died before April 1692. He is counted only in the column for refusal.

Table B-4. Appointment and service of administrative officers, September 1689–April 1692

Offices	Not Reappointed	Reappointed	New	Refused	Service unknown	Service proved	Died	Dismissed	Appointed after Sept. 1689
Sheriffs	5*	5	5	2	2	6	3	5†	8
Clerks	5	5	5	2	0	8	0	1	3‡

* Of these, one sheriff, Robert Doyne of Charles, had died, and a second, Francis Jenkins of Somerset, had already served six years as sheriff. Jenkins was appointed to the bench and served.

† Two, William Pearce of Cecil and Edward Pindar of Dorchester, had served three years when replaced. Pindar was appointed to the bench at once. Pearce held no office again until Nicholson's arrival and probably was basically opposed to the Associators.

‡ County clerks were appointed by the bench, 1689–92, after the initial ordinance of September 4, 1689.

Table B-5. Civil appointments made after September 1689

County	Justice	Sheriff	Clerk	Office under royal govt.	No office under royal govt.
Anne Arundel*	2(1)	1(1)	0	1	2
Baltimore	5	1	0	6	0
Calvert	4(3)	1#	0	3	1
Cecil	5(2)	1	0	2	4
Charles	3(3)	1†	1	5	0
Dorchester	6(5)	1	1	8	0
Kent*	3‡	?	0	1	2‡
St. Mary's*	1	?	?	1	?
Somerset	3(1)	2§(1)	0	3	0
Talbot	5(4)	0	1∥	6	0
Total	37	8	3	36	9

Note: Numbers in parentheses show men appointed at convention of April 1690.

* Information is incomplete.

† Humphrey Warren left the bench to become sheriff. A newcomer was not appointed.

‡ William Lawrence had served in the 1680's and was very old. Not a newcomer.

§ Both William Brereton and Stephen Luffe left the bench to take the sheriff's office. Not newcomers. Both had died before the arrival of Governor Copley.

∥ John Llewellin had been a proprietary clerk. Not a newcomer (*HLP*, 135, 169).

William Parker was appointed justice after September 1689 and then became sheriff. Therefore four men filled five appointments.

Table B-6. Militia appointments, September 1689

County	Dismissed	New appointments	Reappointment			Total appointments	Service			
			Certain	Probable	Possible*		Proved	Probable	Unknown	Refused
Anne Arundel	1	1		5		6	3		1	2
Baltimore	1	2		1	1	4	2	1	1	
Calvert	3	4	3			7	6			1
Cecil	1	2		1		3	3			
Charles	3	3	2			5	5			
Dorchester	2	2	1			3	3			
Kent	1	1		1	1	3	2			1
St. Mary's	2	4	2			6	5	1		
Somerset	1	1	3		1	5	4	1		
Talbot	6	5	3			8	4	1	3	
Total	21	25	14	8	3	50	37	4	5	4

* These men had had militia commissions previously, but not necessarily in July 1689.

County Court Jurisdiction,

1680's

Tables C-1 and C-2 below indicate the importance of county court criminal jurisdiction during the 1680's. In most counties only one or two crimes a year were so serious that trial could not be had locally, and outside St. Mary's County, where the Provincial Court sat, offenses triable in the counties were not often sent to the higher court.

Table C-2 suggests that the new criminal jurisdiction created by act of assembly in 1681 meant a substantial increase in the business of the county courts. The act achieved the increase by reducing the penalties for simple theft of goods valued at no more than 1,000 pounds of tobacco.[1] The expansion of jurisdiction gave the county justices power to try nearly all the offenses that actually occurred within their communities, and they exercised this power.

It should be noted that the county courts had had some of this jurisdiction earlier. From 1649 until 1666 penalties for hogstealing— but no other thefts—had allowed county court trial on the first offense.[2]

Criminal proceedings for the Provincial Court are missing from 1672 until March 1683/84, making impossible a comparison of the

---

[1] Acts 1681, c. 3, *Md. Archives*, VII, 201–3, revived through 1688, 247, 438; XIII, 126, 142, 212. On the third offense, the accused was sent before the Provincial Court.

[2] Acts 1649, c. 7, *Md. Archives*, I, 251; Acts 1662, c. 22, 455; Acts 1666, c. 18, II, 140–41; revived 1669, 216; Acts 1671, c. 7, 277–78, revived through 1688, 338, 413, 466, 556; VII, 84, 215, 246, 328, 436; XIII, 124, 140, 211.

exercise of criminal jurisdiction by this court before and after the act of 1681.

Tables C-3 and C-4 indicate that the county courts of the 1680's were the chief agencies for the enforcement of contractual obligations. In Charles County alone, there were nearly as many such actions brought to judgment at two sessions of 1683 as were heard in two sessions of the Provincial Court during the same period for the whole province. Two-thirds of the Charles County actions, furthermore, could have been brought in the higher court. When creditors preferred the Provincial Court, substantial sums tended to be at stake. Nevertheless, in both Charles and Baltimore counties in 1683 large creditors who took their causes to the county courts equaled or outnumbered the total number of creditors who had debts in those counties but preferred to collect at St. Mary's. For a discussion of the nature of this litigation for debts, based on data for a slightly later period, see "County Government," text, 182–187.

Table C-4 suggests, however, that the enlargement of civil jurisdiction granted to the county courts in 1679 (see pp. 8–9) did not mean a major increase in the number of causes heard in these tribunals. The vast majority of cases were for sums that could always have been litigated in the county.

The new concurrent jurisdiction (post 1679) referred to in Tables C-3 and C-4 covers actions in which the sum demanded was more than 3,000 pounds of tobacco. Old concurrent jurisdiction (ante 1679) covers actions in which the sum demanded fell between 1,501 and 3,000 pounds of tobacco. Exclusive jurisdiction of the county courts was confined to actions in which the sum demanded was 1,500 pounds of tobacco or less.[3]

[3] "County Government," text, 130; C. Ashley Ellefson, "The County Courts and Provincial Court of Maryland, 1733–1763" (Ph.D. diss., University of Maryland, 1963), 43–45, 110–11.

Table C-1. Criminal Charges, Provincial Court, March 1683/84–April 1688 (14 sessions)

County	No. of charges	Triable locally
St. Mary's	20	6
Talbot	6	0
Calvert	14	2
Cecil	15*	1
Dorchester	2	1
Anne Arundel	4	1
Somerset	4	0
Charles	8	0
Baltimore	1	0
Kent	0	0
Total	74	11†

* Seven were indictments, found *ignoramus,* brought in April 1688 for capturing in His Lordship's "forest" wild horses and steers, animals to which the proprietor laid claim under the kingly prerogatives of his charter. Possibly these seven should be listed as triable in the county courts, but the value of the animals was probably thought to be more than 1000 pounds of tobacco. The charges may have fallen for lack of particulars. For the offense, see "County Government," text, 405.

† Total charges triable in the county courts, St. Mary's excepted: 5.

Source: Prov. Ct. Judg., TG, ff. 2–121.

Table C-2. Criminal charges in counties, 1680's (7 sessions)

County*	New juris.	Total	Dates
Talbot	4	21	Jan. 1685/86–Jan. 1686/87
Somerset	12	40	Jan. 1687/88–June 1689
Charles	4	12	Jan. 1685/86–Jan. 1686/87
Baltimore	0	17	June 1684–Nov. 1685
Kent	6	16	Jan. 1685/86–Jan. 1686/87
Total	26	106	

* No criminal proceedings survive for the 1680's in the remaining counties. In Baltimore county there is a gap from November 1685 until 1691; in Somerset, from 1676 until 1687, except for a brief period in 1683.

Sources: Talb. Land Rec., NN no. 6, ff. 1–121; Som. Jud. Rec., 1687–89, ff. 10–121; Ch. Ct. and Land Rec., M no. 1, ff. 67–262; N no. 1, ff. 1–71; Balt. Ct. Pro., D, ff. 150–394; Kent Ct. Pro., I, ff. 131–254.

Table C-3. Civil Judgments,* Provincial Court, March and June–July Terms, 1683

County	Total actions	New concurrent county juris.	Sums demanded unknown	Old concurrent county juris.
St. Mary's	11	6	2	3
Talbot	14	9	2	3
Dorchester	8	5	1	2
Somerset	2	2		
Kent	6	3	1	2
Cecil	2	2		
Baltimore	2	1		1
Anne Arundel	0			
Calvert	1			1
Charles	3	1		2
Total	49	29	6	14

* Only actions for the collection of debts are included.
Source: Md. Archives, LXX, 306–465.

Table C-4. Civil judgments,* counties, at two sessions, 1683

County†	Total actions	New Juris., concurrent	Sums demanded unknown	Old juris., concurrent	Exclusive juris.
Charles	42	7	1	20	14
Baltimore	24	2	1	4	17

* Only actions for the collection of debts are included.
† Records of other counties for this year are insufficient or destroyed.
Sources: Ch. Ct. and Land Rec., K no. 1, ff. 124–248; Balt. Ct. Pro., D, ff. 34–85.

A Note on Sources

Little has been written about the revolution of 1689 in Maryland since the late-nineteenth-century studies of Francis Sparks (*Causes of the Maryland Revolution of 1689*, The Johns Hopkins University Studies in Historical and Political Science, series XIV, nos. 11–12 [Baltimore, 1896]) and of Bernard C. Steiner ("The Protestant Revolution in Maryland," American Historical Association, *Annual Report of the American Historical Association for the Year 1897* [Washington, D.C., 1898], 279–353). Two stimulating articles have appeared more recently by Beverly McAnear ("Mariland's Grevances Wiy The[y] Have Taken Op Arms," *Journal of Southern History*, VIII [1942] 392–409) and Michael Kammen ("The Causes of the Maryland Revolution of 1689," *Maryland Historical Magazine*, LV [1960], 293–333), which discuss the causes of the rebellion; Professor Kammen's share of a documentary edited with Michael G. Hall and Lawrence H. Leder (*The Glorious Revolution in America, Documents on the Colonial Crisis of 1689* [Chapel Hill, N.C., 1964]) has called attention to other aspects of the upheaval. David S. Lovejoy's recent comparative study, *The Glorious Revolution in America* (New York, 1972), appeared after completion of the present book. Its stimulating discussion of Maryland events relies almost exclusively, however, upon printed sources and focuses solely upon developments on the provincial level. Similar limitations characterize Michael David DeMichele's "The Glorious Revolution in Maryland: A Study of the Provincial Revolution of 1689" (Ph.D. diss., Pennsylvania State University, 1967), as well as Richard A. Gleissner's "The Establishment of a Royal Government in Maryland: A Study of Crown Policy and Provincial Politics, 1680–1700"

(Ph.D. diss., University of Maryland, 1968), and two published articles drawn from it ("Religious Causes of the Glorious Revolution in Maryland," *MHM*, LXIV [1969], 327–41, and "The Revolutionary Settlement of 1691 in Maryland," *MHM*, LXVI [1971], 405–19). Otherwise, the events of 1689–1692 have received only passing notice.

This lack of interest in the Maryland revolution has been, in part, the result of the absence of records. Only one ordinance and a few scattered proceedings remain for the Associators' Convention or its Grand Committee. Most of these are hidden among the recordations of the county courts where scholars of the past have missed them. No records whatever survive for the Provincial Court that sat for the last year of the revolutionary interregnum. In the absence of these records, this study has depended heavily on evidence from other sources, many of which have been difficult of access until recently.

Among the most valuable of these sources are the county court records, now housed at the Maryland Hall of Records in Annapolis. These consist of court proceedings (minutes, judgments, and sometimes levy accounts) and such recordations (land conveyances, bills of sale, vital records, cattle marks) as inhabitants were required, or wished, to put in the public record. In the earliest volumes, proceedings and documents are enrolled together. Toward the end of the seventeenth century, the clerks began to create separate series. The records that remain are published through the mid-1670's in the *Archives of Maryland*, edited by William Hand Browne *et al.*, 72 vols. to date (Baltimore, 1883–), LIII, LIV. In addition, Joseph H. Smith and Philip A. Crowl have edited the *Court Records of Prince George's County, Maryland, 1696–1699* (Washington, D.C., 1964) as volume IX of *American Legal Records*. The whole collection is described in Morris L. Radoff, Gust Skordas, and Phebe R. Jacobsen, *The County Courthouses and Records of Maryland, Part Two: The Records*, Hall of Records Commission Publication no. 13 (Annapolis, 1963).

These records have suffered losses. Fires in St. Mary's and Calvert county courthouses destroyed all their colonial records, and the statehouse fire of 1704 consumed those of Anne Arundel county for the seventeenth century, although several volumes of deeds were rerecorded. Dorchester court proceedings remain for the critical years 1690–1692, but otherwise only conveyances and other recordations survive before the mid-eighteenth century. Baltimore County has lost its seventeenth-century court proceedings before 1682, from 1686 through November 1691, and after 1696. In Kent there is a gap from 1676 to 1685 and from 1687 to 1693; in Somerset, from 1676 to 1687 (with the exception of a few months in 1681 and 1682). Civil proceedings begin in Cecil in 1683, but criminal proceedings are missing. Luckily, Charles and Talbot counties have nearly full records for the last quarter of the seventeenth century, but those for Talbot have disappeared from January 1690 through April 1692. Only Charles and Somerset have complete proceedings for the years of the revolution. Those for Somerset are especially valuable, however, because it was the practice of the Somerset clerk to record all the documents he received. Through him we can follow the relations between the county courts and the convention and the Grand Committee.

Where court proceedings are missing, recordations have supplied indirect evidence of local activity during the revolution. Deeds, with their acknowledgments in open court or before pairs of justices, survive for all but St. Mary's, Kent, and Calvert counties. Only St. Mary's and Kent have no records of testamentary business, temporarily within the jurisdiction of the counties during the revolution. Appeals from county court decisions made to the Provincial Court during 1692–1693 also provide information about the preceding years.

The records of the seventeenth-century provincial government are almost all at the Hall of Records, and some of the most important are in print. In the *Archives of Maryland* appear the minutes of the council and the journals of the assembly, the Chancery Court proceedings from 1669 to 1679, and Provincial Court proceedings to 1683. Unfortunately, the assembly journals are incomplete and are missing entirely for the session of 1686. Criminal proceedings of the Provincial Court have disappeared for the period between April 1673 and March 1683/84, and there are no records for the year preceding the revolution. Use of the manuscript Provincial Court proceedings that remain is greatly facilitated by a name index on cards prepared by the Hall of Records.

Fortunately for the historian there is an invaluable collection of Maryland materials for this period in the Public Record Office, London. As English attention became more directed toward the proprietary colonies in the 1680's, the Lords of Trade and Plantations began accumulating more information on Lord Baltimore's government. After the revolution in 1689, the Lords conducted hearings on the overthrow of the proprietary and future royal policy toward the colony, and from 1690 to 1715 a regular file was maintained on Maryland. Much of our knowledge of the interim government, particularly the membership of the convention, derives from reports sent by the Associators and their opponents to the crown, and these files also provide our information on the decision to assume the power of government in Maryland and the appointment of the first royal council. These materials are found primarily in the CO5/713 series, and many of the documents are published in the *Archives of Maryland*, volume VIII. Much relevant material is helpfully calendared and briefly summarized in W. Noel Sainsbury *et al.*, eds., *Calendar of State Papers, Colonial Series, America and West Indies*, 44 vols. to date (London, 1860–) and William John Hardy *et al.*, eds., *Calendar of State Papers, Domestic Series of the reign of William III*, 6 vols. (London, 1908–1937). The Journals of the Board of Trade, a transcript of which is on deposit in the Pennsylvania Historical Society in Philadephia, and William Blathwayt's Journal of 1680 to 1717, a transcript of which is in the Pro-Treasury Papers, Library of Congress, have both provided additional insights into the English deliberations. Blathwayt, secretary to the Lords of Trade, conducted an active correspondence with colonial figures. His complete papers are on deposit at the Huntington Library in San Marino, California, but many helpful letters are available on microfilm at the Research Library of Colonial Williamsburg, Inc.

In addition to sending reports to England, the Associators also maintained correspondence with neighboring colonies in America. The letters to and from Jacob Leisler's rebel government in New York have fortunately survived and are published in two collections edited by Edmund B. O'Callaghan, *The Documentary History of the State of New York*, 4 vols. (Albany, 1849–1851) and *Documents*

Relative to the Colonial History of the State of New York, 15 vols. (Albany, 1856–1887). Maryland had a less cooperative relationship with her immediate neighbor to the south, Virginia, as can be seen in the *Executive Journals of the Council of Colonial Virginia,* edited by H. R. McIlwaine and Wilbur M. Hall, 4 vols. (Richmond, 1925–1945).

There is a disappointing scarcity of private papers for this period of Maryland's history, and what scattered collections do exist are usually of a semiofficial nature like the Blathwayt letters. The Calvert Papers, located at the Maryand Historical Society, unfortunately peter out after 1676 when Charles Calvert became proprietor. Some earlier and more illuminating letters from this collection are printed in *Maryland Historical Society Fund Publication no. 28* (Baltimore, 1889). Edward Randolph was another colonial bureaucrat who left a voluminous correspondence which includes some colorful commentary on the early months of royal government in Maryland. It has been edited by Robert Noxon Toppan and Alfred Thomas S. Goodrick in *Edward Randolph: Including His Letters and Official Papers . . . 1676–1703,* 7 vols. (Boston, 1898–1909). More personal in nature are the letters of Virginian William Fitzhugh, which occasionally comment on Maryland events. Richard Beale Davis had edited those papers in *William Fitzhugh and His Chesapeake World, 1676–1701* (Chapel Hill, 1963). The few additional letters, found in scattered collections and repositories, are identified in the footnotes.

Given the religious conflicts that the revolution dramatized, the church records available for the religious history of seventeenth-century Maryland assume importance. The only extensive collections for the period before 1692 are those of the Quaker meetings. These are at the Hall of Records in the original or on microfilm. Minutes for the Third Haven Meeting on the Eastern Shore begin in 1676; for the Monthly Meeting at the Clifts on the Western Shore in 1677; for the Yearly and Half Yearly Meetings of Friends in Maryland in 1677; and for the Quarterly Meeting for the Western Shore in 1680. Registers of births, marriages, and burials remain for the meetings of both shores. The records are described and catalogued in Phebe R. Jacobsen, *The Quaker Records of Maryland,* Hall of Records Commission Publication no. 14 (Annapolis, 1967).

Correspondence between English and Maryland Quakers and accounts of Quaker travels in Maryland are to be found in the Friends House Library, London.

The information available about the Jesuit mission in Maryland has been discussed and printed in Thomas A. Hughes, *History of the Society of Jesus in North America, Colonial and Federal*, 4 vols. (London, 1907–1917). Aside from a few deeds and grants, the mission records of the seventeenth century have disappeared, but some correspondence with authorities remains at Stonyhurst in England and in the archives of the Vatican in Rome. A visit to the Jesuit Farm Street Residence in London turned up nothing of value that Hughes had not already printed.

The progress of the Anglican establishment after 1692 can be followed in the surviving registers and vestry minutes of the parishes, collected in the original or on film at the Hall of Records and described in their manuscript Catalog of Records of the Protestant Episcopal Church. Indexed transcripts of most are at the Maryland Historical Society in Baltimore. A few registers begin before establishment. In addition, correspondence relating to establishment in Maryland is in the Fulham Palace Papers, Lambeth Palace Library, London, and these are on microfilm at the Library of Congress. Some of the more interesting of these papers have been described by Bernard C. Steiner in the *Maryland Historical Magazine*, XII (1917), 115–41. Many are printed, although not always accurately, in William Stevens Perry, ed., *Historical Collections Relating to the American Colonial Church*, 4 vols. (Hartford, Conn., 1870–1878), IV. Percy G. Skirven, *The First Parishes of the Province of Maryland* (Baltimore, 1923), also prints manuscript sources.

The discussions of social structure are based primarily on career studies of councillors, burgesses, Associators, and major county officeholders. Apart from assembly, council, and court records of all kinds, the materials available for such studies are mainly those of the Prerogative Court and the Land Office. The Prerogative Court was in suspension during the revolution, but otherwise this central agency conducted all testamentary business. Hence probate records remain for all the counties, despite local fires and carelessness. Wills, inventories, and administration accounts reveal much about a man's family, his standard of living, and what property he owned at his death and after his debts were paid. On administration bonds and inventories are found the signatures or marks of administrators and their sureties and of appraisers, which provide our chief clue to the literacy of those who signed. The bonds were not usually recorded in full, being merely noted in the proceedings of the Prerogative Court, but for some counties original bonds remain.

In 1692 probate was somewhat decentralized through the creation of deputy commissaries in the counties, but official recordation remained in the Prerogative Court. The deputy commissaries must have kept their own records, but only six years' worth for Charles County (1716–1722) remain for the whole colonial period. An accident of history, however, has left partial collections of probate records by county, which are useful in studying particular areas. In 1777 the assembly created the county orphans' courts and ordered that the papers of the Prerogative Court be returned to each county of origin. Once there, the register of wills, who was also clerk of the orphans' court, was to copy them into volumes. These rerecorded documents provide quick and convenient reference, insofar as they survive, and the original papers are the surest proof available of signature literacy, since the carelessness of a clerk cannot conceal a signature made with a mark. All of these records are indexed on cards at the Hall of Records. The indexes are explained in regularly issued bulletins. The records themselves are discussed in Elisabeth Hartsook and Gust Skordas, *Land Office and Prerogative Court Records of Maryland*, Hall of Records Commission Publication no. 4 (Annapolis, 1946).

The Land Office records are also at the Hall of Records. This office, the central agency for land grants, was closed from 1689 until 1694, when Lord Baltimore wrested from the new government recognition of his rights to control grants. Seventeenth-century Land Office records consist of volumes of rent rolls, of warrants, and of proofs of rights, warrants, surveys, and patents in a series called the Patent Libers. There are volume-name indexes to the warrants, to the proofs of rights, and to the rent rolls of 1659; there are card indexes to the surveys and patents both by tract name and by patentee. Rent rolls compiled from about 1699 to 1707, after fire destroyed most earlier sets, are indexed only for tracts, but copies among the Calvert Papers at the Maryland Historical Society (on film at the Hall of Records) are indexed for possessors also. These rent rolls are indispensable for counties in which deeds have been destroyed, since they offer the only clues to changes of land ownership through sale after the original grant. All the Land Office records are described in the Hartsook and Skordas volume.

Numerous secondary sources have contributed to our understanding of events and developments in Maryland during the late seventeenth century; these are cited in the footnotes.

Index

Maryland's Revolution of
Government, 1689–1692

Designed by R. E. Rosenbaum.
Composed by York Composition Co., Inc.,
in 11 point linotype Janson, 3 points leaded,
with display lines in Weiss italic.
Printed letterpress from type by York Composition Co.
on Warren's 1854 text, 60 pound basis,
with the Cornell University Press watermark.
Bound by Vail-Ballou Press
in Columbia book cloth
and stamped in All Purpose foil.